BECOMING CAJUN, BECOMING AMERICAN

SOUTHERN LITERARY STUDIES

Fred Hobson, *Series Editor*

BECOMING CAJUN, BECOMING AMERICAN

THE ACADIAN IN AMERICAN LITERATURE FROM LONGFELLOW TO JAMES LEE BURKE

MARIA HEBERT-LEITER

Louisiana State University Press   Baton Rouge

Published by Louisiana State University Press
Copyright © 2009 by Louisiana State University Press
All rights reserved
Manufactured in the United States of America
First printing

Designer: Laura Roubique Gleason
Typeface: Minion Pro
Printer and binder: Thomson-Shore, Inc.

Library of Congress Cataloging-in-Publication Data

Hebert-Leiter, Maria.
    Becoming Cajun, becoming American : the Acadian in American literature from
Longfellow to James Lee Burke / Maria Hebert-Leiter.
        p. cm. — (Southern literary studies)
    Includes bibliographical references and index.
    ISBN 978-0-8071-3435-1 (cloth : alk. paper) 1. American literature—History and
criticism. 2. Cajuns in literature. 3. Acadians in literature. I. Title.
    PS173.A26H43 2009
    810.9'529410763—dc22

                                                                        2008050688

Chapter 4 contains material published in an earlier version as "A Breed Between: Racial
Mediation in the Fiction of Ernest Gaines" in *MELUS: The Journal of the Society for
the Study of the Multi-Ethnic Literature of the United States* 31. 2 (Summer 2006). It is
reprinted here with the permission of *MELUS*.

To my Hebert family

CONTENTS

ACKNOWLEDGMENTS

This project stems from my own Cajun identity and my interest in researching the Cajun narrative that arose once I left Louisiana. Like many Cajuns before me, I realized upon leaving that my home and its people are indeed still unique. During my time outside of the state, I have met people who have become the community that supported me throughout the writing and various revisings of this study.

This book extends from my University of North Carolina, Chapel Hill (UNC-CH) dissertation, which I wrote under the direction of Fred Hobson. His direction, his encouragement, and his faith in the project have been invaluable to me over the years. In addition, I would like to thank William Andrews, Robert Cantwell, Joseph Flora, Patricia Sawin, Linda Wagner-Martin, and Tyler Curtain, all of whom served as readers and responders to the project as it evolved. I would especially like to thank Connie Eble, who offered me a suggestion that grew from an idea into a book.

I owe a debt of gratitude as well to the various UNC-CH academic and administrative units for their support of my research, especially the Center for the Study of the American South and the Graduate School. Both provided me with the means of completing archival research in Louisiana, which greatly benefited my understanding of certain texts. I would like to thank the librarians at Dupré Library and the Howard Tilton Memorial Library for their patience and support while I completed this research. I also thank Wilkes University and its financial support, which allowed me to travel to conferences and present portions of this manuscript.

Additionally, I thank Carl A. Brasseaux, who provided me with a copy of *Trois saisons;* Marcia Gaudet, whose suggestions regarding early twentieth-century literature greatly helped me expand chapter four; Tim Gautreaux, who agreed to an interview that proved invaluable to my understanding of his characters and their Cajun journeys; and Jason Wiese, who answered my questions regarding John Banvard's "A Panorama of the Mississippi."

I would also like to extend my gratitude to certain people who have dedicated countless hours to reading and rereading this work. I could not have revised without the support and guidance of Emily Rosenbaum and David Davis, whose feedback continually reminded me to step away from my writing and allow for fresh, new readings of my work. Over the last couple of years, I have also shared my ideas and my writing with Marcia Farrell, who has become yet another valuable reader of my work. In addition, I thank everyone at LSU Press who has helped me prepare this book for publication.

Like many Cajuns before me, I have come to realize how Cajun I am only by leaving Louisiana. I thank my family for giving me the passion necessary for seeing this project to completion. I especially thank my father for sharing his love of Cajun literature with me and for introducing me to the wonderful work of Ernest Gaines and James Lee Burke, among many other contemporary Cajun writers. Finally, I thank Andrew Leiter for his continual support and patience. His advice and encouragement have made my years of research and writing possible. And his gumbo proves that he is indeed an honorary Cajun.

BECOMING CAJUN, BECOMING AMERICAN

Introduction: From Acadian to American

THE PARADOX OF CAJUN AMERICAN IDENTITY

In *The People Called Cajuns: An Introduction to an Ethnohistory,* James Dormon describes Cajun literary representation as "America's love for the exotic and unusual" producing "grotesque caricatures of the reality" (viii). For any study of Cajun fiction, one must address the way in which these representations create a lineage, literary and cultural, for contemporary Cajun authors while also exposing the stereotypical images that arose when past works incorporated representations of Cajuns into their pages. Although "few [ethnic groups] have been the subject of greater fascination to outside observers than Louisiana's 'Cajun population,'" which has led to "distortive myths, fictions, and lore" (viii), these distortions and myths are part of contemporary renderings of Cajuns because they have come to frame our present understanding of Cajuns.

Demonstrating this point, the New Orleans Historic Collection exhibited paintings from December 2001 through January 2002 that reflected life in south Louisiana around the time represented in Henry Wadsworth Longfellow's *Evangeline* (1847), one of the most popular and powerful of Acadian literary representations. To tie the various works together under one title, and to demonstrate the continuing power of the poem as a heading for Cajun culture, the collection named the show "Still Stands the Forest Primeval." The accompanying pamphlet, which directed viewers from one painting to the next, also reminded the audience of Longfellow's work by using quotations from *Evangeline* to introduce, guide, and conclude the movement of the viewer from beginning to end of the exhibit. The pamphlet acknowledged the literary and cultural framework in which Longfellow wrote and the significance of this framework as a connection to Acadian history.

The Acadian exile is probably best known through Longfellow's poem *Evangeline* (1847). As the most prominent American literary figure of his day, Longfellow devoted much of his poetry to the description of North American landscapes in a concerted effort to forge for a nation of immigrants a spiritual connection with their new land. Longfellow understood that while Americans were busy surveying, mapping, and finding economic use for the frontier they were also searching for a deeper relationship with the land.... By using the story of the Acadian expulsion, he spoke to this sentiment in *Evangeline*. (*Still Stands* 1)

This pamphlet introduction not only frames the exhibit through the Evangeline myth, but it also reminds the exhibit's viewer of Longfellow's place in American literary history while demonstrating how *Evangeline* acts as a bridge between an Acadian and an American past.

Longfellow wrote for a new nation still expanding and still searching for an identity distinct from its colonial motherland's. *Evangeline* captures a people at the beginning of their American settlement, making it an origin myth not only for a native ethnicity, but also for the larger nation. The Historic New Orleans Collection's exhibit demonstrates an American understanding of the Acadian dispersal through the words of New England's Longfellow, an understanding that stems from a mythical memory replacing a lost past for Americans and Cajuns alike. Even though today's Cajun scholars critique this mythic portrayal of the Acadian past, no one can deny Longfellow's position as preserver of a memory of this past, because his work made Acadians American characters worthy of the notice of a developing publishing world.[1] His poem depicts them as English-speaking heroes of a romantic and pastoral American tale, regardless of their French language and identity and their Catholic religion. In many ways, *Evangeline* relates the story of a people indistinguishable from most Americans in their quest for a new home complete with family bonds and spiritual ties, guaranteeing their assimilation into the popular American imagination.

From Henry Wadsworth Longfellow's fictional narration of the *Grand Dérangement*, the 1755 expulsion of the French community from Acadia by the British governor Charles Lawrence, stems a mythical memory of communal survival for contemporary Cajuns that begins a literary process by which Acadians became Cajun Americans by becoming both Cajun and American, simultaneous processes that built upon each other. Moreover, the educational, social, and economic advances that allowed Cajuns to become American throughout the nineteenth and twentieth centuries instigated the present need for remembering Cajun difference in conjunction with studying such issues as translation and self-representation as framed through a larger study of a particular American ethnic population. While such issues have remained prevalent in studies of various American ethnic literatures, including both African American and Native American fiction, an examination of Cajun representation reveals interesting assumptions about American racial and social structures that have allowed for Cajun Americanization in ways not always offered to other ethnic groups, providing further insight into national assimilation. In conjunction with other ethnic communities, Cajuns have also remained different within this Americanization process and have begun embracing their differences within the pages of American literature that once attempted to capture and contain such Otherness.

The study of Cajun literature is the study of the very movement from assimilation to differentiation that mimics the path Cajuns took from their Acadian identifications to an all-American, yet different, notion of self. From Longfellow through Tim Gautreaux, Cajun literature captures the stages of this fascinating cultural dynamism, making it a pivotal part of any study of American ethnicity in general and Cajun culture in particular because it records the means by which an Other empowers itself by embracing difference in the midst of an already enacted assimilation process.

Before delving into any study of Cajun literature, one must first understand what it means to be *Cajun* both today and in the past. Louisiana racial, class, and ethnic categories are unique in comparison to national race and class categories. These unique divisions continue to diverge from those regarded as standard by the rest of the nation, but they have come to reflect more closely national standards as Louisiana became more Americanized over the last hundred and forty years or so. The national bipartite racial system, for example, conflicts with the Louisiana tri- or even quadpartite system that takes into account such categories as Cajuns, Creoles, and Creoles of Color. As Barbara Ladd explains, "Prior to the Louisiana Purchase in 1803, racial classification in the creole Deep South was much more complex than in the Anglo Upper South, where the status of a mixed-blood child followed that of the mother" (21). This difference extended from the fact that children of "European colonists and African women constituted a separate caste," as demonstrated by New Orleans's free persons of color population (21). Miscegenation complicated racial divisions and testified to their arbitrary nature all over the South, but Louisiana society included a legal and social space for these intermediary figures, which further tested the boundaries of difference. Cajuns became an ethnic group in the midst of, and possibly because of, this unique social structuring. Cajun and Creole identities remain complicated, as demonstrated in American fiction and in today's continued confusion over how comprehensively to define each. This complexity, especially in terms of outside and national views of Louisiana difference, leads American authors to rely on stereotypes and allows them to address controversial and, sometimes, taboo subjects through the ambiguity of Louisiana class and race divisions.

In the simplest of terms, Cajuns are the descendants of the Acadians, although there are people of non-Acadian descent who also identify themselves as Cajun today. Karen Tobin Bernard and Shane Bernard complicate this simple definition with a clear explanation of the cultural complexity present in the Acadian fold, including "English, Scottish, Irish, Spanish, Basque, and even American Indian" ("Cajun"). Nevertheless, the majority were of Old World peasant stock, with "[f]ifty-five percent . . . hail[ing] from the Centre-Ouest region of France" and settling in the present-day Maritime Provinces of Canada (Nova Scotia, New Brunswick, and Prince Edward Island) ("Cajun"). Following the *Grand Dérangement,* the Acadians adapted to their new situations and to the continued threat the British held over those who remained behind. Thus, the Acadians became a people ruled by various imperial powers, part of separate colonies, and in need of adopting new cultural ways. By 1764,[2] Acadians were settled in Louisiana, and the changes wrought by new environmental conditions and government policies produced a people now known as *Cajuns,* a group made up of particles of various cultures, including Spanish, German, Creole French, American Indian, and even Anglo-American (Ancelet et al., *Cajun Country* 33–34).

Dormon takes Cajun studies a step further by concluding that the Cajuns are an American ethnic group: "They *became* an ethnic group—indeed they became several different ethnic groups, including the group known as Cajuns—only after their fateful exile and diaspora took them to assorted farflung places, including Louisiana, where they found themselves regrouped in constant situations within larger social frameworks" (*The People* 7). In Louisiana, Cajuns continued their use of French and their practice of Roman Catholicism. They also developed new foodways, producing dishes such as gumbo, which combines the French *roux* (a mix of oil and flour) with African okra and other unique seasonings, and new musical traditions as they adopted such instruments as the diatonic accordion and made them vital to Cajun music. Louisiana offered a land on which Cajuns formed strong family and community bonds that aided in their ethnic formation around traditional Acadian and evolving Cajun cultural ways. The Cajuns exist today as an ethnic group in part because of the Acadian dispersal of 1755, which encouraged their settlement in Louisiana. Their present American geographical location made their ethnic formation possible. This location also caused conflict because the national government, after purchasing the Louisiana Territory in 1803, had the power to demand adherence to national and state laws. Considered American by the government that established the laws by which they lived, Cajuns began to assimilate to such standards as the use of English to merit and maintain rights and privileges. Simply put, they became more American. For this reason, a study of Cajun literary representation is a study of multiple displacements, since Cajun formation and change depend on geographical boundaries and linguistic conditions.

Clearly, Cajuns demonstrate the possibility of an "American melting pot," resulting in "Cajun children practically indistinguishable from Anglo-American children" by the 1960s (Bernard, *Americanization* 84). Furthermore, the term *Cajun* "suggests that it was employed by *outsiders,* not insiders, for it is fundamentally an anglicized form of the contraction *'Cadien* (or phonetically, 'Ca'jin'), long in use among the French Acadians to refer to themselves. 'Cajun' is an Americanized form of the term" (Dormon, *The People* 33, emphasis mine). Ironically, Cajuns take pride in an American-corrupted term used to label themselves, an excellent example of cultural recovery. Like present Cajun identity, the term's origin lies in the Acadian past. *Cajun* is a powerful example of the double bind in which contemporary Cajuns find themselves, tied to an American present and an Acadian past.[3] Cajuns can empower themselves through this double bind only if and when they realize that it is within the space between their Acadian and American identifications that their Cajun identity was formed, thus making any study of Cajuns an examination of their interstitial position.

My study of this Cajun interstitial position stems from Homi Bhabha's introduction to *The Location of Culture* in which he argues that it "is in the emergence of the interstices—the overlap and displacement of domains of difference—that the intersubjective and collective experiences of *nationness,* community interest, or cultural value are negotiated" (2). In his introduction to *Nation and Narration,* Bhabha further postulates that "What emerges as an effect of such 'incomplete signification' is a turning of boundaries and limits into the *in-between* spaces through which the meanings of cultural and political authority are negotiated" (4). Specifically, I am drawing from this notion of these "in-between spaces" as the places of negotiation and connecting this idea back to the Cajun situation in south Louisiana.

As a French Catholic people, the Acadians were other than typical Americans following the 1803 Louisiana Purchase, which made them inevitably part of the United States. Throughout their history in the nation as both Acadians and Cajuns, they have remained *in between* racial, social, and economic categories, making them interstitial figures in both history and fiction. Charles Stivale establishes the ability of Bhabha's postcolonial theory to speak to the formation of Cajun cultural identity in the late twentieth century in terms of authenticity in Cajun dance and music in his work *Disenchanting Les Bons Temps: Identity and Authenticity in Cajun Music and Dance.* In this work, he argues that the Cajun "struggle for authenticity" demonstrates the shift of this authenticity into "something altogether hybrid, in-between, and quite extraordinary" (31). He explains, "The musical self-representation and affirmation of Cajun identity . . . continuously reconstitute the hybrid ground of what Homi Bhabha calls 'an in-between' reality," a borderline or crossroads (64). Such an example demonstrates that Cajun interstitial positioning refers not only to literary representations of an ethnic Other, but also to the Other's current attempts to remain different. The study of Cajun literature is thus a study of such "in-between spaces" that allow for both cultural assimilation and differentiation.

The Cajuns' impulse toward accommodation for survival, which led to the formation of their position between Acadian and American cultures, actually originated with their ancestors before the 1755 dispersal. In *A Great and Noble Scheme,* John Mack Faragher credits the survival and success of the New World Acadian settlement at least in part to the "intercultural conversation" between the French settlers and the Micmaq Indians, their neighbors (6). This interdependence led to "mutual accommodation" between the two communities, which made the New World situation a fascinating one because of its cultural implications (16). Not only did the French and natives live in mutual respect, but some of the French males married native females and fathered *métis* children, making future Acadians a somewhat mixed people. According to Faragher, "Dozens of church-registered interethnic unions were a significant factor in the making of the Acadian community" (46). They were also a complicating factor during the imperial conflict between the French and British since the Micmaq were decidedly anti-British, and the Acadians maintained a mantle of neutrality (160, 221–22). The mixed ethnicity of the Acadians made neutrality difficult and somewhat questionable as the Micmaq continually challenged British domination. The double bind of contemporary Cajuns can be studied in relation to this earlier double bind of French and native identifications, which made the Acadians a group apart and in between, interstitially situated between Old and New World cultures. Like their ancestors, the Cajuns also use this double identification as a means of surviving American change and progress. Their interstitial place, between an Acadian past and an American present, allows them to hold on to a unique ethnic identity while also taking pride in their American history and cultural ways. The French and Micmaq interethnic breeding also predates the intermixture of the Acadians with other Louisiana settlers, again complicating any notion of simple historical definition of Louisiana Cajuns. But it is this complexity that makes the Cajuns more interesting in their ability to adapt to and survive imperial and American conflict and change.

Like *Cajun,* the word *Creole* also presents an interesting and complex example of Louisiana ethnic categories. In 1952, Joseph Tregle Jr. recorded the use of the term in accordance with "the religious belief that all those who bore the name were Louisiana born to descendants of the French and Spanish, that they were almost uniformly genteel and cultured aristocrats, above the lure of money, disdainful of physical labor, and too sensitive to descend into the dirty business of political and monetary struggle with the crude *Américains*" (228), a self-identification that George Washington Cable captures in his Louisiana stories. Addressing an earlier period in Louisiana colonial history, Shane Bernard explains the origins of the term:

> After the New World's discovery, Portuguese colonists used the term *crioulo* to denote a New World slave of African descent. Eventually, the word was applied to all New World colonists, regardless of ethnic origin, living along the Gulf Coast, especially in Louisiana. There the Spanish introduced the word as *criollo,* and during Louisiana's colonial period (1699–1803) the evolving word *Creole* generally referred to persons of African or European heritage born in the New World. (Bernard and Bernard, "Creole")

While both Tregle and Bernard discuss an original basis for the ethnic Louisiana group, these more general definitions would become complicated following the Civil War because of postbellum racial implications. Even though Tregle explains that *Creole* was "generally used in Louisiana to designate *any* person native to the state" during the 1820s and 1830s (230, emphasis mine), *Creole* came to signify a white identification, and *creole* was used by the white population to designate Creoles of Color following the war. Virginia Domínguez dates the use of *creole*, with a lowercase *c*, as a racial identity only after the Civil War (134), and Barbara Ladd explains post–Civil War southern fears of being labeled "black" as the reason for distinguishing between *Creole* and *creole* (xv).

Making such categories even more complex, the term *Creole of Color* was created even before the outbreak of the war, proving an already shifting notion of the variety of Creole identification along racial and social lines. With the rise of free persons of color who were born in the New World and who could claim European descent, Dormon explains how "[t]he growing community of Afro-European miscegens who were descended from colonial free persons of color and who occupied a special, intermediate place in the racial and social order of antebellum Louisiana and the Gulf port cities began referring to themselves as 'Creoles of Color'" (*Creoles* x), as a means of distinguishing themselves from both the Creoles who identified as white and the slaves of African descent, proving that the label already implied social and racial assumptions.

During the second half of the twentieth century, *Creole* again shifted to include a broader and more diverse population. Ironically, Louisianians who consider themselves Creole today are "generally descendants of French-speaking slaves who were emancipated during or immediately after the Civil War" and are "almost universally Catholic and largely French-speaking," adding both another significant meaning to the definition of Louisiana Creole and a refutation of Creoles as white only (Brasseaux, *French* 112). Presently, *Creole* can refer to all of the above, both black and white populations. This tangled history demonstrates the complexities of Louisiana social and racial categorization, which also affected Cajun identity in the state, especially since "the descendants of the Acadian migrants . . . were ruled out of this select society—they may be Cajuns, but never Creoles," according to Tregle (229).

Along with the difficulties in addressing Louisiana ethnic and racial categories, which prove the complex issues involved in any cultural study of Louisiana ethnic literature, comes the challenge of defining Cajun literature, which has also shifted in history. According to *The Companion to Southern Literature: Themes, Genres, Places, People, Movements, and Motifs,* Cajun fiction is marked by a nonidealized, but always pivotal depiction of land, an assessment of "difficulties resulting from cultural stigmas, racism, economic hardship, and modern industrialization," a continuation of religious and secular cultural traditions, and the bonds of family and community (122). This entry in *The Companion* continues to demonstrate these traits by listing the most popular, and, thus, powerful, writers of Cajun fiction: George Washington Cable, Kate Chopin, and Ernest Gaines. It also mentions Cajuns who choose to represent their cultural ways in print, which include Barry Jean Ancelet, with his folklore and poetry collections, Albert Belisle Davis, Chris Segura, and Tim Gautreaux.

Although *The Companion to Southern Literature* recognizes outside representation as part of Cajun literature, it does not address the central role external representation plays in contemporary Cajun literature written by Cajuns. Through successful relocation, Acadians proved their ability to survive through adaptation and their power to defy a British enemy set on destroying community bonds. In contemporary Cajun fiction, pride stemming from survival becomes the key to Cajun endurance in the midst of American assimilation, an embrace of difference from within an already realized American identification. It becomes the answer to the tension caused by the Cajun double bind.

The work of Carl Brasseaux, James Dormon, and Shane Bernard, among others, offers an accurate historical account of the process by which French settlers became Acadians, Cajuns, and Americans over the last four centuries, while Glenn Conrad, Mathé Allain, and Marcia Gaudet examine the role that American fiction has played and will continue to play in the representation of Acadians and Cajuns. Specifically, Glenn Conrad argues that such depictions fall into two categories, both too simplistic to address fully the complexity of Cajun culture:

[The Cajun] is either depicted as an ignorant, cunning, superstitious swamp dweller, living in squalor in a moss-draped, reptile-infested wilderness which is truly a backwater of American civilization; or, he is interpreted as being a creature of simple virtue, somewhat religious, easily amused by bouree, beer, and quaint music and who occasionally blurts out (in his 'usual patois') unexpected words of wisdom. (1)

According to this statement, the representation of Cajuns falls into either *The Waterboy* variety or the *Evangeline* one.[4] *Evangeline* is so well embedded in Cajuns' conceptions of themselves, as well as in outsiders' images of them, that Longfellow's epic continues to speak through contemporary Cajun history and culture, and thus through Cajun fiction. If the Cajun "diaspora—their Grand Dérangement, as it later came to be called—has provided the basis of epic legend, myth, folklore, and endless historical controversy, even now still unresolved" (7), then Evangeline's fame grows from her place as a basis for Cajun myth. *Evangeline* symbolizes the origin of Cajun Americanization, both literally and historically.

By becoming American in 1803, the Cajuns experienced the same push for modernization and upward mobility that has characterized America's gift of class flexibility from the beginning. In the midst of this assimilation to mainstream American culture, Acadians refused to lose their unique identity as other than Anglo-Americans, a refusal that preserved the need and the desire for actual, as well as mythical, memory, which remained a bond, although an illusive one, with the past. Cajuns today are products of this interstitial location between Americanization and an Acadian past, making them just one example of American minorities that through American literature have searched for their own voices while acknowledging the national literary framework in which they write.

In fascinating ways, the history of the national literary industry speaks directly to the history of Cajun fiction because the two parallel each other. A postcolonial people attempt to establish a literature for and about themselves by adopting and adapting previously established literary techniques and genres to fit their own conditions and situations in life. Also, a regional location becomes a symbol for the overall conditions of a people, with the particular speaking for and to, as well as sometimes against, the universal. Cajuns remain a specific piece of the American cultural landscape, and their development into Americans has the fortune of being recorded in American literature perhaps because of their interesting position between a unique culture and an American identity.

The authors who dominate this work do so because of their continuing significance to American literature and because of their contributions to the international, national, and Cajun literary imaginations. The history of Cajun literary representation can best be examined through the national process by which outside representation turned inward, a process that appropriately begins with Longfellow and that uses English translation as its framework, because such translation demonstrates how Cajuns have adapted to and incorporated cultural changes to empower themselves in their quest for self-representation in literature.

When Longfellow wrote *Evangeline* in English, he set a precedent that even contemporary Cajuns follow in their fiction. This poem is a product of its time, written to create an American epic complete with a hero and heroine who, although Other, represent an American nativity; thus, the publication of this particular work has serious implications for Cajun literature and identity as they exist today. The Acadian Americanization process as recorded in literature continues through the work of George Washington Cable, a southerner whose written words argue for national unity and public education following the Civil War and Reconstruction. In *Bonaventure* (1888), Cable relates the process by which Cajuns became more American through English education, a foreshadowing that would have serious consequences for Cajuns throughout the twentieth century. *Bonaventure* acknowledges the national changes occurring as the North enacts a reconstruction process that allows such interstitial communities as the Louisiana Acadians to choose between remaining different or becoming American and benefiting from national unification.

At the close of the nineteenth century, Cajuns were continuing to assimilate in various ways to a mainstream, white American culture complete with some English usage. Cajuns were caught between the cultures, no longer fully Acadian and not fully assimilated Americans. In *The Awakening* (1899) and "The Storm" (published in 1969), the world of Cajuns and their racial and class ambiguity constitute Kate Chopin's embodied literary space of freedom from the genteel publishing standards that controlled depictions of female sexuality, a space she created by using Cajuns to question contemporary notions of identity. Chopin's fiction records the popular confusion during the late nineteenth century over how to label the Louisiana Acadians, now becoming Cajuns, because of their potential for social and racial flexibility. Using this confusion to her advantage at a time when genteel publishers disapproved of any notion of women's sexual desire in fiction, Chopin chose to employ a stereotype as a tool to create an ideological space for herself as an author.

By the twentieth century, *Evangeline,* through tourism, became a link between the Acadian settlement of Louisiana and American identity, even as pressure increased for Cajuns to become American because of national debates regarding assimilation. At the very moment when national distrust arose based on notions of ethnic and cultural difference, St. Martinville, Louisiana, began to embrace *Evangeline* to promote pride that stemmed from a fictional character, proving to what degree Longfellow's poem affected Cajun memory and how Cajun culture was becoming more

American while Acadian culture was becoming more symbolic. During the early twentieth century, Cajuns struggled with forced and self-determined assimilation, a struggle that is recorded in the work of Ada Jack Carver, Elma Godchaux, Shirley Ann Grau, and Ernest Gaines. As represented in Grau's *The Hard Blue Sky* (1955), twentieth-century Cajuns found themselves between American modernization and their cultural past by the 1930s, creating a desire among some Cajuns to leave their Cajun homelands behind in search of better opportunities, a movement that would continue throughout the twentieth century.

By the middle of the twentieth century, divisions were already occurring between generations within Cajun communities, which caused conflict and tension to arise. Ernest Gaines analyzes this tension within and between Louisiana's ethnic populations from an African American perspective of the midtwentieth century, a time of tremendous industrialization and mechanization that greatly affected both African Americans and Cajuns. His stories of racial and social conflict offer insight into an Americanization process that altered an agrarian way of life forever, leaving older African Americans with deteriorating homes and Cajuns desiring the American education endorsed by Cable a hundred years earlier. Ironically, this education system provides the potential for racial cooperation in *A Gathering of Old Men* (1983), making assimilation a reminder of loss and an instrument for positive change. Regardless, Gaines's fiction remains a look backward that acknowledges an already enacted assimilation to American mainstream culture among the younger generation of Cajuns, with their English speech and their interest in an all-American recognition of themselves.

Following Gaines's depictions of cultural change and ethnic conflict, James Lee Burke emphasizes the reality of such changes through his use of the detective fiction genre, which reflects cultural tensions in literature. In *The American Roman Noir: Hammett, Cain, and Chandler,* William Marling specifically argues that the motif of the prodigal son remains central to American detective fiction because of its sense of resolution of such tensions. Burke incorporates this motif in order to reverse it by addressing the impossibility for such resolution, that is, the homecoming of the prodigal son, to occur in late twentieth-century America. Dave Robicheaux, Burke's Cajun detective, may desire a return to his father's earlier Cajun way of life, but such a backward movement is now impossible due to Cajun Americanization. Detective Robicheaux (1987 through today), is a type of contemporary ethnic son searching for a return to a cultural world that has already assimilated to American standards.

As the twenty-first century progresses, Tim Gautreaux and other contemporary Cajun authors represent the Cajun movement away from traditional cultural ways in their work to illustrate the difficulties facing today's Cajuns as they struggle to maintain pride in their ethnic difference in the midst of their continuing assimilation to Anglo-American standards, a paradox that dominates contemporary Cajun literature. Gautreaux resolves this paradox by illustrating in his first novel, *The Next Step in the Dance* (1998), how Cajuns can live as both Cajuns and Americans since Cajun identity is located between an Acadian history and an American present. In other words, the survival of Cajun difference and pride depends on an understanding of the Cajun interstitial position and how it has been formed and informed by both cultural outsiders and insiders. Twenty-first-century Cajun literature embraces difference while also acknowledging that such difference exists from within an already enacted assimilation to mainstream American culture, making differentiation possible in the midst of Americanization. Contemporary Cajun authors, such as Gautreaux, write in the English language, demonstrating how Cajuns, an American Other, have empowered themselves through American education to represent difference.

As American literature and national publishers evolved over the nineteenth and twentieth centuries to fit the needs of a growing nation, so too did Cajun literary representation. Combining a study of literary history with an examination of ethnic history and theory, one can begin to explain the national fascination with Acadians and their descendants, the Cajuns. This national fascination guaranteed continued interest in Cajun culture, which eventually led to contemporary Cajun literary representation by Cajuns.

As recorded representations of Cajuns illustrate shifts in the meaning of the terms *Acadian* and *Cajun*, they also portray shifts tied to American development and national dynamics. The history of Cajun fiction is the history of Acadians becoming Americans, which also made them Cajuns. For this reason, the history of Cajun representation in literature and its evolution follows American literary history and its development over the last hundred and fifty years. Literature becomes the vehicle not only for the Americanization of the Cajun ethnic minority, but also for the struggle to embrace and reclaim ethnic pride, and the need to do so, through differentiation from an Anglo-American norm.

1. Longfellow's *Evangeline*

THE ORIGINS OF AMERICAN MYTH AND CAJUN MEMORY

In 1927, Huey P. Long visited St. Martinville, Louisiana, on his gubernatorial campaign tour. As he stood under the Evangeline Oak along the shore of Bayou Têche, he invoked the romanticism of the Evangeline myth to frame his campaign promise of better times for Louisianians: "Evangeline wept bitter tears in her disappointment, but it lasted through only a lifetime. Your tears in this country, around this oak here, have lasted generations. Give me a chance to dry the tears of those who still weep here" (Long). This moment in history demonstrates how completely an American author's character became not only the dominant image of an ethnic group for the rest of the nation and the world, but also the reference for selfhood among Louisianians. *Evangeline*'s prominent place in American, Louisianian, and Cajun memory extends from its author's significant role in the New England publishing world, but it also arises from the ashes of cultural representation. At a time when the representation of ethnic minorities in American literature signified a need to create an American self as not Other, *Evangeline* produced a separate notion of Other as American, changing the face of Acadians in Louisiana and of Americans forever in the national literary imagination.

By writing *Evangeline* (1847), Henry Wadsworth Longfellow created a unique American tale and established a new American literary character while claiming a place for Acadians in the history of the United States. According to Barry Jean Ancelet, Longfellow "clearly sought to be the interpreter of the new American adventure" at a time when the "Acadian exile was not a matter of early United States history" ("Elements" 119). The poem introduced American readers to their Acadian neighbors, which Charles Calhoun emphasizes when he argues that *Evangeline* "put the Acadians, and the plight of the Acadians, on the map" (259), an American map. Longfellow chose the Acadians as his vehicle for portraying new developments in national literature both to claim them as fitting native characters on which to place American identity and to make this identity absolute by assimilating native differences to Anglo-American culture. *Evangeline* remains a reminder not only of the cultural formation of American literature, but also of the Acadian journey to Louisiana and of Acadian assimilation to American identification, a journey that led to the formation of a people called Cajuns.

In *Sensational Designs: The Cultural Work of American Fiction, 1790–1860,* Jane Tompkins questions the formation of the literary canon by positing that readers should reconsider certain popular nineteenth-century novels because of their contemporary cultural impact. Tompkins reevaluates such works as James Fenimore Cooper's *Leatherstocking Tales* and Harriet Beecher Stowe's *Uncle Tom's Cabin* in terms of the cultural context in which they were written and to which they were addressed. Even though his reputation has declined (only to be revived every so often), Tompkins reminds us of Longfellow's position as one of the "cultural spokesmen at mid-century," when all three of these American authors wrote bestsellers (28).[1] Tompkins's thesis sheds light on Longfellow's work and its popularity, especially because he was a cultural arbiter of literary merit through his position in Boston and his contributions to the *North American Review,* which supported such careers as Nathaniel Hawthorne's.[2] If one agrees with Tompkins that "*looking* is not an activity that is performed outside of political struggles and institutional structures, but arises *from* them" (23), and if one chooses to study literature in its cultural context, then Longfellow's work, especially *Evangeline,* takes on a whole new meaning. By pushing Tompkins's theory a step further to assume that literature continues to do cultural work beyond its original era and that this work can evolve to address any present moment, then one can argue that *Evangeline* not only affected both the American public that originally read it and the Louisiana Acadians of which it speaks, but also affects to this day the descendants of these Acadians and the national imaginary space in which they reside.

While Tompkins's study sheds light on the cultural context within which American literature thrived, Richard Bauman adds another dimension to any reading of Longfellow's work through his examination of the nationalization and internationalization of folklore. Bauman studies the process by which an Indian dream narrative of oral origin became part of Longfellow's *The Song of Hiawatha* (1855). This study extends from Bauman's interest in "the political economy of folklore in the service of nationalist ideologies" and "international cultural spheres" which guides the path along which such folklore is decontextualized and recontextualized (248). Bauman's study of Henry Rowe Schoolcraft's "Gitshee Gauzinee" implicates not only Longfellow's *Hiawatha* but *Evangeline* as well since both make certain cultural assumptions even as they address such assumptions for slightly different purposes.

Through the insights of both Tompkins and Bauman, the study of *Evangeline* develops into a multilayered process with significance that reaches across a hundred and sixty years of literary and national development. What began as an American tale has become the foundation for national and international recognition of a unique American ethnicity, while simultaneously reshaping Cajun cultural memory through an American image of self-identity. The history of this particular nationalist myth captures the literary world's struggle to claim a national vision of self even as it reveals the process by which assimilation affects ethnic identity, sometimes by replacing native legends with national myths, creating an ethnic struggle to claim one's own vision of self.

Evangeline began as an oral tale that became a piece of literature when Longfellow chose to revise it through his American perspective, following a pattern similar to Schoolcraft's recording and revising of American Indian tales. This pattern remains significant to the study of the poem since, as Bauman concludes, "[t]here is no collection of folklore in which the texts are not already national and international" (268), because to collect such stories already assumes a meaning for them and a reason for them to be collected in the first place. *Evangeline's* history emphasizes this point. According to Carl Brasseaux, H. L. Conolly, a Maine clergyman, repeated a parishioner's story of the Acadian dispersal to Longfellow at a dinner party on May 2, 1844 (*In Search* 9). Conolly had already shared the story with Hawthorne in 1839 and had encouraged the American short story writer and novelist to use the story as the basis for a tale, although Hawthorne never did so. Longfellow felt inspired to create a poem about the Acadians based on this story of two lovers divided by the Acadian dispersal of 1755, so he wrote to Hawthorne, "If you really do not want this incident for a tale, let me have it for a poem" (S. Longfellow, vol. 2, 70). The finished product is the tale of Evangeline and Gabriel and their fated division from each other and from the Acadian community of Grand-Pré because Governor Lawrence, the colonial governor who enforced British rule in once-French Acadia, decided that the French Catholic Acadians were a threat in the British colonial war against the French. Placed on different vessels, Evangeline and Gabriel sail away from each other. Evangeline arrives in Louisiana only to discover that Gabriel has recently departed. The rest of the poem follows her search for him and ends in Philadelphia, at his deathbed, where the two are finally reunited.

This beginning reveals much about Longfellow's literary situation and his purpose for writing such a poem. Longfellow's close association with Hawthorne testifies to his position in the American literary world of his time. That he asked Hawthorne for permission to use the folktale to create a literary piece points to Hawthorne's growing literary reputation. After all, Conolly first shared the tale with Hawthorne with the intention that the author would use it in his own work. Finally, Longfellow's interest in the story points to the significance of this particular tale as an American folktale because of its place in the search for "resources for the development of an American national literature" (Bauman 261).

Evangeline's typological framework, its expansive geography, and its regional focus made it an ideal poem for a new nation still in search of a national literature and mythology. Longfellow's appeal to readers, both national and international, translated into an ability to sell, which publishing houses realized as profits for themselves as more copies were produced and sold, which encouraged the spread of the Americanized Acadian myth.[3] Richard Bauman argues that the nationalization and internationalization of folklore occurs because of its transformation into "a commodity," and he points out this is the reason Schoolcraft "did not publish another collection of Indian tales until 1856, when he attempted to cash in on the popularity of Longfellow's *Hiawatha*" (260). American publishing companies and authors were not only seeking out a native literature but also searching for the next bestseller, making American literature and the companies that dominated its distribution as much an endeavor to affect national consciousness as a means of commercialization, as *Evangeline's* history demonstrates.

Ticknor and Fields, a major Boston publishing company, showed much interest in Longfellow's *Evangeline,* proving their faith in his poetry's appeal and their confidence in the tale's national popularity. The publishers not only offered Longfellow the most advantageous deal to date but also benefited from this deal when *Evangeline* "far outsold any previous book of American poems" (Buell, *New England* 407). Not long after its publication, *Evangeline* became "America's first best-seller in verse since Michael Wigglesworth's *The Day of Doom* (1662)" (Buell, Introduction, *Selected Poems* xix), which guaranteed a growing American familiarity with the Acadian story. *Evangeline* was already in its sixth printing during the summer of 1848 (Calhoun 190), a success that not only confirmed Longfellow's place in the American literary world but also signaled its audience's interest in native tales, an interest echoed in the development of the literary world of the time.

In a journal entry dated January 6, 1847, Longfellow recorded his theory of national literature, confirming his interest in the already established debate regarding the formation of a native literature:

> Much is said now-a-days of a national literature. Does it mean anything? Such a literature is the expression of national character. We have, or shall have, a composite one, embracing French, Spanish, Irish, English, Scotch, and German peculiarities. Whoever has within himself most of these is our truly national writer. In other words, whoever is the most universal is also most national. (S. Longfellow, vol. 2, 73–74)

With the publication of *Evangeline*, Longfellow evolved into his ideal of a national writer. If, as Edward Wagenknecht argues, "Longfellow champions and exemplifies nationalism in literature, but it should be understood that his nationalism is clearly of the eclectic variety" (135), then *Evangeline* exemplifies this eclecticism with its oral basis in Acadian dispersal lore supplemented by the author's studies of American geography and memories of European literature, folklore, and scenery.[4]

Although *Evangeline* combines various literary techniques already established by European tradition, such as its meter,[5] it also rewrites the history of a particular ethnic group in typological and allegorical terms in order to claim a folktale for the nation at large.

At a time in American literary history when authors represented slaves and American Indians as Other in order to establish American identity as white, Longfellow represented Acadians as possible Americans, complete with English-language usage and nationalistic impulses toward geographical expansion and settlement. For this reason, *Evangeline* remains a powerful example of a nineteenth-century literary work that speaks from a somewhat different position in the larger discussion of American immigration and nationalization. John Seelye claims that "in its sympathetic treatment of the refugee, Roman Catholic Acadians, *Evangeline* may be read as a pioneering work of ethnic interest" (31). The poem does treat Acadian Roman Catholicism sympathetically. More important, it treats a French Catholic Other not only with sympathy, but also with a sense that such an Other can be assimilated to American literary identification.

Longfellow's Acadian characters reflect an American movement at the time for authors to use histories that were not their own to assimilate Others into American literary and cultural frameworks by incorporating them into a New World mythology that distinguished itself from the Old World. This movement reflects Benedict Anderson's argument in *Imagined Communities* that "from the start the nation was conceived in language, not in blood, and that one could be 'invited into' the imagined community" (145), which for Acadian folklore in the United States meant a baptism into American literature through the English language.

During this period in American literary formation, American Indians became a vehicle for claiming American nativity, as already demonstrated by Schoolcraft's interest in publishing American Indian folktales in English. Ironically, this very nativity extends from an ethnic Other, a tension that needed to be resolved. As part of this expanding national consciousness, Longfellow later wrote *The Song of Hiawatha* (1855). Lawrence Buell describes the poem as a "[n]ineteenth-century literary complacent-sympathetic construction of Indian culture as noble, exotic, and doomed" (Introduction, *Selected Poems* xxix), and it was written at a time when authors were focusing on Indian legends, such as William Gilmore Simms in his short story collection *The Wigwam and the Cabin* (1856)[6] and Cornelius Mathews in his *Big Abel and the Little Manhattan* (1845).[7] James Fenimore Cooper had already established the nation's interest in "savages" with his Natty Bumpo novels, including *The Last of the Mohicans* (1826).

Hiawatha, along with the work of Cooper and Simms, represents the American need for understanding and controlling national formation. It also speaks to Anderson's argument that "more and more 'second-generation' nationalists, in the Americas and elsewhere, learned to speak 'for' dead people with whom it was impossible or undesirable to establish a linguistic connection," and that this "reversed ventriloquism helped to open the way for a self-conscious *indigenismo*" (198). By appropriating the nativity of the Other in fiction, American authors were, in a sense, containing the threat presented by these strange Others through the creation of stereotypes, such as the "savage" Indian, even as they were attempting to claim as their own the Other's identity as Native Americans.[8] Their interest in American Indians testifies to an American fascination with the exotic and the nation's need to exhibit "aspects of Indian culture . . . under the domination of the nation-state" (Bauman 257). The act of writing and publishing such stories, whether originally based on folklore or not, testifies to the process by which the nation claims such native stories for itself by nationalizing them (258). Jane Tompkins argues that during the 1820s and 1830s, "[w]ith independence and national status achieved, the nation's continued westward expansion and the growth of the slave-dependent plantation system required a rationale for dealing with non-white peoples" (109). Thus, between "the War of 1812 and the Civil War, Americans wrote seventy-three novels dealing with Indian-white relations" (110). The desire for a national literature appears to have directed Anglo-American writers to the most native of subjects, and the least British, as a means of creating a literature independent of European influence.[9]

This process of collection and recontextualization extends from national fears and insecurities regarding these native Others. "Cooper's Leatherstocking novels," Tompkins explains, "establish the racial identity of Americans . . . by positing the Indians as 'not us' in a general sense" (111). The Indians represent "qualities that white America lacked that motivates the nostalgia for Indianness pervading these fictions, even as they affirm the impossibility of union with the 'dusky' race and acquiesce in its extermination" (111). When expanded to confront the representations of African slaves and Acadians in American fiction, Tompkins's study proves useful in determining why these representations were popular during this period of American history. Cooper's fiction captures the paradox of American identity formation of the time: if Americans wanted to distinguish themselves from their European roots, then they had to establish a native identity for themselves, an identity represented simultaneously through and in opposition to American Indians and their "exotic" culture.

American representation of the African slave in literature again demonstrates how American writers captured non-Anglo subjects while attempting to create a national sense of identity in fiction because slaves, like American Indians, represent a darkness against which white America could better identify itself.[10] This dark shadow grew into a force larger than simply the opposite of white identity as the North and South continued to debate the institution of slavery. Both Simms and Longfellow address the slave along with the American Indian in their fiction, but they do so in a way that illustrates the growing divisions occurring in the nation at the time. As a white southerner, Simms supported slavery and the plantation system. His use of African American stereotypes throughout *The Wigwam and the Cabin* reflects his white paternalism. On the other side of the slavery argument, Longfellow published *Poems on Slavery* (1842), a thirty-page pamphlet including "The Quadroon Girl," to voice his strong objection to the peculiar institution.[11] By writing slaves into American fiction, authors chose to present one of two sides of this particular American story. Southern authors such as Simms created depictions of a plantation life that benefited the slaves by teaching them organization and discipline and that grew out of the paternalistic desire to civilize slaves in order to save them. Longfellow and his fellow northerners refuted the institution of slavery while complicating white/black demarcation through the character of the "tragic mulatto," a figure that appears in both Longfellow's "The Quadroon Girl" and in abolitionist Lydia Maria Child's short story "The Quadroons" (1842), as well as in Stowe's *Uncle Tom's Cabin* (1852), the novel that further divided an already torn nation. As reminders of a culture that evolved on American soil into an identity separate from Africa, American slaves provided another possible Other as a topic of fiction, but they caused much division as the battle between North and South began to gain strength.

After publishing his slavery poems, Longfellow chose to work on a story that would not divide the nation but would in fact record the geographical expansion of the United States through assimilation. Longfellow stands apart in choosing to write about the Acadians and the tragedy that led some of them to the United States, and he created his heroine as an uncomplicated white figure more than capable of attaining American identification, regardless of Acadian difference.[12] By creating such an American character, Longfellow, "like Whittier, like Whitman on a different scale, is one of the founders, through *Evangeline,* of a North American consciousness in poetry," according to Henri-Dominique Paratte (Foreword).

Within the lines of *Evangeline,* Longfellow maintains his Acadians' distance from their African slave neighbors to create an uncomplicated and nondivisive image of a native American people. Slaves exist in only one subtle line of *Evangeline* and their presence is but an abstract one: "Shaded by china-trees, in the midst of luxuriant gardens, / Stood the houses of planters, with negro-cabins and dove-cots" (761). As a New England Unitarian, Longfellow was averse to slavery of any kind.[13] *Evangeline,* however, retains its distance from the North-South tension, perhaps to mimic the regional situation of the 1760s and to maintain Evangeline and her people's uncomplicated image. As Evangeline evolved into the symbolic image of Cajuns, she retained her pure white skin, regardless of future Cajuns' struggles to claim the full privileges of identifying as white Americans.

Evangeline may remain distant from the African American population of her new homeland, but her relationship with American Indians does not follow the same pattern. Longfellow in fact wrote his white heroine as similar to her American Indian counterpart. His concept of a national nativity written as an Acadian-American nativity perhaps gained credibility through a bond with more native sources, such as the American Indians. Ironically, Longfellow does not address, and may not have realized, the degree to which the Acadians were an interethnic people through their close relationship with the Micmaq Indians in Acadia. As John Mack Faragher makes quite evident in *A Great and Nobel Scheme,* the Acadian settlers not only interacted, but some also intermarried with their Micmaq neighbors, contributing to their survival in the New World. While the factual evidence points away from ethnic purity, Longfellow's poem, which dominated American notions of Acadian identity, enforces the claim of whiteness, thus allowing for the possibility that a French-Catholic Other can become American, making her folktale and history part of a national consciousness.

In his poem, Longfellow frames Evangeline's meeting with a Shawnee woman during her search for Gabriel through a romantic lens that confirms their common bond of suffering and loss. This passage reinforces the use of American Indians in national fiction even as it demonstrates Longfellow's imperialistic, if somewhat sympathetic, view of American Indian life. The "Indian woman . . . Wore deep traces of sorrow, and patience as great as her sorrow" (1117–18). Her sorrow stems from her loss of love since "her Canadian husband, a coureur-des-bois, had been murdered" by Comanches (1121). Evident in this passage is the connection of loss to its cause by Comanche hands, placing blame firmly on the darker, violent ways of the American Indians. The above line also reinforces Cooper's conclusion, located in his Leatherstocking novels, that "the ideal form of human society consists . . . in a proper respect for the 'natural' divisions that separate tribe from tribe and nation from nation" (Tompkins 116), since the Shawnee woman loses her white Canadian husband.

Such loss does not reside only among the American Indians, which *Evangeline* makes clear:

> Then at the door of Evangeline's tent she sat and repeated
> Slowly, with soft, low voice, and the charm of her Indian accent,
> All the tale of her love, with its pleasures, and pains, and reverses.
> Much Evangeline wept at the tale, and to know that another

Hapless heart like her own had loved and been disappointed. (1129–33)

The Indian maiden repeats to Evangeline the story of Mowis, "the bridegroom of the snow, who won and wedded a maiden, / But, when the morning came, arose and passed from the wigwam, / Fading and melting away and dissolving into the sunshine" (1140–42). By comparing the sorrow of Evangeline with the suffering of the Shawnee woman who echoes the Acadian maiden's sad tale of love lost, Longfellow in effect parallels the displacements of the two American peoples and writes both as native material for a national folklore.[14] Simultaneously, he refuses the marriage between Shawnee and Canadian, even as he distances his Acadians somewhat from other white Americans by focusing on their own community within Louisiana and on their interaction with those already on the fringes of the new nation, such as American Indians.

Evangeline does not simply contain Acadians within the margins of the new nation, as it does the American Indians. Its geographical area and its contribution of American ideas of westward settlement and expansion to Acadian culture point to a more complicated relationship between Longfellow and his Acadian characters. The typological and allegorical nature of the poem frame it as a national tale of assimilation. Evangeline even finds a new "home and country" in Pennsylvania (1259), where she interacts with the citizens of the United States. As such examples demonstrate, Acadians do seem to become citizens by default in and through the poem itself. This literary assimilation extends from Longfellow's creation of unrealistic but mythic and biblical characters and settings.

From its "murmering pines and the hemlocks," to the "Druids of eld, with voices sad and prophetic," this "forest primeval" reflects its biblical and mythical precursors (*Evangeline* 1). Actually the "forest primeval" never existed in Grand Pré, where the land is flat and treeless, but Longfellow's Eden supercedes reality to paint a more romantic image of a lost land. As Tompkins writes in relation to Stowe's *Uncle Tom's Cabin* and other such typological narratives, "The setting does not so much describe the features of a particular time and place as point to positions on a spiritual map" (135).

Longfellow's work becomes sentimental when it emphasizes the central theme of patience and faith: "Ye who believe in affection that hopes, and endures, and is patient, / Ye who believe in the beauty and strength of woman's devotion, / List to the mournful tradition still sung by the pines of the forest" (*Evangeline* 16–18). The Prelude further asks of the "forest primeval," "Where is the thatch-roofed village, the home of the Acadian farmers,— / . . . Darkened by shadows of earth, but reflecting an image of heaven?" (9–11). And the peasant maiden's last words echo Acadian faith in God: "Meekly she bowed her own [head], and murmured, 'Father, I thank thee!'" (1380). *Evangeline* remains a lesson of Christian faith and hope for all Americans.

The vision of land as sacred, as illustrated in Longfellow's portraits of Canadian and Louisianian Edens, also utilizes religious images to frame the settlement of North America as a spiritual quest of a chosen people, again promoting American notions of land ownership. John Locke's theory of labor as the means of ownership is fulfilled in Longfellow's poem as the Acadians settle in Louisiana:

> Much they marvelled to see the wealth of the ci-devant blacksmith,
> All his domains and his herds, and his patriarchal demeanor;
> Much they marvelled to hear his tales of the soil and the climate,
> And of the prairies, whose numberless herds were his who would
> take them;
> Each one thought in his heart, that he, too, would go and do like-
> wise. (970–74)

Longfellow portrays the Acadians as settlers of virgin lands, similar to other New World colonists, who are given the right to own land full of promise.

Although Longfellow used the Acadian dispersal as a framework in which to write this poem, his main focus remains on Evangeline and her saintlike patience and endurance. Her name marks her ancestry with biblical associations of Eve and of angels. On November 28, 1845, Longfellow writes of his project: "Set about 'Gabrielle,' my idyl in hexameters, in earnest. I do not mean to let a day go by without adding something to it" (S. Longfellow, vol. 2, 25). "Gabrielle" was the original name of the heroine, but Longfellow quickly found himself debating which name would be best, a name that would come to signify, after a complicated history, *Cajun* in future years: "I know not what name to give to,—not my new baby, but my new poem. Shall it be 'Gabrielle,' or 'Celestine,' or 'Evangeline'?" (25). He decided upon Evangeline within a month, as evidenced by a January 8, 1846, entry that mentions the poem by that name. "Gabrielle" then became the hero's name Gabriel Lajeunesse, reminding readers of the angel of the biblical Annunciation of the birth of Christ. Both names reflect the author's typological project because they interpret Acadians as Christian models. By combining a tale of American settlement with biblical names and images, Longfellow marks Acadians as a people led by God to settle Louisiana. The Acadians' quest for a new home also mimics the Hebrews' exodus from Egypt and journey to the Promised Land.

In the Eden of the Acadians, Evangeline is the anti-Eve, ready and willing to undo the sin of her foremother by refusing temptation and by symbolizing heaven through her "celestial brightness" and "ethereal beauty" (*Evangeline* 78). In one passage, Longfellow even bestows Evangeline's saintliness onto the rest of the community: "Thus dwelt together in love these simple Acadian farmers,— / Dwelt in the love of God and man" (52–53). Clearly, Longfellow uses the Acadians as models for Christians everywhere. Lawrence Buell places this morality firmly within the framework of nineteenth-century American literary culture since the "growth of native literature and institutions after 1820, . . . especially in New England, was carried on with a degree of public vigilance and authorial self-consciousness about the *moral and social responsibility of art*" (*New England* 39, emphasis mine). Furthermore, the establishment of Evangeline, the faithful woman, as the reader's spiritual guide through the text and through life in general also follows from the literary context of Longfellow's time. After all, domestic fiction firmly entrenched women and children as the spiritual leaders through their lives and their deaths.[15]

From the title of the poem to its final words, Evangeline shines as a faithful and strong woman who refuses to allow circumstances to end her search for Gabriel. She "does not hesitate to roam throughout all of the known Americas in her quest" (Paratte, Foreword). Furthermore, "men do not have the main, nor the most beautiful role" in the poem (Foreword). An American ethnicity finds its ultimate image in the literary body of a woman who is "the embodiment of pride," "the soul of l'Acadie" (Foreword). By placing a woman character as the central focus of his work, Longfellow bestowed Cajuns with an origin myth complete with roots in female courage and faith. He also addressed the masculine notion of "Manifest Destiny" by placing a feminine face on the issue of national expansion. Once more Longfellow subtly addressed the national conflict with American Indians and slaves that abounded during his writing career through his creation of the seemingly uncomplicated and universal Evangeline.

Longfellow establishes his work on a spiritual plane that consistently frames the movement of the poem from Grand-Pré, Acadia, to Louisi-

ana, or from an initial Eden to a second Eden. In formulating her examination of Harriet Beecher Stowe's work in terms of a "typological narrative," Tompkins asserts that "this novel does not simply quote the Bible, it
rewrites the Bible as the story of the Negro slave" (134). One could as easily claim that *Evangeline* rewrites parts of Genesis and Exodus as the story
of the Acadian. Evangeline's purity and saintliness provide an example
for all readers since "human history [as depicted in these stories] is a continual reenactment of the sacred drama of redemption" (Tompkins 134).
During the 1840s and 1850s, sentimental fiction gained fame as a spiritual
guide for the American people. This work helped set cultural standards
and provide cultural guidance for its time. *Evangeline*'s message and its
popularity at the time of publication reflect this function of sentimental
fiction. Longfellow's purpose in creating such a heroine and in framing
her in Acadian garb addressed a similar cultural and spiritual function.

    Evangeline also illustrates its national scope by mapping the geo-
graphical expanse of the United States. H. L. Conolly, the minister who
told Longfellow the tale of divided Acadian lovers, confined his version
within New England boundaries, but, as John Seelye notes, Longfellow
"extend[ed] Evangeline's wanderings to include the geographical limits [in
1846] of the United States" (39). Longfellow's use of the United States' geographical expanse echoes journalist John L. O' Sullivan's Young American
promotion of "Manifest Destiny," a belief in America's God-given duty to
settle the West. In Part II.iii of *Evangeline,* Basil, the Acadian blacksmith
and father of Gabriel, speaks of Louisiana in terms of expansion: "Here,
too, numberless herds run wild and unclaimed in the prairies; / Here, too,
lands may be had for the asking, and forests of timber" (993–94). Here,
Acadians are already becoming American by claiming land as their own
and settling it regardless of the others who may have lived there before the
Acadian migration. As Seelye points out, "it is the blacksmith of Grand-
Pré, Basil Lajeunesse, who lends the first part of *Evangeline* a measure of
vital force, for he is the only Acadian who advocates resistance against the
British tyranny, a distinctively American note" (26). And it is Basil who
experiences a "characteristic American metamorphosis" by becoming an
"American Abraham," leading his people through his words of "expan-
sionist propaganda" (37). Finally, Longfellow chooses two names for his
main families that symbolize the newness and native hopes of America:
Lajeunesse, "youth," and Bellefontaine, "fountain of beauty."

    Evangeline may travel across the United States, but Longfellow relied
on histories and geographical studies, not direct experience, to create his

heroine's expansive journey. On January 7, 1847, Longfellow wrote, "Went to the library and got Watson's Annals of Philadelphia, and the Historical Collections of Pennsylvania. Also, Darby's Geographical Description of Louisiana.[16] These books must help me through the last part of Evangeline, so far as facts and local coloring go. But for the form and the poetry,—they must come from my own brain" (S. Longfellow, vol. 2, 74). Longfellow never claimed that his story of the Acadian dispersal was historically accurate. He simply placed Conolly's inspiring story into a new framework that spoke to the American desire for a national literature and the Acadian wanderers' place in it. About a year later, Longfellow writes, "I see a panorama of the Mississippi advertised. This comes very *à propos.* The river comes to me instead of my going to the river; and as it is to flow through the pages of the poem, I look upon this as a special benediction" (S. Longfellow, vol. 2, 67–68). This source for depictions of the Mississippi River itself and for the West was John Banvard's painting, "A Panorama of the Mississippi" (Wagenknecht 106).[17] The path the Acadians take to Louisiana in Longfellow's poem, although historically inaccurate,[18] remains significant because it places them on the Mississippi River, the body of water that became the core of the nation as the United States expanded westward. It also reflects the Louisiana Purchase and the importance of this purchase to national history because of the value of the river's mouth to the economic and military control of the nation.

Critics such as Carl Brasseaux have spent time researching the facts behind the Acadian dispersal and have detailed Longfellow's creation of what can be considered an "imaginative geography," a geography that relied on library sources and the author's imagination. Edward Said discusses imaginative geography as a process by which an outside imperial power assumes geographical knowledge of a culture or a place in order to control the colony, regardless of real distance between the colonizer and the colonized, by naming the indigenous population as Other to claim superiority over the colonized and to maintain boundaries of difference. Through the presence of this distance, the "mind's geography" can create its own meaning for the foreign place it has chosen to study (58). These discourses take the form of maps, historical documents, and literature. Longfellow's *Evangeline* uses a form of imaginative geography, not to set aside Acadians and their lands as strange and different, but to claim this people and their lands as American. *Evangeline* inverts the postcolonial impulse to define difference by assimilating Acadians into American culture.

By covering the entire geographical area of the nation, Longfellow

carefully constructed a work that spoke to contemporary American readers. Evangeline travels "Far in the West," where "Westward the Oregon
flows and the Walleway and the Owyhee" (1082). In this passage Longfellow recalls biblical images to address the plight of American expansion: "Over them [the lands of the West] wander the scattered tribes of
Ishmael's children, / Staining the desert with blood" (1095–96). Evangeline's journey finally ends in Philadelphia, "In that delightful land which
is washed by the Delaware's waters" (1252). Longfellow writes of the city as
a haven and a home for the wandering Acadian woman: "There from the
troubled sea had Evangeline landed, an exile, / Finding among the children of Penn a home and a country" (1259).[19]

Even before the Louisiana Purchase of 1803, Longfellow places Evangeline in the first capital of the newly formed nation and claims an American identity for her. In Philadelphia, Evangeline finally completes her
quest when she finds Gabriel, who is dying. Gabriel's last moments on
Earth are filled with memories of his Acadian home, but the lovers' journey has taken them far from their simple Acadian lives. As a "Sister of
Mercy" (1288), Evangeline nurses the sick through the "pestilence" that
"fell on the city" (1298). Through her nursing work she finally finds Gabriel, who is suffering from Yellow Fever. Upon his death, Gabriel "be-
held, in a dream, once more the home of his childhood; / Green Acadian
meadows" (1364–65). Longfellow solidifies his Acadian characters' American identity by carrying them to Philadelphia, choosing the birthplace
of the nation as the final resting place for the two Acadian lovers, solidly
binding Acadians to America:

> Still stands the forest primeval; but far away from its shadow,
> Side by side, in their nameless graves, the lovers are sleeping. . . .
> In the heart of the city, they lie, unknown and unnoticed. (1381–84)

The graves are unnamed and unnoticed because they rest in a Philadelphia churchyard, far from the community of Acadians in south Louisiana
from which Evangeline began her search for Gabriel.

Also binding Acadians and Americans together, Longfellow's poem
begins before and ends after the American Revolution but never hints that
the war took place. The Acadian dispersal occurred in 1755, and the "pestilence [that] fell on the city" signifies the Yellow Fever epidemic that at-
tacked Philadelphia around 1793 (*Evangeline* 1298). Evangeline's presence
in the capital city of the newly formed nation, especially because of her
own witnessing of British tyranny, actually speaks to her past and acts as a

foreshadowing of the coming war and the future democracy under which America would be built.

Although Longfellow created his own American version of Acadians in *Evangeline,* he did choose to portray some of their folkways, a move that Bauman would argue is a means of "salting [published] texts . . . to add a bit of [native] flavoring" (263). In truth, the passages that relate Acadian and Cajun folklore do add a bit of factual culture to an otherwise imagined people. In the poem, LeBlanc, an influential Acadian in Grand-Pré, "told [the Acadians] tales of the Loup-garou in the forest, / . . . And of the white Létiche, the ghost of a child who unchristened / Died, and was doomed to haunt unseen the chambers of children" (*Evangeline* 280–83). This passage includes the two folktales that Lyle Saxon's *Gumbo Ya-Ya* would record a hundred years later as popular among Cajuns around the middle of the twentieth century:

> There are even werewolves in Louisiana! Here they are known as *loup-garous,* and are the most dreaded and feared of all the haunts of the bayouland. . . . The *letiche* is the soul of an unbaptized infant who haunts small children in their beds at night, a wandering, restless young spirit from whom there is no peace. (190–91)

Evangeline's inclusion of these tales demonstrates Longfellow's familiarity with Acadian folklore. The poem also represents the translation of folklore to the written page in the same way Longfellow translates the story of the Acadian dispersal, as told by Conolly, to the pages of American literature. This translation can be a way of considering *Evangeline* as more than a misrepresentation of a people because it follows the common path by which folktales are decontextualized and recontextualized as demonstrated by Saxon's own focus on collecting and publishing folklore in English and for national and international audiences. So like all written and, thus, recontextualized folktales, *Evangeline* remains a reminder of the Acadian past regardless of Longfellow's creative revisions.

Although Cajun critics refute Longfellow's mythic portrayal of the Acadian past, no one can deny Longfellow's position as preserver of memory. Longfellow's work awoke the American publishing world to the history, however related, of the Acadian dispersal of 1755 and the consequent settlement in Louisiana. Ethnic criticism of the poem extends from its portrayal of the Acadians as English-speaking heroes of a romantic and pastoral American tale, regardless of their French language and identity and their Catholic religion. It is because of *Evangeline*'s story of a people almost indistinguishable from most Americans in their quest for a new home complete with family bonds and spiritual ties that the poem provided not only a basis for the assimilation of these different people into the popular American imagination, but also a foundation for regional identification with the tale.

Based on the popularity of the Evangeline myth in Louisiana, the poem remains a reminder of the Acadian past and as such has continued to evolve in south Louisiana into the symbolic memory of Acadian settlement in Louisiana, either because Louisiana authors were influenced by Longfellow's tale and its publishing success or because they wished to address the popularity of the poem as flawed because it does not rely on fact. Following the poem's publication in 1847, Louisianian Sidonie de la Houssaye wrote *Pouponne et Balthazar* (1888), which also relates the dispersal of the Acadians but does so from a perspective of Creole superiority.[20] Pouponne, the heroine of the story, is separated from her lover, Balthazar, during the deportation. After settling in Louisiana, Pouponne gains the friendship of a Creole woman who transforms Pouponne into a Creole lady. Balthazar returns and is reunited with Pouponne, but they both dismiss their Acadian past and accept the more elevated Creole way of life. De la Houssaye's literary significance arises from her work's claim as "family legend" and its less than flattering portrayal of Cajuns. This portrayal led Felix Voorhies to create *fakelore* through his publication in 1907 of *Acadian Reminiscences: The True Story of Evangeline* (Brasseaux, *In Search* 15).

According to Rita Ross and Carl Brasseaux, the Evangeline myth reached *fakelore* status when Voorhies's fictional tale was accepted as the factual story of the two Acadians Emmeline Labiche and Louis Arceneaux (Brasseaux, *In Search* 19; Ross 15–16).[21] Ross quotes Richard Dorson's explanation of *fakelore* as the "claiming of oral tradition to lend legitimacy to some other end," which includes the creation of cultural images that are necessary for the national identity of an inferior people, a category Acadian descendants filled by the end of the nineteenth century (15–16). Twentieth-century Cajuns faced ridicule that confirmed that any national respect for Evangeline did not extend to all of her descendants. By writing his own version of the Acadian dispersal myth, Voorhies refuted the concept of Cajuns as inferior and gave them a story of pride.

Voorhies claimed that his story of the Acadian dispersal came from his grandmother's oral account of the tragedy, an account that claimed a prominent place for south Louisiana, especially St. Martinville, as the meeting place of the divided lovers and the burial place of Emmeline, otherwise known as "Evangeline, or God's little angel" (Voorhies 84). This version of the Evangeline story not only demonstrates the process by which one claims authenticity through an oral origin, but it also guarantees for Cajun Louisiana recognition as a tourist destination. Through his study of Longfellow's influence on both Voorhies's creation and popular concepts of Cajuns, Brasseaux claims *Evangeline*'s significance for contemporary Acadian and Cajun identity even as he refutes its basis in actual Acadian history.

The path from *Evangeline*'s publication to the formation of Cajun memory marks the significance of a literary author's work to an ethnic community's need for national inclusion and cultural differentiation. An important point in this evolution of Longfellow's American myth is that Acadians in Louisiana had their own folktales and folk heroes long before Longfellow wrote the first word of this one poem. In his notes on Warren Perrin's study of *Beausoleil,* an Acadian and Cajun folk hero, Chris Segura argues, "In the beginning [Acadians] had many heroes and knew them quite personally, but the distances of time and geography, continuous ethnic persecution by humiliation and fragmented isolation had eroded their history" (Editor's Notes vii). He describes this loss as "a reluctance to remember" (vii), a reluctance that left Acadian descendants in Louisiana with only a memory of myth created by an American. With the growing national interest in Evangeline and her home in Louisiana, Acadian descendants began to recreate and revise the tale of Acadian dispersal and consequent settlement in Louisiana. When Voorhies published *Acadian Reminiscences,* complete with metaphors of paradise and a central theme of divided lovers, he offered the Louisiana Acadian descendants a means by which they could claim Evangeline without erasing personal pride in their Louisiana homeland and their cultural differences. Voorhies's work demonstrates the Cajun need to address the Acadian passage to Louisiana and their reliance on *Evangeline* to do so. Even if Voorhies's tale is an example of *fakelore,* as Brasseaux claims, it and other narratives of the dispersal remain significant examples of the need to remember and the loss of Cajun memory, or perhaps the need to alter memory to address contemporary issues, which follows a pattern similar to the decontextualization and recontextualization of folklore.[22]

Like Longfellow, Voorhies describes Louisiana as a paradise, but he also chooses to detail the beauties and plentiful bounties of Louisiana in contrast to the lands of Acadia. Longfellow establishes this perfect vision in order to parallel Grand-Pré with Louisiana and to mirror the previous Acadian situation in Nova Scotia because "They who dwell [in South Louisiana along Bayou Têche] have named it the Eden of Louisiana" (862). Departing from this mirror structure, Voorhies has the narrator name Louisiana the "Eden of America" and divides this perfect place from the "desolate" land from which the Acadians came (100). By confirming his homeland's and his culture's place in the nation, Voorhies was, in essence, depicting the Cajuns' American identity and their need to experience a spiritual connection with their Louisiana land. Longfellow created this bond to reflect American notions of spiritual righteousness in settling the future state of Louisiana, but Cajuns now view this bond as part of their identity since they became Cajuns by traveling to Louisiana and establishing a new homeland. By inverting the emphasis on place, Voorhies's work revises *Evangeline* by framing the dispersal narrative as a particularly Cajun tale, and not just as an Acadian and American story. His emphasis on Louisiana as a paradise and a new home for the dispersed Acadians relates the origins for Cajun ethnicity and makes such narratives demonstrative of twentieth-century Cajun perspectives of settlement and history.

With *Acadian Reminiscences,* Voorhies created a tale that he hoped would "awaken cultural pride" (Brasseaux, *In Search* 19) and ended up initiating a specifically Louisiana interest in the Evangeline myth. In Voorhies's version of the tale, "The narrator is a worldly wise matriarch who seeks to impress her young and impressionable grandchildren whom she considers guilty of ignoring their cultural and historical heritage and of embracing American materialism" (18). As *Evangeline* addressed the native literature argument and literary culture surrounding a New England poet, Voorhies's tale also speaks to a cultural situation, specifically the cultural surroundings of Cajuns fifty years later and the growing process of American assimilation.

Together Longfellow and Voorhies have shaped a myth of the Acadian tragedy of 1755, a myth that has encouraged the growth of tourism and other industries that benefited from national recognition. In St. Martinville, Louisiana, tourists can visit the Evangeline oak (where in his story Voorhies has Emmeline meeting Louis and learning of his marriage to another);[23] a statue of Evangeline; and, perhaps, a tour guide who is willing to repeat the story of the two lovers. Leona Guirard, the former curator of the Acadian House Museum and Evangeline State Park in St. Martinville, added her own ending to Voorhies's tale to create a more pleasing story for her tours. In her version, "the sound of the wind in the oaks behind the house is actually the reunited lovers whispering to each other" (Ancelet, "Elements" 126). This ending not only emphasizes Voorhies's change of *Evangeline*'s culmination by placing the burial mounds of the lovers in Louisiana, thus allowing for a boost to the tourist industry and for Louisiana's larger claim in Longfellow's tale—but it also shapes the ending to reflect a sense of continuity, even immortality, between the Acadian tragedy and the Cajun present. As far as Guirard is concerned, her changes are part of the history of the Evangeline myth "pointing to Longfellow's exercise of poetic license" (126). They also portray "[t]he continuing evolution of the Evangeline myth . . . indicat[ing] the legend's continuing vitality, even in the face of numerous, recent scholarly publications contradicting Longfellow's account of the Acadian migration" (Brasseaux, *In Search* 51). The story of Evangeline, in whatever form, has grown beyond any original tale or American author as it has become the dominant folktale of the Acadian dispersal and settlement in Louisiana. As Longfellow revised the tale to assume his own American agenda, so too have the Acadian descendants reshaped it to fit their own memories, or lack thereof, of a distant history.

Both within and without the community of Acadian descendants, in Canada and the United States, various adaptations of *Evangeline* exist as proof of Longfellow's continuing power over the imaginations of artists. A number of films based on the tale have been released, most famously Edwin Carewe's *Evangeline* (1929),[24] starring Dolores del Rio, who was the model for the Evangeline statue in the St. Martin de Tours churchyard (Brasseaux, *In Search* 41). Plays, operas, novels,[25] and many other artistic forms have captured Evangeline in a variety of representations. Longfellow may have used the Acadian tragedy to entertain a national public and guarantee fame for himself, but the Evangeline statue and Voorhies's tale of Emmeline Labiche address Cajun reclamation of the dispersal tale, a reversal that has made the bond between Longfellow and contemporary Cajuns both complex and necessary to understand Cajun identity. Carl Brasseaux argues, "Longfellow was self-consciously creating a usable past for Americans" (13). To prove how powerful this "usable past" is, all one has to do is travel to south Louisiana to witness the iconic Evangeline's story as the "memory" of a tragedy that led Acadians to Louisiana over two hundred and fifty years ago.

The criticism Longfellow's work faces among the Cajuns of south Louisiana proves that his patient, pure Evangeline may not sit well with everyone in the nation. This critique also proves, however, that even Cajuns cannot discuss their own history without referring in some sense, for better or worse, to the poem that began a flood of tourist activity and that created an American myth. Acadian descendants have also come to realize that their expulsion from Nova Scotia (1755) and their initiation into American citizenship via the Louisiana Purchase (1803) have encouraged them to become mainstream Americans. Acadians chose to settle in Louisiana, and Longfellow chose for them to become American literary characters because of this settlement. Through his work, Longfellow created an American myth that not only spoke to a unique New World experience and people, but that also remains a source for Cajun memory as an origin myth. If "No one can fully comprehend the literary culture of nineteenth-century America without coming to terms with [Longfellow's] work" (Buell, Introduction, *Selected Poems* xxxii), then no one can fully comprehend Cajun literary representation without coming to terms with Longfellow's *Evangeline.*

2. How to Become American

THE IRONY OF GEORGE WASHINGTON CABLE'S
BONAVENTURE

At a pivotal moment in George Washington Cable's *Bonaventure: A Prose Pastoral of Acadian Louisiana* (1888), the title character claims, "[I]n America you mus' be American!" (114). *Bonaventure* clearly promotes English language usage and public education as the means of guaranteeing Acadian assimilation to an American way of life, a necessary Americanization process in the mind of Cable, especially following the divisive Civil War and process of Reconstruction. This assimilation agenda pertains not only to a little known culture that would soon feel the aftereffects of national exposure, but also to the South in general. While Henry Wadsworth Longfellow chose to depict Acadians as American in many ways, Cable more accurately describes a people who remain different within their Louisiana boundaries, a difference placed at risk by the consequences of the war and Reconstruction. While writing to aid in the advancement of lower class Louisiana Acadians, Cable actually records popular notions of Acadian backwardness and simplicity alongside his descriptions of folkways and rituals. Although his intention may have been to improve the lives of Louisiana Acadians, Cable's novel, with its romantic notions of freedom through English usage, places the Acadian community firmly within American boundaries and endorses an assimilation process that ironically foreshadows the process by which Acadians became Cajun Americans.

Bonaventure claims that "Knowledge is power" (88), and knowledge of the English language is the greatest power of all in the nation. As the title character endeavors to spread this message to the Louisiana Acadians, many of the adults he confronts refute his instruction because of distrust of the assimilation process such education promotes. Not all adults are automatically against change, however. In the novel, one father who speaks in "strange French" tells his son Claude St. Pierre that he must attend school daily for two reasons: for his own future and for his father's future, because he passes his knowledge on to his father in the evenings. St. Pierre falls under Bonaventure's spell and so believes that education in English brings, in the teacher's words, "light, libbutty" (90), which points to an already shifting cultural foundation for the Acadians of Louisiana.[1] Framing English education as the means to liberty in the United States, Cable addresses American assimilation as a pathway to empowerment, not only for the Acadians, but also for the South. Through St. Pierre, an older Acadian man who readily recognizes the benefits of learning English, Cable allows this community a choice regarding such empowerment. By placing this recognition within the Acadian community itself, Cable promotes assimilation through education by choice, not by force, emphasizing his impulse to provide encouragement for improvement. This passage also emphasizes why Acadians were prime candidates for the assimilation process Cable promotes. Their "strange French" automatically establishes them as Other, as different not only from Americans in general, but from other southerners, including the Creole populations of Louisiana. According to Cable, Acadians could, if they chose to do so, elevate themselves beyond what he considered a backward and isolating past to become part of the American population. While he may have been offering empowerment, Cable foreshadowed the very shifts that would lead future Cajuns further away from their Acadian past, making cultural loss a central part of this assimilation process.

Cable's Acadian novel overlooks or romanticizes such realities of assimilation because of its place within the author's larger agenda of southern improvement. With its emphasis on American assimilation and its determination that English education is the key to this necessary process, *Bonaventure* argues for the betterment of the South through the negation of southern sectionalism. As he wrote in "Literature in the Southern States," Cable believed that the solution to southern economic and racial woes lay in national unity, in the dissolution of the "New South" and the promotion of the "No South" complete with no geographical or imagined boundaries between North and South ("Literature" 44).[2] To achieve this end, he argued that the South had to recognize itself as part of the United States. Public education, according to *Bonaventure,* is the central means of guaranteeing such recognition. The lower class and "strange" Acadians in the novel do begin to assimilate to American ways without resorting to claims of southern identification, a process made possible through English education. By claiming that such a people could become American, Cable was further admonishing the rest of the South for not doing so.

Cable's use of the Louisiana Acadians as an example for the South in general and for aristocratic Creole New Orleans in particular may stem from his previous experiences with Creole disdain. *The Grandissimes* (1880), his most famous novel, exemplifies Cable's daring critique of his home because it emphasizes Creole superstition and racism to endorse change in race relations. As he compounded his fictional and nonfictional protest into more daring stories and essays, Cable found himself ostracized more and more by the South. By 1885, Cable's depictions of race relations in New Orleans and his critique of Creole culture had gained him enemies among the Creoles in the city, especially the historian Charles Gayarré.[3] Cable, however, refused to leave Louisiana completely behind him even as he moved his family to the North.[4] Realizing the power of his previous work to incense the southern world, Cable did not abandon his message as much as he veiled it behind his representation of Acadian simplicity in *Bonaventure*.

In his endeavor to save his fallen homeland, Cable utilizes Acadian difference to promote American assimilation for the entire South, which he depicts through his translation of Acadian folkways and his encouragement of English usage as south Louisiana's first step toward becoming American. At the height of Cable's career, the South became a major setting for American regional fiction because of northern fascination with the area following the years of sectional conflict and the national need for unity. Northeastern publishers encouraged the southern local colorists to portray their homes in print, through which the North could then assume knowledge of the southern other. Richard Brodhead concludes that regionalism was a "means to acknowledge plural Americas. . . . this fiction produced the foreign only to master it in literary terms" (137), making it either American or Other.

While northeastern publishers endorsed local color as a means of understanding the South, the South itself still faced uncertain times as the North determined who and what would be identified as American. This identification caused shifts in Louisiana's unique social and racial systems. Virginia Domínguez dates the use of *creole* as a racial identity only after the Civil War (134). Before the war, the term referred to all people of French or Spanish descent born in Louisiana as a means of distinguishing Anglo-Americans from French-Hispanic Louisianians after the Louisiana Purchase in 1803. Barbara Ladd explains, "the white southerner's insistence that *Creoles* are 'white'—and only *creoles* (lowercase) are mixed—is intended to protect the southerner from being aligned too closely with former slaves or with colonialism in the New World" (xv).[5] She addresses these southern fears in conjunction with northern images of the dangerous southerner: "[T]he creole metaphor also marks the southerner as a dangerous border figure, someone who might look like an American and claim to be so (with greater fervor than other Americans at times) but who carries within him- or herself traces of the displaced and who might at some point act traitorously to undermine the progressive nation" (xvi). Although Ladd makes this argument through her discussion of southern writers and their redemptive narratives, this point also sheds light on the American publishing world following the Civil War and its interest in local color's representation of the South in fiction. The South and its Creoles (and even more so, creoles) threatened American nationalism for two reasons: they "represented an intermediate stage between European 'encroachment' in the New World and the development of a New World nationalism on British foundations," and they signified "linked black and white and red populations," with hints of interethnic identification (xvi). Ladd explains that the "newly intensified debate in the 1880s and afterward over the definition of *creole* reminds us that once again, in the post–Civil War era, the question of who might be or become an American had resurfaced, and the implicit racism of the US national mission made it once again necessary that the color line be reaffirmed" (29). Her assessment of Cable's fiction arises from his influence on other writers (who also wrote of a defeated South) through his representations of Louisiana racial and social divisions. By addressing such defeat through the Other, he distances it from the American past by claiming it as foreign: "In George W. Cable's postbellum generation, and perhaps largely through Cable's work and influence, there developed a tendency to represent the defeated South as 'creole,' and to attempt to read the reconstruction of the post-bellum white southerner in terms of the nationalization of white Creoles during the cession years" (28). Reconstruction pertained not only to the economic and political agenda by which the North punished the South in an attempt to reunify the nation, but it also involved the reconstruction of racial and ethnic boundaries, which shifted to allow for reunification through Americanization, according to northern norms, of a fallen South.

While Cable's theory of Acadian Americanization through English education endorses assimilation, his novel also records Acadian folkways and celebrates the sincerity and communality of the people. He fills his novel with phrases such as, "these illiterate and lowly ones" (24), while also claiming that "the day's coming when the Acadians will be counted as good French blood as there is in Louisiana! They're the only white people that ever trod this continent . . . who never on their own account oppressed anybody" (197).[6] Cable, in essence, found a means to save the Acadian people from their poor and lowly lives by giving them, in fiction, the opportunities provided by English education, which they could choose to embrace. This romantic notion of American uplift that acts as a veiled metaphor for the South in general taints Cable's version of life among Louisiana Acadians, but it also presents a telling history that will lead inevitably to the very Americanization process Cable promotes in his novel.

By employing his notes and ideas, collected in his Acadian Notebook, to translate Acadian culture into English for a national audience, Cable began to Americanize the group in his fiction. From his personal observations and recordings of Acadian folkways, taken while vacationing among Acadian communities throughout Louisiana in 1880,[7] Cable decontextualized, through transcription and translation, and recontextualized, through publication and distribution for an American audience, cultural ways in order to inform the American public about a particular Louisiana ethnic group.[8] Unlike Longfellow who relied on printed maps and oral stories removed from context, Cable studied the Acadians of Louisiana firsthand and took notes in his own handwriting, making his novel, which he claims "is my only fiction in which a well-filled notebook proved of any direct service" ("After-Thoughts of a Story-Teller"), a more immediate depiction of Acadian life as viewed by the author.

Through the use of his notebook, Cable framed *Bonaventure* as he had previously framed Acadian folkways, through English translation that had larger implications for the Acadians than realized by the American Cable. In *Lost and Found in Translation,* Martha Cutter focuses specifically on ethnic writers who use the trope of translation from their native tongues into English in literature as a means of bridging ethnicity and American identification. She concludes that such writers do so "to speak in a double voice that finally attempts to dismantle the line between a process of translation that colonizes and a process of translation that enriches" (16). This "double voice" that extends from "translation as trope" "concerns a struggle to transcode the meaning of ethnicity itself so that one can be both ethnic and 'American'" (5). Cutter's examination of this trope may revolve around ethnic writers, but it also enlightens our understanding of literature written by Anglo-Americans who began this translation process by collecting folklore and songs, translating such stories into English, and publishing such collections for mass distribution, making the Other part of American literature, a colonization process of which *Evangeline* is an example.

Cable wrote *Bonaventure* with the intention of enriching the lives of Louisiana Acadians since he believed that liberty in the United States extended from speaking English and identifying oneself as American. While Cable's promotion of English education extends from a desire to encourage Acadians, and the South, to become American as a means to empower them, his white, paternalistic perspective does not extend from within the ethnic community of which he writes. His promotion of English usage reminds today's readers of English-only debates that tore their native tongue from Cajuns in the early twentieth century[9] and that still plague ethnic groups in America today.[10] Cable's tale seems to colonize through Americanization. His translation of his character's native French dialect into an English dialect in the novel further promotes Americanization by making the Louisiana Acadian novel of assimilation an American story in the dominant language of the time.

The process by which Cable advocates for translation, through English education, may remind readers somewhat of the historic treatment of American Indian education. In his history of the American Indian boarding school experience, David Wallace Adams explains that "[i]n 1871, Congress officially confirmed the altered status of Indians: they were now deemed to be wards of the government, a colonized people" (7). No longer autonomous, the various American Indian groups now belonged, by law, to the United States government. According to Eric Cheyfitz, the process of colonization began with the transfer of Indian lands into European property through legal, contractual language used basically to steal the land from native groups (60). Translation can be and was used to colonize an Other in North America. Due to this new understanding of the colonized Other, the United States government began its promotion of American Indian assimilation through education, most evidently in off-reservation boarding schools such as the Carlisle School, founded by Colonel Richard Pratt in 1879, in Carlisle, Pennsylvania. Following the Civil War, white American attitudes toward American Indians began to shift as "Indian sympathizers who dubbed themselves 'Friends of the Indian'" began to envision a means by which to save the "savages" through education in American ways (Enoch 121). While the off-reservation boarding school was just one option, "Taking the Indians from the reservation, Pratt argued, was the only way for them to begin the three-step process toward civilization that required Indians to exchange 'savage' ways for 'civilized,' to forget their tribal ways to become individuals, and to silence their Indian voices and speak English" (121). In her discussion of Zitkala Ša's writings on her experience both as a student in a reservation school and as a teacher at the Carlisle School, Jessica Enoch argues that such letters and essays prove the power of one's ability to voice opposition in English, but they also demonstrate the consequences of such education. Zitkala Ša admits that her education leaves her with "no place in nature," as if she is "located somewhere on the borders of white and Indian worlds" (129), between her ethnic identity and American identification.

The belief in assimilation through education following the Civil War that the nation endorsed to "civilize" American Indians appears in Cable's novel as the key to improving upon not only Acadian simplicity, backwardness, and isolation, but also national unification in general. Whereas Colonel Pratt and others felt that to force assimilation was to save "savages" from themselves and "to silence their Indian voices," a true colonization process, Cable's agenda diverges in its more sympathetic and somewhat less critical representation of Acadians. Such differences in beliefs exist because while American Indians were always Other, Acadians, labeled "white" by Cable (*Bonaventure* 197), had the potential and the means to gain access to all things American, including upward mobility as already demonstrated in upper class Acadian society.[11]

To emphasize this point, Cable has Bonaventure converse in English with "a tattered negro," although "[f]ifteen years earlier these two men, with French accents, . . . would hardly have conversed in English" (73). This African American describes the Acadians for Bonaventure:

> Oh, dey good sawt o' peop', yes. Dey deals fair an' dey deals square. Dey keeps de peace. . . . Dey *does* love to dance, and dey marries mawnstus young; . . . I don't see fo' why folks talk 'gin dem Cajun'; on'y dey a lil bit slow. (76)

These words reflect popular stereotypes of the time regarding African Americans and Acadian descendants. The African American's words emphasize the misconception of *Cajuns* as ignorant and incapable of attaining education, and his dialect reflects popular notions of the time regarding African American ignorance, as captured in minstrel shows. This passage also touches on the close proximity between lower class Acadians and their African American neighbors. The use of *Cajun* in this passage reflects the dialect of African Americans and mimics their pronunciation of *Acadian,* a corruption that also follows Acadian dialect since, as Cable later points out in the novel, some Acadians' "English has been acquired from negroes" when both races worked the same jobs in sugar houses and such (139). Cable's field notes on Acadian speech include this connection between Acadian English and African American dialect: "Some of their inaccuracies may be attributed to the manners of the French-speaking black man" (Cable, Box 97, Folder 1).

Cable's novel captures the word *Cajun* in print to copy, as well as possible, the sound of Acadian and African American dialect and to indicate changes that are already occurring in south Louisiana.[12] As this usage of *Cajun* signifies, English became more dominant in Louisiana following the Civil War and Reconstruction. Realizing this already inevitable shift, Cable places Bonaventure in a position to offer Acadians the choice to learn standard English in a school setting, instead of using nonstandard phrases and words picked up by noneducated folk. By choosing such an education, the Acadians would be more recognizable as both "white" and American, two categories put into flux by the war and Reconstruction. This encounter confronts the realities of cultural change while also emphasizing the necessity of the Acadians to empower themselves through assimilation to American ways, and not to a southern past where such corruption of the national language occurred.

Cable's work does not necessarily extend from a typical colonization impulse since the assimilation process his fiction encourages seems to arise not from a need to control and to silence an ethnic other, but from a desire to provide the means by which such a group could improve its situation in life. Off-reservation boarding schools for American Indians enforced students' complete disavowal of their native culture;[13] however, Cable's method of assimilation, which still presented serious consequences to an ethnic community, offers English education as a choice for those who wished to be identified as American. While the public education system would be used in the twentieth century as a place for forcing Cajun assimilation through English usage, through an amendment to the Louisiana Constitution in 1921, Cable's fictional assimilation process endorses suggestion over force to convince the people that such improvement will work to empower them. Such a perspective on the Acadian situation may have developed through Cable's interaction with the people of whom he wrote.

While no one can deny that Cable's position as recorder places him firmly outside the ethnic community of Louisiana Acadians, his novel does attempt to teach the nation about Acadians by including in his fiction actual sections of his notes. The beginning of the novel even repeats the actual story of Governor Mouton's grandmother and her survival in Nova Scotia, a family history recorded in the notebook.[14] Governor Mouton's grandmother was affected by the Acadian exile by the British in 1755 (Acadian Notebook 131). As a widow with children, she "[h]eard of ensnaring of the people in the church, [so she] fled to woods where she lived on roots and berries for ten days" (Acadian Notebook 131). She then traveled to Louisiana and married and settled in Carencro, where she continued to be always hospitable to *Américains,* but never to English (Acadian Notebook 131).[15] *Bonaventure* begins with this same note of Acadian survival and strength stemming from memories of the dispersal:

> On that dreadful day, more than a century ago, when the British in far-off Acadie shut into the chapel the villagers of Grande Pré, a certain widow fled with her children to the woods, and there subsisted for ten days on roots and berries, until finally, the standing crops as well as the houses being destroyed, she was compelled to accept exile, to these prairies. Her son founded Vermillionville. Her grandson rose to power,—sat in the Senate of the United States. (3)

By opening his Acadian novel with the reminder of how and why this particular people have become part of the Louisiana landscape, Cable both records Acadian dispersal lore and carries it a hundred years into the future when a new challenge, the Civil War, faced the now settled and content Acadian descendants who were definitely Louisianians but not yet Americans.

To further mark the simplicity of Acadians, and thus their need for improvement, Cable writes in the novel that they were "living in unpainted houses, rarely seeing milk, never tasting butter; men who at call of their baptismal names would come forth from these houses barefooted and bareheaded in any weather, and, while their numerous progeny grouped themselves in the doorway one behind another in inverse order of age and stature, would either point out your lost way, or, quite as readily . . . ask you beneath a roof where the coffee-pot never went dry or grew cold by day" (*Bonaventure* 6). Such a people may be poor and simple, but they are also friendly and helpful, making them worthy and capable, in Cable's view, to become truly American while also remaining connected to their Acadian notions of community. Such a people were ripe for the improvement Cable prescribed.

The Louisiana Acadians offered the nation an image of a people in need of assimilation because of their un-American way of life. According to Carl Brasseaux, outsiders viewed Acadians as backward and ignorant for a multitude of reasons, including their lack of English usage:

> Because they were Southerners, they were 'debased and tainted' by their archaic and unjust social system as well as their climate; because of their different cultural and linguistic characteristics, they were perceived as inherently inferior; . . . because of their Catholicism, they were priest dominated . . .; because of their lack of formal education, they were ignorant (often stupid); because they failed to embrace materialism, . . . they were backward. Worst of all, because they refused to assimilate, they were un-American. (*Acadian to Cajun* 100)

Cable's solution to the disparaging national stereotypes of Acadians is simple: Americanization through English education. Instead of being "inherently inferior," he writes of a people more than capable of upward mobility; instead of being "ignorant" or even "stupid," he depicts a French-speaking ethnic group who can embrace English education if the use of English does not refer them back to their colonial days under the British empire; and, instead of being "un-American," he claims the potential for such a people to become American through English education. That he can imagine this process as advantageous for the people of whom he writes proves his honorable intentions, but his romantic and still limited depiction of Acadian Americanization fails to portray the actual consequences of assimilation on a people who were becoming Cajuns.

With a history "all poetry and pathos" and a character that is "brave, peaceable, loyal, industrious, home-loving" (197), Acadians, with their goodness and simplicity, are an ideal vehicle for Cable's message of assimilation and unification, perhaps because of their distance from Creoles and other dominant southern communities. He located a white ethnicity in America that he could praise even as his fiction raised them to higher status through assimilation and education, claiming them as future Americans through English translation. By using an ethnic community who refused to assimilate to either southern or American mainstream culture, Cable represents his nationalistic agenda without directly offending southerners in general, such as the Creoles, while still proving his theory of unification through Americanization. While others were disparaging the isolated Acadians, Cable chose to elevate them in national literature, while constructing a larger message of identification that favored an American way of life over a fallen southern culture.

Bonaventure is, in essence, the story of how Acadians could improve their economic and social status in life through assimilation. Cable focused on a lower class people who would not be offended, until decades later, with his representation of their culture because they were, for the most part, illiterate and French-speaking, thus incapable of reading his English work.[16] Cable, therefore, describes the people in both his notes and his novel as being full of "helpless ignorance" with "no spirit of adventure" (Acadian Notebook 152), building the basis for his story of uplift.

This tale of improvement also describes an innate pride within the people themselves. Much like the Creoles, Cable's Acadians share a pride in their heritage, as illustrated when the Acadian governor in the story meets Bonaventure Deschamps's mother as she enters Carancro.[17] Their exchange demonstrates Creole disdain for Acadians and Acadian pride in the face of this disdain:

> The ex-governor asks, "Widow, are you? And your husband was a Frenchman: yes, I see. Are you an Acadian? You haven't the accent." "I am a Creole," she said, with a perceptible flush of resentment. . . . "Yes, and, like all Creoles, proud of it, as you are right to be. But I am an Acadian of the Acadians, and never wished I was any thing else." (*Bonaventure* 3)

When he realizes that the mother can no longer care for her child alone, the ex-governor suggests she find residence in Sosthène Gradnego's home, which she does. She dies shortly after arriving in the town and her son Bonaventure is adopted by the Gradnegos. This tale of the orphan child is somewhat ironic in relation to Cable's other works because it suggests that the Creole Bonaventure is the redeemer of the Acadian people. This notion of Creole superiority over Acadians may stem from Cable's friendship with Sidonie de la Houssaye, whose own Acadian tale, *Pouponne et Balthazar* (1888), relates the story of the dispersal from the perspective of the author's Creole identity. In 1885, Cable conversed with de la Houssaye, a good friend, a Creole, and "his authority on the Acadians" (Turner 236). Departing from his earlier condemnation of the Creole population because of its love of ritual over progress and class over equal rights, Cable actually holds one of them up as a model for Americanization, but such a position only becomes possible because the Creole has been raised among

Acadians. Bonaventure develops into a model for Acadian improvement when the ex-governor suggests, "He ought to go to school" (8). "And Sosthène, half to himself, responded in an hopeless tone: 'Yass.' Neither Sosthène nor any of his children had ever done that" (8). The ex-governor, like Sosthène himself, recognizes Bonaventure as the "little Creole" (8), maintaining the child's different status even though he lives as an Acadian.

Such difference allows him to move safely between Acadian folkways and American progress, which is again ironic considering Cable's earlier depictions of Creole stubbornness to do so. By placing the Creole in an Acadian world and proving that he can belong, Cable's novel promotes cultural exchange and harmony, which have larger implications for Bonaventure as he becomes an educated man. As a Creole, Bonaventure also becomes a part of the Acadian community in which he lives. Through his situation within the community, he realizes the significance of becoming American, a realization that may not have been possible if he still lived among wealthy Creoles. His interstitial position within the community thus leads to his ability to bridge Acadian and American worlds, making his situation complicated and ironic on many levels. Such critics as Marcia Gaudet argue that *Bonaventure* depicts Cajuns "from the viewpoint of a cultural outsider" ("The Image" 77). She further explains her displeasure with Cable's placement of Cajuns below Creoles, because such a representation influenced later writers' depictions of the people as such, including Kate Chopin (77). Her argument arises from Cable's placement of the Creole Bonaventure as the savior of the Acadian people, which seems to confirm popular notions of Acadian inferiority of the time. While Bonaventure's Creole origin leads him to become the educational model for Acadians, Cable does not forget to admonish New Orleans Creoles for their aversion to assimilate, which he depicted in earlier works. At the end of the novel, Cable even places Acadian pride above Creole wealth and position as significant in the development of an American future for Louisiana. Through his story of a Creole who leads Acadians to a knowledge of English, and thus to American assimilation, Cable converts Creole stubbornness into leadership and proves, in general, the ability to become American, thus reversing the trend he witnessed and disparaged in the South. By doing so, a Creole, a member of the very group protesting change, becomes the symbolic leader of Americanization, in an ironic twist of Cable's pen.

Education and the national advances it promises first appear in the novel juxtaposed fittingly against the background of the Civil War, in which the character 'Thanase Beausoleil finds himself embroiled.[18] The Civil War proved to be the beginning of powerful changes in the South that greatly affected the lives of Louisiana Acadians, and later Cajuns. 'Thanase volunteers for Confederate duty, but only after soldiers attempt to conscript his father into service (*Bonaventure* 26).[19] In reference to this action, Cable condemns Confederate conscription when he has Sosthène name the forces of the army "*Diable!*" (25).[20] Thus 'Thanase fights for a losing cause only to save his father from fighting, and not for any loyalty to either side of the Civil War.

Bonaventure captures the changes occurring in the South following the Civil War, especially in its depiction of the Americanization process that affected Acadians on many levels.[21] Carl Brasseaux explains that "[s]corned by rival groups, abandoned by their own natural leadership element, and under mounting pressure to conform to the Anglo-American norm, poor Acadians were ill-equipped to meet the challenges of life in the postbellum South" (*Acadian to Cajun* 151). Forced to assimilate to some degree or remain economically impoverished and socially rejected, Acadians faced a period of great change in their cultural ways. Brasseaux argues that Reconstruction, in fact, "serve[d] as a major watershed in the society's metamorphosis from an imported culture into a distinctly local and modern cultural synthesis now called Cajun" (xii). The name *Cajun* even extends from the collision of Acadians and Americans since it "is fundamentally an anglicized form of the contraction ''Cadien,'" according to James Dormon (*The People* 33). By becoming more American, Acadians of south Louisiana became Cajuns, a unique ethnic group formed on United States soil. This ethnic formation occurred, to some degree, through exposure to American ways because Acadian assimilation caused cultural shifts that merged an Acadian past with an American present. As Shane Bernard explains, "Cajuns can be viewed, ironically, as the product of Anglo-Saxonism" because their forced dispersal from Nova Scotia by the British colonial government led to their eventual settlement in Louisiana, their interethnic relations with various other groups there, and their eventual American identification (*The Cajuns* xix). Bonaventure's role as Acadian leader through his support of education in English thus foreshadows the future national and ethnic identity of Cajuns.

During the war, 'Thanase is lost somewhere in the North, so Bonaventure sets out to find him and lead him home. This search for the Acadian man becomes a larger quest for Acadian improvement, a mission the curé understands, as represented in his advice to Bonaventure: "And learn English, my boy; learn it with all speed; you will find it vastly, no telling how vastly, to your interest—I should say your usefulness. . . . Make haste to know English; in America we should be Americans; would that I could say it to all our Acadian people!" (*Bonaventure* 44). Instead of viewing the Civil War as a dividing wall between North and South, the curé realizes the significance of unity and nationality in his Acadian parish. His plan for Bonaventure is for him to become a leader of the Acadian people, a position he can reach through his adventure outside of Acadian and Creole lands during his search for 'Thanase, which symbolizes Bonaventure's initial Americanization through his developing knowledge and usage of the English language. As he continues his journey further and further away from his south Louisiana and French-speaking borders, Bonaventure becomes fluent in English, a skill he is destined to share with his adopted Acadian people (45).

'Thanase eventually returns safely to his Acadian home and marries Zoséphine, Sosthène Gradnego's daughter. Following the wedding, Zoséphine becomes the model Acadian wife who was "her own housekeeper, chambermaid, cook, washerwoman, gooseherd, seamstress, nurse, and all the rest" (*Bonaventure* 66). Once interested in education along with Bonaventure, Zoséphine focuses all of her time and energy on 'Thanase and their household until, after three children and only a handful of married years together, 'Thanase is stabbed in a fight. Like every action in the novel, this death complements Bonaventure's opportunity to leave Carancro in order to teach another Louisiana community of Acadians. The first third of the novel ends with Zoséphine's solution of returning to the schoolroom, which frees Bonaventure not only to leave Carancro, but also to spread his message of American education. Her mother says, "You can go ahead and repair the schoolhouse now. Our daughter will want to begin, even to-morrow, to teach the children of the village" (72). Through the death of 'Thanase, Zoséphine and Bonaventure return once more to their educational vocations.

The death of 'Thanase opens a door to Acadian Americanization in the novel. His last name, Beausoleil, represents folk culture and heroism based on past struggles to escape British tyranny in Nova Scotia. Joseph Broussard *dit* Beausoleil, an Acadian folk hero, was called such because of his flaming red hair. After the 1755 dispersal, some Acadians remained in Nova Scotia, with as many as five thousand hiding in the woods (Dormon, *The People* 13), while others simply lived in areas where deportation did not occur. As one of "5,000 in all [who] escaped into the wilderness" instead of answering the demand of Governor Lawrence to gather in wait for forced deportation, Beausoleil led militia forces against the British army in the area (15). In 1764, he led a group of Acadians forever from their homes, finally settling in Louisiana in 1765, one of the first Acadian settler groups to reach that area (Perrin 38). According to Warren A. Perrin, "*Beausoleil* emerged from the Acadian expulsion as the only Acadian folkhero" (57), a hero who consistently fought to prevent assimilation. This battle against assimilation becomes symbolic in Cable's work because of his promotion of translation to English as the cornerstone of his larger Americanization agenda. Cable's novel does not remain trapped in this past battle between British forces and Acadian folk in which assimilation became a means of domination and cultural oppression, but turns instead to his present concerns and solutions to Acadian illiteracy and backwardness through the move from Acadian French to standard American English. By murdering the fictional Beausoleil in the first third of the novel, Cable chooses to put away the Acadian past represented by their native language so that the people may move into an American, thus English-speaking, future. As the model for folk culture and its struggle against assimilation through the reminder of the Acadian past within his surname, 'Thanase must die so that education in English, and thus assimilation, can become a reality for the community and replace this "Acadian ruggedness" (*Bonaventure* 71).

Ironically, the Beausoleil of the novel does not live up to his namesake's adventurous spirit and rebellious actions: 'Thanase chooses settlement. Meanwhile, Bonaventure, whose name means "the good adventure," refuses to settle by questing after better conditions and higher educational opportunities. Cable may kill off the Acadian past, but he rewrites the historical Acadian quest for home as Bonaventure's quest for improvement, which leads him toward English education and away from Acadian isolation. In essence, Cable's novel advocates for Americanization and the change it offers for what he considered an improved way of life for the people. Unfortunately, such Americanization did change Acadian culture in ways that may have offered advantages to the people but that also erased or altered irrevocably past folkways.

While the first third of the novel promotes Acadian assimilation through education in English, the second part, "Grande Pointe," addresses the Acadian community's reaction to such change. When Bonaventure enters the town and greets the Acadians he immediately reveals "his preference for the English tongue, and to this many could only give ear" (*Bonaventure* 82). He is determined to teach the town to read and speak in English because it is the national language. He even considers his profession as a duty to one's country: "[I]s not the schoolmaster the true patriot? Shall his honor be less than that of the soldier?" (83). Once again, Cable places the future above the past by favoring the educator over the soldier, in essence attempting to push the Civil War aside for the betterment of the people, which can only occur, in his mind, through Americanization.

Cable does not make Bonaventure's quest unproblematic by acknowledging local distrust of English-only public education through certain characters. In his notebook, he explains that Acadians harbor an "old resentment against English [that] prompts withholding the child[ren] from public schools where English is taught" (Acadian Notebook 165). Furthermore, the Acadians "[d]on't trust or follow *Américains,* save exceptionally" (Acadian Notebook 111). Following the tensions faced while living in Nova Scotia and the 1755 forced dispersal by the British government, Acadians had a legitimate reason for feeling skeptical about anyone who claimed authority over their lives, especially English speakers. Such distrust of English stemmed from memories of past horrors and injustices served based on French usage and a Catholic belief system. In reality, many Acadians did not view such assimilation, and especially English usage, as a source of freedom. James Dormon confirms that the Cajuns themselves "persistently refused to make the necessary compromises and concessions to Anglo-American ways that would enhance the potential of their upward mobility" (*The People* 43). Such skepticism regarding the Americans and their English education as threats to Cajun culture arises as well in the community portrayed in Cable's novel of Acadian life, obstacles he has Bonaventure overcome through such romantic notions of freedom and salvation that pertain to an American, not a Cajun, point of view. Cable attempts to resolve such tensions by claiming English as the American language, and one that offers users a sense of freedom, although such a notion extends from an Anglo-American nationalistic understanding.

In the novel, an Acadian critic named Chat-oué, a man who "saw no harm in a little education, but took no satisfaction in the introduction of English speech" (*Bonaventure* 95), demonstrating the deep distrust of English among Acadians, calls Bonaventure a "*socier!*—Voudou!—jackass!" and leads the battle against the school (97). In answer to this battle cry, Bonaventure realizes his duty as in relation to a "protector's care for his Acadian sheep. . . . He believed a sudden overdose of enlightenment would be to them a real disaster, and he proposed to save them from it by the kind of management they had been accustomed to" (98). Like Chatoué, the priest from College Point becomes Bonaventure's most dangerous critic. He refuses to understand English education as anything other than "American ideas" that will place the Acadians under the control of "Yankees!" whom he claims write the very books used to educate the Acadians (98). Furthermore, he argues that education breeds "Discontent. Vanity. Contempt of honest labor. Your children are going to be discontented with their lot" (99). When he realizes that he has still not convinced an Acadian neighbor that English education will harm the community, he threatens to "preach somewhere else on the thirteenth Sunday of each quarter, and let Grande Pointe go to the devil" (100). If, in accordance to Cable's notes, Acadians are "All Roman Catholics. . . . Great church-goers even in bad weather" (Acadian Notebook 111), then a priest's threat to abandon the community's spiritual guidance has major consequences.

In the face of this threat, Bonaventure holds to his belief in the coming of American education as the long-awaited moment of freedom for the Acadians:

> [T]he day of liberty which had come to the world at large a hundred years before had come at last to them; that in France their race had been peasants; in Acadia, forsaken colonists; in Massachusetts, Pennsylvania, Maryland, Virginia, exiles alien to the land, the language, and the times; . . . and for just one century in Louisiana the jest of the proud Creole . . . and the competition of unpaid, half-clad, swarming slaves. But that now the slave was free, the school was free, and a new, wide, golden future waited only their education in the greatest language of the world. (101)

By writing this catalogue of discrimination, Cable reveals his own sympathy for a people who have suffered throughout the past generations and his own version of redemption for such a people. He names them as "forsaken," until this "golden" moment of freedom presented by the Civil War and made accessible through the English language. This passage in the novel reflects Cable's understanding of Acadian suffering while also establishing such suffering as a basis for future advancement, one defined by American standards. His answer to Acadian discrimination and abuse remains secure within his belief in English education. According to Bonaventure and his creator, the greatest hope for Louisiana Acadians resides in their becoming American by choice. What Cable viewed as salvation for the Acadian people is an American perspective not auto-matically shared by those of whom he wrote. Bonaventure is his vision of the nineteenth-century hero for Acadians because of his ability to bridge Acadian and American cultures. By writing that English is the "greatest language in the world," Cable offered Acadians what he believed was the means of achieving American identity, and thus American freedom.

Although the priest threatens Grande Pointe with spiritual abandon-ment to the devil, an even greater threat to tradition and ritual hovers in the background. When a surveyor speaks to St. Pierre about the ad-vantages of education, "you can't keep railroads away from a place long, once you let in the public school and teach English" (*Bonaventure* 112), the town protests in English, although they protest English education, that "Ed'cation want to change every thin'—rellroad—'migrash'n [migration]" (113). Such use of an English dialect represents both Cable's translation of Acadian French to English for his American audience and the already changing linguistic practices of the ethnic group as it becomes, inevita-bly, more American. Bonaventure disagrees by holding strong to his mes-sage that "in America you mus' be American! Three Acadians have been governor of Louisiana![22] What made them thus to become? . . . 'Twas Eng-lish education!" (114). Bonaventure claims Acadian history as a founda-tion for Americanization through English education because he offers Acadians as testimony to knowledge's power, specifically the knowledge of the English language. Cable clearly confirms his message that transla-tion into English can empower Acadians in social and economic ways that may benefit the community at large. Such knowledge does not have to be used against Acadians if the people can wield it for themselves by gaining positions of authority. In such cases, the Acadian no longer remains "the jest of the proud Creole" because he can become the governor of the same Creole.

In truth, these Acadian governors, including Mouton whose family history of the 1755 dispersal opens the novel, win power by dividing from their lower class and poorer Acadian brethren. Dormon even argues that such leaders "were systematically co-opted by the Anglo-dominant hege-monic system that controlled the larger system of which they were part. They could cross the boundary, learn the English language and accept the ways of 'others,' gain status and prestige by process of Americanization" (*The People* 43). The Mouton family is even Dormon's example of such an upward rise in status. Cable's argument for Americanization through English education as the means of achieving upward mobility proves accurate, but as an American he failed to understand the cost to the ethnic group of this assimilation process.

While Bonaventure firmly argues for an identification of the Acadians as American if they wish to remain within the boundaries of the United States, the townsfolk are not yet convinced by his message. Instead of throwing Bonaventure immediately out of the town, the Acadians agree to a challenge. If the superintendent of schools appears in the schoolroom one day, Bonaventure and his students must perform perfectly for him. If but one mistake is made, the school will be closed. Bonaventure gladly takes up the challenge and wins it, but his students do not perform for the superintendent.

In an attempt to trick the schoolteacher, the townspeople bring in George Washington Tarbox, a traveling salesman of the "Album of Universal Information," to play the role of the superintendent. This character's name signifies both the first president of the United States in a novel of Americanization and the name of the author himself and his role in the modernization of Acadians through the dispersal of knowledge.[23] Cable uses Tarbox to confirm the necessity of English education to Acadian culture. Tarbox acts the part and passes the students, finally admitting, "I came out here to show up that man as a fraud. But what do I find? A poor, unpaid, half-starved man that loves his thankless work better than his life" (*Bonaventure* 135). As his reward, Bonaventure remains in Grande Pointe educating the children and marries his prize pupil. Through Bonaventure, Cable has won at least a fictional victory for these Louisiana people by making them finally accepting of change through their knowledge of the English language, a knowledge they have gained by choice.

"Au Large," the third part of *Bonaventure,* recalls the story of Claude St. Pierre and the consequences of American education and English usage on the once-isolated Acadian community that is becoming American, a process that creates a double bind for future Cajuns and immediate consequences for the Acadians of whom Cable writes. This section of the novel also relates the marriage of the American Tarbox to the Acadian Zoséphine. Her first marriage was one of Acadian tradition and ritual, but her second marriage crosses the Acadian-American boundary and proves her acceptance of Americanization. Once again, the novel places the folk culture and hero in the past in favor of an American future as the surname *Beausoleil* is replaced with *Tarbox.* This marriage proves that the Acadian and the American can live in harmony to the benefit of both.

Cable promotes the same message of harmony through the character of Claude St. Pierre. Through Claude's experience outside of his hometown and his rise in social status, Cable further emphasizes the benefits of English education. Claude finds employment under a surveyor, who instructs him in mapmaking. St. Pierre had long known the geography of the area, which he passed on to his son. With the surveyor's skills, Claude combines his father's practical lessons with formal means to create maps of south Louisiana areas (*Bonaventure* 174). Although his father's pirogue was his first schoolroom, since St. Pierre "knew every spot of land and water for leagues around, like a bear or a fox would know the region about his den" (276), now Claude moves beyond the swamps to learn larger lessons of life. "Claude, who did not know his letters then, was rising—nay, had risen—to greatness! Claude, whom once he would have been glad to make a good fisherman and swamper, or at the utmost a sugar-boiler, was now a [*sic*] greater, in rank at least, than the very schoolmaster" (182). By marrying the practical and experiential wisdom of his father with his English education, Claude succeeds in his mapmaking position. His success stems from this between space, this overlap of knowledge from his Acadian upbringing and his English education, making it a prime example of how such overlap could benefit Acadians.

Progress does indeed lead to better opportunities, but these opportunities lead to divided families as the younger generations move away from their homeland to improve their situations in life. Although proud of his son and supportive of English education, St. Pierre, nevertheless, asks Bonaventure, "Why you di'n' tell me ed'cation goin' teck my boy 'way from me?" (183). After talking to Bonaventure about the need to give one's education back to the larger community, St. Pierre agrees to allow Claude to rise in the world and decides, "I goin' *quit* Gran' Point' and give myself, me, to Claude" (187–88), which he does. And so Cable resolves the tension between generations through the simple solution of having the father follow the son outside of his Acadian home, a solution that does not address the significant consequences felt as Acadian and Cajun youth became more American in later decades. The earlier statements of the townspeople, such as "Your children are going to be discontented with their lot!" (99), proved true through history as more and more Cajun children grew up and moved away from home and away from traditional Cajun occupations of fishing, hunting, and farming.[24] Cable may gloss over this reality with his pastoral sense of the father-son bond, as depicted through Claude and St. Pierre, but historians such as Brasseaux and Shane Bernard, among others, prove the fictional townspeople's words to be more accurate through their studies of the emergence and Americanization of Cajun culture, again highlighting Cable's romantic notions and American agenda.

The lower class Acadians are not the only Acadian descendants mentioned in the novel. Marguerite, Zoséphine's daughter, travels to New Orleans where she resides with a family who may speak perfect English and take "great pains to call themselves Creoles," but who "knew well enough they were Acadians" (*Bonaventure* 204). In separate notes on Acadians that are not included in the Acadian Notebook, Cable writes of a host who says of Acadians, "They are a good people. . . . Honest, peaceable, sober, but unaspiring and . . . improgressive!" In response, the guest "is somewhat surprised to hear, next day, a little farther up or down the coast, that his host of the night before might have mentioned, but probably forgot at the moment, that on one side of his house—possibly on both—he is, himself, Acadian" (Cable, Box 97, Folder 1). The story of Marguerite's rise in social status through her involvement with New Orleans society is thus framed within the story of one Acadian family's rise to upper class status through sugar and rice plantations (*Bonaventure* 204–5). Never forgetting his previous rejection of and by New Orleans society, Cable has Marguerite assess her newly discovered associates as sometimes "unaccomplished fathers, stupid mothers, rude sons and daughters" (206), reminders that maintain her rural goodness and family piety. In a later chapter, Tarbox even warns Claude, "But don't go into the down-town part [of New Orleans]; you'll not like it; nothing but narrow streets and old buildings . . . unprogressive—you wouldn't like it. Go up-town. That's American" (236). Through a portrait of the Acadian rise to Creole status that is juxtaposed against Claude's rise to American status, *Bonaventure* promotes American identification above and beyond the "old-timey" Creole ways (236). Even after living amid Creoles in New Orleans society, Marguerite emphasizes, "*Je suis Acadienne*," capable of becoming an American in Cable's view but never to recognize herself as Creole, or even southern (296).

With its American themes and story of assimilation, *Bonaventure* remains Cable's concept of the "No South," dominated by English education. In many ways, the Acadians were his test case, his key to proving the opportunities that would extend to those southerners who finally identified themselves as American. By making Acadians capable of assimilating to an American way of life through English usage, Cable not only used them for his own purposes, but also wrote them into American literature in a way that reached beyond Longfellow's idealistic poem. Like Longfellow, however, Cable also wrote from an American perspective of an ethnic group barely understood by the nation. While Cable pulled from personal observation and translation to build a story of uplift for the Louisiana Acadians, his notebook and his novel still remain controlled by American notions of difference and assimilation, foreshadowing the process by which an isolated ethnic community would indeed become American in future years. From Cable, Chopin would take the next step in transforming Acadians to Americans, even as she, like Cable, continued to do so from an outside perspective that always recalls the Acadian status as Other capable of becoming American, a process by which Acadians in south Louisiana became Cajun.

3. *The Awakening* Awakened
CAJUN IDENTITY AND FEMALE SEXUALITY IN THE FICTION OF KATE CHOPIN

Beginning in the late 1880s, Kate Chopin created a literary Louisiana abounding in class and race tensions. Focusing on the intersections of Creole, Acadian, and African American cultures, she wrote of a complex social structure affected by the process of Americanization following the Civil War. Although her depictions of Creoles, Creoles of Color, and African Americans remain interesting to critics studying ethnic representation in literature, her Acadian characters are particularly fascinating because of their racial and class ambiguity, which allows them to shift between identity categories.[1] Acadians, now calling themselves 'Cadians by the time Chopin began her literary career,[2] could and did shift in Chopin's literature in a way that African Americans and Creoles, black or white, could not. Chopin's fiction benefited from her recognition of the interstitial subject position of 'Cadians, somewhere between white aristocratic Creole and black Louisiana cultures, questioning both social and racial classifications.[3] Through her 'Cadian characters, Chopin also discovered a space of literary freedom for herself. In a climate of American confusion over how to code Acadian descendants, Chopin used this ambiguity to create her stories of female desire, which questioned the boundaries set by genteel publishers of the time. By incorporating Acadian characters into her fiction, Chopin joined Longfellow and Cable in recording shifts in the literary Americanization of Cajuns while simultaneously utilizing this character to reflect her own conceptions of human freedom. Chopin turns a romantic stereotype into a tool for creating a space in which female sexuality can be discussed in American fiction through her use of the Cajun interstitial position.

National confusion over how to categorize Cajuns by class and race stems from the collision of French and Spanish Louisiana colonial social divisions with the American bipartite structure of white and black racial categories. With the Louisiana Purchase in 1803, Americans began to settle in larger numbers in the new territory. Following the Civil War, these numbers increased. American settlement caused conflict over how to redefine such terms as *Creole* and *Cajun,* since exposure to Americans encouraged Louisiana's mixed population to identify as American.

Before the Civil War, Louisiana contained various subdivisions within racial categories.[4] These various categories further complicated clear class divisions since Creoles of Color were usually economically above Cajuns. In this complex categorization, the Cajuns also arose as interstitial figures who fell between categories because of their nonblack but definitely lower class status, thus questioning the social structure of racial and ethnic divisions. Chopin's racial and social representations allow for movement between categories, which then allows for her ultimate questioning of social constructions of feminine desire. To comprehend Chopin's purpose in representing Cajuns, one must first understand her racial representations and their power to deny the reality of strict categorization. Bonnie James Shaker notes that "what [Chopin] was rushing to achieve was the designation of whiteness for specific groups of people, a designation that conferred not only social preferment but also civil protections and political enfranchisement" (*Coloring Locals* xii). To better emphasize why this distinction is significant during Chopin's literary career and during this period in Louisiana history, one must first understand the shift in meaning of the term *Creole* between antebellum and postbellum years. According to Shaker, *Creole* was a "term [that] was used to describe people along the entire spectrum of the color line. [It] bespoke no particular social or economic class, either," until after the Civil War.

> Louisiana's "white" French and Spanish American population set into motion the fiction that the term "Creole" only ever referred to those (white) Louisiana residents of pure Gallic or Spanish descent. Because Louisiana's formerly legalized tri-caste system of white/free colored/ slave had been abolished, people of virtually all shades . . . engaged in a frantic claim to "whiteness" to guarantee their social preferment and political entitlement. (Shaker 29)[5]

Before the war, Louisiana's multi-caste system complicated the simple division of people into white or black categories. Chopin's work not only captures this unusual system but also uses it to question further social standards of her time.

Following the Civil War, Louisiana's unique social system was overwhelmed by the need to assimilate to American standards, which George

Washington Cable describes in *Bonaventure,* and this change caused much confusion over how to code Louisiana communities that fell between American divisions. Creoles fought through this confusion by claiming the purity of their white, upper class status, regardless of their loss of wealth because of the war.[6] Upper class Acadians also established their white identity by assimilating to Creole ways even before the Civil War, as demonstrated in Cable's Acadian Notebook and novel.[7] Meanwhile, Cajuns, who were lower class and French speaking, fell prey to American and Creole labels and became an ambiguously categorized people. In Chopin's fiction, Cajuns find themselves located between racial and class divisions, and their only means of rising in either division is to identify as American and white.

Cajun location somewhere between white and black and between class categories shifted Acadian representation from Longfellow's saintly Evangeline, from Cable's depiction of American assimilation, and from both Longfellow's and Cable's definitely white categorization of Louisiana Acadians, since it complicated the figure of the Acadian in literature. Chopin's 'Cadian characters enact a rebellious battle that veils one of their creator's ultimate purposes: to question social constructions of female desire. By pushing against gender and social boundaries, these characters also, perhaps inevitably, question racial identifications in their shifts among supposedly concrete categories.

Significant to any study of the literary Americanization of Cajuns, Chopin's 'Cadians also record in literature a shift in meaning and in identification as Acadians came to be called *Cajuns*[8] by the American public while maintaining their own pronunciation of Acadian, 'Cadian or 'Cadien (pronounced Ca'jin), to refer to themselves (Dormon, *The People* 33). As is evident in Chopin's work, Cajun interstitial social and cultural positioning also refers to popular American identifications of the Acadian descendants as they evolved from Acadians to Cajuns in American history and fiction.[9] Between the nineteenth and twentieth centuries, this interstitial subject position refers as much to the temporal space between Acadian and Cajun identification as to racial and social spaces. Chopin's use of *Cajun* as a pejorative word in the stories "In Sabine" and "A Gentleman of Bayou Têche" begins to shift the definition of Longfellow's Acadians in terms of both American familiarity and categorization as they evolve into more ambiguously racial and social characters than those revealed in earlier fiction.

Born in St. Louis to a Creole French mother and an Irish father, Kate

O'Flaherty grew up in a society that included Catholic school and French lessons. After marrying Oscar Chopin in 1870, Kate Chopin moved to New Orleans with her husband to begin a new life as a wife and mother. Still maintaining close ties to her mother in St. Louis, Chopin nevertheless absorbed the Creole ways in the Crescent City, filing away memories that she used in later tales. In 1879, Oscar Chopin decided to move his family back to his childhood home in Cloutierville, Louisiana, where his family owned a plantation, once complete with slaves.[10] Oscar suddenly died on December 10, 1882, leaving his wife with six children and a $12,000 debt to pay (Toth 93). Strapped to the land, Kate Chopin became a plantation mistress who fulfilled her family's financial needs before returning to St. Louis for good in 1884.[11]

Chopin may have left Louisiana and its people behind her, except for annual visits, but she retained affection for the place and its rich mixture of cultures. Although her husband's debt had been paid in full, Kate Chopin continued to think and act as a businesswoman when she began depicting her husband's homeland for national entertainment. With the rise of local color, due in part to national endeavors to unify the recently torn nation after Reconstruction ended, and a fascination with regionalism, writers including Mark Twain, Joel Chandler Harris, Grace King, and George Washington Cable staked literary fame on their portraits of life in the South. With the conjunction of regional space and ethnic identity in contrast to the dominant image of Americans, 'Cadian characters provided Chopin with a perfect trope to comment on themes otherwise regarded as improper by American publishers of the time. Since Cajuns were not a part of the higher social order, they did not directly threaten societal norms; therefore, they provide possible spaces of freedom from societal restraints. Louisiana itself offered her a backdrop of liberality and exoticism that allowed for rebellious renderings of female desire.

Chopin's stories remain examples of regional fiction, but they also contain larger implications for the nation in terms of literary movements and identity debates. Kathryn McKee's "Local Color" entry in *The Companion to Southern Literature* states that as a literary genre local color "appealed to women nationwide because it sanctioned an interest in what they knew best—everyday life in the area in which they lived" (451). This was soon categorized as a feminine interest along with the rise of realism and naturalism, as captured in the novel. This literary movement occurred in conjunction with the rise of class friction, which Amy Kaplan demonstrates through her discussion of the railroad strikes of 1877 and the Haymarket riot of 1886 (20). In the midst of this class conflict, Chopin writes of Cajun assimilation and racial confusion. With labor agitation followed the notion that the agitators were foreign, Other, making it even more necessary for Chopin to depict south Louisianans as American so that they would not be associated with "all things *different* from a standard, middle class, white, Anglo-Protestant 'American' code of conduct" (Shaker, *Coloring Locals* 21). Simultaneously, William Dean Howells, an influential magazine editor during Chopin's career, "was in fact actively feminizing short story writing as he worked concomitantly to masculinize novel writing" (6).[12] By the 1890s, Howells, in essence, determined that writing short stories constituted a hobby for women, and he emphasized the literary merit and more outstanding achievement of male novelists, making Chopin's endeavor to name Louisianians as white even more significant because it also became her means of claiming a fictional space free of these male-dominated notions of literary achievement. Chopin used the romantic stereotype of the Louisiana Acadian, made popular by Longfellow, and turned it into an ideological opportunity for herself to refute Howells's diminishing concept of women's fiction. The Cajun became her space of freedom from patriarchal publishing standards.

Chopin may have foregrounded the theme of female desire in her fiction, but she also addressed racial and social divisions in south Louisiana. Her 'Cadian characters move between these divisions and in doing so, question social structures. Today's readers may be confused by this movement, but Chopin constructed 'Cadians as interstitially situated among Creoles and African Americans to reflect racial and social uncertainty that abounded in post-Reconstruction Louisiana. Today's literary debates regarding Chopin's racial sympathies and ethnic categories parallel the confusion among Louisianians themselves following Reconstruction and the necessity of claiming *whiteness* for those who finally answered to American identification.[13] Chopin's work also reflects changing notions of female identity in the late nineteenth century. By first clarifying her 'Cadian characters' ambiguity in relation to American social and racial norms, Chopin establishes her means of voicing personal disagreement with popular contemporary notions of American womanhood. Calixta, the heroine of "The Storm," achieves sexual freedom through adultery while married to a 'Cadian, which allows her to move across racial and social boundaries because of her ambiguous social and racial position as a 'Cadian wife. Calixta illustrates Chopin's use of popular American notions of Acadian identity at the end of the nineteenth century as a tool for addressing female desire.

Chopin's use of Cajun interstitial subject positioning reinforces her message of female desire by questioning socially accepted gender and racial roles. This interstitial position can also refer to Chopin herself because of her own rebellion against simple definition as a local colorist. Addressing Chopin's rebellion, Judith Fetterley and Marjorie Pryse distinguish between women's regional writing and local color in their introduction to *American Women Regionalists, 1850–1910,* in order to encourage more complex readings of American women's fiction. With this work, Fetterley and Pryse demonstrate how women's writing denies male definition, which reflects Chopin's creative use of regionalism to address daring issues, such as women's sexuality. They use Chopin's refutation of the local color category,[14] along with their own bases of beliefs, to organize a feminine literary tradition separate from, yet similar to, the masculine local color genre. They title their new division "American woman regionalism," a female literary tradition beginning with Catherine Sedgwick and continuing through the work of Willa Cather (xiii–xiv). Fetterley and Pryse, in essence, identify a tradition and heritage of American women's writing, in which Chopin plays a significant part. In various ways, this establishment of a possible new division in literary history acknowledges how Chopin's literary course diverged from typical male categories because of her need to express a deeper meaning of freedom for women, a need perhaps initiated by the American women writers who came before her.[15]

It is necessary to address American women's regionalism in conjunction with local color's popularity in order to place Chopin in relation to the literary and historical context of the Genteel Tradition, in which she refused to be contained because of its limiting male-dominated notion of proper literary themes.[16] Richard Brodhead notes that by the 1870s, the *Atlantic Monthly,* first published in 1857, "had established itself as the premiere organ of literary high culture in America" (77, 79). Howells, the editor of the journal from 1866–1881, guaranteed a reputation for the *Atlantic,* along with *Harper's Monthly* and *Century,* as a "quality journal" of the time (124). Howells, Henry Mills Alden, editor of *Harper's,* and Richard Watson Gilder, editor of *Century,*[17] all voiced support and published according to the dictates of the Genteel Tradition. They also guided American literary tastes and embraced regional fiction as a threefold solution to national issues: to unify the nation by emphasizing interest in the South;

to remember a simpler way of life passing in the face of industrial prog-ress; and to "tell local cultures into a history of their supersession by a modern order now risen to national dominance" (Brodhead 120–21).

Howells and his supporters did not foresee certain results of this pro-motion of local interest literature. According to Brodhead, regionalism "made the experience of the socially marginalized into a literary asset" (117), opening literary opportunities to women and African Americans, including Charles Chesnutt. If regional devices became a recourse for the oppressed as exemplified through Chesnutt's *The Conjure Woman* (1899) through its mimicking of Joel Chandler Harris's Uncle Remus and Thomas Nelson Page's Mars Chan, then the work of Kate Chopin can also be viewed as a means of liberation. Her battle to portray realistically fe-male desire parallels Chesnutt's writing as his weapon against portray-als of "all of the many Negroes . . . whose virtues have been given to the world in the magazine press recently [that] have been blacks, full-blooded, and their chief virtues have been their dog-like fidelity to their old mas-ter" (Brodhead 206).[18] With Chesnutt and Chopin, local color shifted from prescribed themes and messages to the utilization of these prescriptions to mask the authors' ulterior motives: to write what they chose. This shift oc-curred even as local color began to decline in popularity in the minds of American publishers. Now capable of reflecting division as much as unity, local color no longer demanded the full attention of an American audi-ence.[19]

In the midst of an evolving literary world, Chopin wrote stories about women's sexuality and framed them against a Louisiana backdrop.[20] Ex-tending American fiction by women to encompass themes and topics con-sidered "taboo" for women to write about at the time,[21] including female sexual desire and childbirth, Chopin dared American literature to address themes popular in the European literature she read, including works by George Sand, Byron, Thomas Hardy, Victor Hugo, Maupassant, Flaubert, and Zola.

Today's critics readily acknowledge Chopin's use of marginally placed characters to address the social oppression of women, but they do not focus on her specific use of 'Cadians as interstitial characters as a possible means of rebelling against this social oppression. Demonstrating this ar-gument, Emily Toth writes:

> Like most local color women writers of her day, she was really writing
> universal stories about women, men, marriage, children, loyalty, and

much more. She was saying very frank things about the power of men to limit and punish women. But when she set her stories in a distant, unusual locale, she deflected criticism—which enabled her to sail into print and even be praised by male publishers, editors, and reviewers in the Northeast. (150)

Toth relates Chopin's use of Louisiana settings to establish Chopin's rebellion. Through her daring use of 'Cadian characters in such settings, Chopin created a new meaning for the Acadian and did so through the accepted boundaries of local color.[22]

The confusion over how to categorize Chopin's work extends to discussions of her Louisiana characters, especially 'Cadians and Creoles of Color. In "Kate Chopin and the Lore of Cane River's Creoles of Color," Marcia Gaudet illustrates the difficulties facing critics in reading Chopin's Louisiana characters correctly because of Chopin's ambiguous identifications.[23] Her reading of Chopin clarifies ethnic markers that readers should use in classifying characters. The mistake she corrects in her article addresses the racial identity of Ozème in "Ozème's Holiday," first published in Century in 1896, and later published in A Night in Acadie (1897). Chopin writes, "His eyes were blue and mild; his hair was light, and he wore it rather long; he was clean shaven, and really did not look his thirty-five years" ("OH" 349). Gaudet reads this description differently from Sandra Gunning and Per Seyersted who identify the character as Cajun.[24] As Gaudet clarifies, the blue eyes and light brown hair that form Ozème's physical features usually signify other than Cajun identity. She argues that "Cajuns typically have dark eyes and dark hair," although some do have lighter features (50).[25] Once physical characteristics become too slippery to hold up under intense ethnic scrutiny, one must search in Louisiana history to locate Ozème's heritage. Gaudet does just that as she recalls for the reader the Isle Brevelle history and its place in Louisiana race issues and identifications.[26]

Supporting her reading, she explains, "Since the Cajuns were not slave owners and the free people of color were," Ozème identifies as a "Creole of Color" (Gaudet, "Kate Chopin" 50). Moreover, Chopin's 'Cadian is usually portrayed as a "stupid, lazy, or bumbling person—a stereotype that Cajuns resent" (50). But Ozème "is not the typical Cajun as portrayed by Chopin. In addition, a Cajun would not be likely to be taking a holiday on Isle Brevelle, since they were typically looked down upon by the Creoles of Color" (50). In essence, Gaudet's article is as much a lesson on racial categories unique to south Louisiana as it is an instruction on how to read Chopin's character. The confusion over how to categorize Chopin's fiction and how to label her characters exemplifies the difficulty present in reading Chopin's 'Cadians, who remain between race and class categories throughout her fiction. This article also addresses the difficulty in reading race in Chopin's fiction, a popular topic among critics that may be understood more fully through a more comprehensive recognition of Cajun culture during Chopin's career and its meaning in her work.

Gaudet's article demonstrates the necessity of discussing how Chopin codes her 'Cadian characters. Chopin's characters diverge from Longfellow's and Cable's Acadians with her depictions of Acadian class and racial ambiguity, reflected in her use of the term *'Cadian,* which demonstrates the move toward American identification and away from more traditional Acadian culture and reflects an interstitial moment between *Acadian* and *Cajun* identification. Chopin's 'Cadians usually have dark complexions, do not own slaves,[27] and can be rather "stupid, lazy, or bumbling" people (Gaudet, "Kate Chopin" 50). They are also social creatures, participating in balls that convene the community to partake of food, drink, and music. In class status, they rest below Creoles and are closer to the African American servants' social status as laborers. Chopin further divides Creoles and 'Cadians through her depiction of their dialects. Similar to 'Cadians, Creoles speak a mixture of French and English that has been influenced by French. Creoles use less slang, however, and have a clearer pronunciation than their lower class neighbors, displaying their educated status. Finally, Creoles employ African Americans who then look down on 'Cadians and their poverty. Chopin also emphasizes 'Cadian ignorance by characterizing African American women as wiser than their 'Cadian counterparts. This wisdom, however, does not help its possessors to bridge the racial gap as far as social events are concerned, as evident in the "whites only" attendance at the balls.

The above code reflects, to some degree, Longfellow's and Cable's Acadian codes. In Chopin's fiction, Acadian simplicity, however, has evolved into ignorance. Chopin's representation also records the social and racial ambiguity of Acadians as they shift to 'Cadians in American history, an in-between state of identity formation. No longer simply Acadian because of the Louisiana Purchase of 1803, which made them American, yet not quite American in their own conceptions of themselves, 'Cadians signify the shifting notions of race and class in Chopin's fiction, which makes her racial representations difficult to access. Through her work, she reinforces this overarching image in order to question further social constructions of identity.

In several of her short stories, Chopin creates images of 'Cadian racial and social flexibility. "In Sabine," located in *Bayou Folk* (1894), is the completion of Grégoire Santien's story that began in Chopin's first novel, *At Fault* (1890). Grégoire rides away to Texas only to reencounter 'Tite Rein, a woman he met "at the 'Cadian balls that he sometimes had the hardihood to attend" ("IS" 206).[28] Chopin writes the story around her already blossoming critique of marriage demonstrated by 'Tite Rein's relationship with her abusive Texan husband who does not even identify his wife as white.[29] Using *Cajun* as a derogatory form, Bud Aiken, the Texan, says, "That's the way with them Cajuns, . . . ain't got sense enough to know a white man when they see one" (207). Carl Brasseaux explains that as "the negative inference of the term suggests, *Cajun* was used by Anglos to refer to all persons of French descent and low economic standing, regardless of their ethnic affiliation" (*Acadian to Cajun* 104), a popular use of the term during Chopin's literary career. The story ends with the Creole gentleman successfully helping the 'Cadian woman to escape her abusive husband and return to her family. Her concern for the welfare of her family, and her dialect, as recorded by Chopin, code her as 'Cadian as much as does her husband's identification of her as such. Interestingly, this story also codes her as racially ambiguous according to her husband, who remains a Louisiana outsider—a reminder of American ignorance of south Louisiana ethnicities. Bud does, however, recognize Creoles as white, demonstrating that their middle to upper class status color codes them differently from their 'Cadian neighbors.

"A Gentleman of Bayou Têche," also published in *Bayou Folk*, again demonstrates Chopin's awareness of popular views of *Cajuns* by the 1890s,[30] and their social status as decidedly lower class people of French descent, by the end of the century.[31] Beginning the story with an explanation of Mr. Sublet's desire to capture Evariste, a 'Cadian, in a picture, the narrator agrees with Sublet that "the 'Cadian was rather a picturesque subject in his way, and a tempting one to an artist looking for bits of 'local color' along the Têche" ("AG of BT" 158). Evariste agrees to sit for the picture and tells Sublet that he will fix himself up for the sitting, but the artist says, "He want' [Evariste] like [he] come out de swamp" (158–59). Although Evariste and his daughter "could not understand these eccentric wishes on the part of the strange gentleman, and made no effort to do so," it is their black friend Aunt Dicey who explains the exploitation of their culture by the artist (159). Aunt Dicey tells Martinette, Evariste's daughter, "An' you know w'at readin' dey gwine sot down on' neaf dat picture? Dey gwine sot down on' neaf: 'Dis heah is one dem low-down 'Cajuns o' Bayou Têche!'" (159). Moreover, Aunt Dicey and her African American neighbors live well compared to Evariste and his daughter whose "low, homely cabin of two rooms . . . was not quite so comfortable as Mr. Hallet's [the land-owner's] negro quarters" (158). Chopin's depiction of Louisiana life reflects the lower class position of 'Cadians, a position that rests somewhere be-tween white and black society.

Further illustrating racial confusion, Aunt Dicey's behavior demon-strates her vision of social equality with the 'Cadians, but she cannot act as they do when associating with the white gentleman. For example, Mar-tinette enters Mr. Hallet's dining room and "laid the two silver dollars be-side [the 'stranger gentleman's'] plate and motioned to retire without a word of explanation" ("AG of BT" 162). No African American would have been allowed to enter the living quarters of the plantation owner on these terms and to treat the stranger in such a negative, if humble, manner. In fact, unlike her black counterpart who is often silent in upper class white company in Chopin's fiction, Martinette is invited to speak by the planter himself: "Speak out, little one" (162). Treated as a simple-minded girl, in-stead of the woman she is, Martinette reacts with excitement and explains in a "shrill" voice her refusal to let Mr. Sublet exploit her father or her peo-ple. Then, Evariste enters the room, and everything changes.

Deciding to go fishing to escape Mr. Sublet's pens and papers, Evariste discovers a little boy drowning in the Carencro lake, and he proceeds to save him. Realizing that the boy is the son of Mr. Sublet, Evariste quickly returns him to the big house and advises the father not to let his son "go no mo' by hisse'f in one pirogue" ("AG of BT" 163). The planter and his guest acknowledge the heroism of the act and invite the 'Cadians to eat breakfast with them. This invitation does not sit well with Wilkins, the black servant, who serves them with "visible reluctance and ill-disguised contempt" (163), again demonstrating the black perspective of superiority over the lower white ethnicity, even as the landowning white class offers the 'Cadians a place, if a superficial one, in white society. The story ends when Evariste agrees to sit for his portrait and ensures his control over the wording under the picture: "You will put on'neat' de picture, 'Dis is one picture of Mista Evariste Anatole Bonamour, a gent'man of de Bayou Têche'" (164). Chopin's story ends with a confirmation of 'Cadian posi-tioning between white landowners and African American servants, and it reinforces 'Cadian simplicity and ignorance while demonstrating the 'Cadian ability to rise in social status. Aunt Dicey, however wise, remains in her racial place as an African American servant throughout the story.

This revealing story looks closely at race in Louisiana. Aunt Dicey and Wilkins assume their superiority over the 'Cadians, and as the servants of a prosperous plantation, they do, in some sense, live above their poor and simpleminded neighbors. Aunt Dicey even says to Martinette, "I jis studyin' how simple you an' yo' pa is. You is bof de simplest somebody I eva come 'crost" ("AG of BT" 159). Her conversation with Martinette and Wilkins's reluctance to serve the 'Cadians at the end of the story demonstrate the open relationship between the Acadian descendants and their African American neighbors, complicated, however, by the subjective notion of "color" that pervades white and black society in Chopin's fiction. 'Cadians are white because they are of French descent, and not because they look white. As such, they shift between racial and social categories. For example, they are allowed to eat with the planter and his guest, but they live in lowlier homes than their black counterparts. Chopin's use of *Cajun* as a negative title for lower class, white people reflects her understanding of Louisiana social structure and its positioning of the Acadian descendants between rungs on the social ladder.[32]

Chopin's creation of the socially flexible Lolotte, in "A Rude Awakening," confirms the arbitrariness of class and race categories, which Chopin further rebels against in her later depictions of female sexuality, as represented by the 'Cadian wife, Calixta, in "The Storm." In "A Rude Awakening," Acadian descendants can and do reach an upper tier in society and are identifiable as white "based on characters' subscription to middle-class codes of behavior" (Shaker, *Coloring Locals* 49). Chopin uses this ambiguity to create a literary space for female desire because proof of racial and social ambiguity leads to a questioning of these constructed categories, an argument that also alludes to the formation of gender roles. Chopin's 'Cadians "float between racial fields," but their African American neighbors are "fixed" societal signifiers (Shaker, "Lookin'" 117). Chopin's use of the 'Cadian as an interstitial figure presents "ethnicity . . . [as] a floating signifier of identity that is eternally re-presentable," as far as this specific people are concerned (117). Shaker's study of Chopin's *Youth's Companion* stories leads her to conclude that Chopin created a successful shift in color coding because her work "mediates for a northern-based periodical press Louisiana's specific, complex social and racial history," in order "to color local Creoles and Cajuns white" for this audience (*Coloring Locals* 27). By doing so, Chopin opened a path into a literary magazine with wide circulation that gained more notice for her work even as she created a new image for Louisiana ethnicities for an audience unfamiliar with the various meanings—racial and social—of these peoples. Moreover, she wrote 'Cadians as upwardly mobile through "A Rude Awakening," continuing Cable's message of assimilation, although Chopin's Americanization process emphasizes social conformity and not English education.

First published on February 2, 1893, in *Youth's Companion*, "A Rude Awakening" never states that Lolotte and Sylveste Bordon are 'Cadians. Chopin codes them as such by addressing their darker complexions, by describing their poor conditions and close proximity to African Americans, and by depicting their dialect in print. The progression of the story is one toward higher class status, which in turn colors the 'Cadian characters as white according to Shaker's thesis that adhering to social norms colors one as white: "the brown-skinned, underprivileged Lolotte has the potential to be read as black until and unless she and her father adhere to bourgeois gender norms" (*Coloring Locals* 48). Thus, the "bare brown feet" become "neatly shod feet" through social assimilation ("ARA" 232, 238). This particular story complicates the implication of Chopin's 'Cadian identification as possibly nonwhite in the story "In Sabine" by "construct[ing] Cajun as a white ethnic category of American identity" (*Coloring Locals* 48), which will have further consequences in "The Storm."

"A Rude Awakening" begins with a description of the poverty in which the Bordon family lives and the reason for this lack of provisions: Sylveste's laziness. When Monsieur Duplan, his Creole neighbor and a plantation owner, offers him work, Sylveste fails to fulfill his responsibilities, leaving his daughter Lolotte to take on the burden. Lolotte discusses her decision with Aunt Minty, the African American servant who remains close to the Bordon family, who immediately criticizes the idea of a woman doing a man's work: "Git down f'om dah, chile! Is you plumb crazy?" ("ARA" 233). Obviously, Aunt Minty feels equal enough in status to address Lolotte in such a casual manner. This familiarity will change, however, as both Sylveste and Lolotte learn to conform to gender and social norms.

While replacing her father in the workplace, Lolotte has an accident that sends her to the hospital. Sylveste finally realizes why and how he must take on the responsibility for his family while Lolotte simultaneously understands her place as a white woman during her recovery. In the end, Sylveste and Lolotte agree to assimilate to social standards that color them white both racially and socially. The final confirmation of this "whiteness" comes from the mouth of Aunt Minty who exclaims upon seeing Lolotte after her recovery, "An' dah you is! . . . dah you is, settin' down, lookin' jis' like w'ite folks!" ("ARA" 239). Lolotte replies, "Ain't I always was w'ite folks, Aunt Mint?" (239). Aunt Minty's final words mark her newly found respect for Lolotte's place as white even as they forever change the relationship between the two women from one of equality to one between a superior and an inferior: "You knows me. I don' mean no harm" (239). As she has always treated Monsieur Duplan, so now Aunt Minty speaks to her 'Cadian neighbors, demonstrating their closer proximity to upper class, white landowners by the end of the story.

Chopin confirms through literature the placement of Creoles and, more significantly, 'Cadians as American to guarantee their identification by non-Louisianians as white, in essence placing African Americans even further from any notion of equality or upward mobility. Her fiction illustrates "Cajun assimilability into hegemonic white middle class American culture, while concomitantly reinscribing African exclusion from such cultural entitlement" (*Coloring Locals* 48). She does so by "assimilat[ing] Louisiana Creoles and Cajuns into the dominant culture by preserving them as distinct ethnic categories that nonetheless, through class and gender conformity, are part of the white race" (25). Lolotte's ambiguous racial identification allows for this movement upward. Neither white nor black, Lolotte can become one because she is not automatically defined as the other. This story demonstrates this ambiguity in reference to class status and roles.

Although these stories clarify Chopin's codification of 'Cadians and her recognition of them as socially interstitial characters in terms of race, these stories do not question, and definitely do not refute, gender roles established for women by patriarchal society, the same society that guided the work of genteel publishers. In many ways, Chopin's earlier stories familiarize northeastern publishers and readers with south Louisiana's unique ethnic and cultural mix. With *The Awakening* (1899) and "The Storm" (1969),[33] Chopin utilizes 'Cadian racial and social ambiguity to create her most daring argument against strict adherence to social rules.

With *The Awakening* and "The Storm," Chopin presents adultery as the ultimate critique of marriage. Through their adulterous behavior, Edna Pontellier and Calixta deny patriarchal structuring of marriage and of female desire, a rebellion framed through Chopin's use of the socially interstitial 'Cadian position. Both women appropriate 'Cadian ways and, in doing so, create a space of desire for themselves. These stories demonstrate Chopin's construction of a literary space of freedom, one in which she could and did portray female desire.

Edna's story of rebellion begins on Grand Isle[34] and with Madame Antoine, the 'Cadian woman who recites tales of pirates and lost treasure to Edna while she rests on Chênière Caminada.[35] In Chopin's fiction, the residents of Chênière Caminada are socially below the higher class vacationers who populate the larger island during the summer months. Because of its social marginality, this place can and does become Edna's refuge. In this story, the interstitial position of 'Cadians becomes the ground for Chopin's subtle critique of patriarchal structures because this between space allows Edna's imagination to reach a place beyond Creole society and its dictates.[36]

In a moment of ultimate surrender to and realization of 'Cadian freedom, Edna credits Madame Antoine with a story that she herself has created. After dinner one evening, Edna tells her father and her husband the tale of a woman "who paddled away with her lover one night in a pirogue and never came back. They were lost amid the Baratarian Islands, and no one ever heard of them or found a trace of them from that day to this" (*Awakening* 70). The story shocks her audience, so she quickly "said that Madame Antoine had related it to her" (70). The reader knows that Edna invented the story because Edna's thoughts reveal this fact. Her crediting Madame Antoine demonstrates the 'Cadian woman's influence on Edna's imagination. Through Antoine's tales of the Baratarians, Edna's mind is opened to new places, new opportunities, and new spaces for self-revelation and freedom. As Edna uses Madame Antoine's folklore as a means of voicing her hidden desires, so, too, does Chopin use 'Cadian characters in her work to create a literary space for her daring message of female sexuality.

Madame Antoine offers Edna a moment of freedom with her myths and legends. Michele Birnbaum reads significance into Edna's day on Chênière Caminada and her use of Madame Antoine as a liberating experience. Birnbaum writes, "Edna first discovers the erotic frontiers of the self by exploiting the less visible constructions of sexual difference associated with the blacks, quadroons, and the Acadians in the novel" (321). Unlike "A Rude Awakening," *The Awakening* actually maintains Acadian descendants' lower class, racially ambiguous social position. The silence of the blacks in the novel and the distance from Acadian speech, demonstrated by Madame Antoine's use of French since "[s]he could speak no English" (*Awakening* 83), represent Edna's "escape from gender convention through the rhetoric of racial oppression," allowing her to "reinforce rather than raise class and race differences" (Birnbaum 322). Everyone remains exactly where society has placed him or her, at the end of *The Awakening*. Although Edna attempts to escape her place by usurping the roles of other races and ethnicities, she finally finds herself trapped within her own world, the one she has helped to make. Edna, not Madame Antoine, invents the story of illicit love, but her construction of Antoine as the teller forces onto the lower culture the same assumptions that plague African Americans: myths of promiscuity and undisguised passion. As such, Edna's claiming Madame Antoine as the creator taints her liberating experience with the 'Cadian woman. Ultimately, Edna is not free, either within herself or within society, to express her own passions and desires. Nevertheless, 'Cadians remain images of freedom for Edna, images she uses for her own purposes.

With "The Storm," Chopin completes her utilization of the 'Cadian position between social categories to subvert social notions of female desire. She does so by mimicking, to some degree, Edna's utilization of Madame Antoine in *The Awakening*. This story was not printed until 1969, in Per Seyersted's *The Complete Works of Kate Chopin* (Toth 139), because Chopin "never offered [the story] to a publisher" (Thomas 41).[37] Heather Kirk Thomas writes, "the last story's depiction of a sensuous southern adulteress suggests a newly amoral revisioning of Edna Pontellier's situation" (41). This amoral revision stems from the 'Cadian presence in the story. The 'Cadian wife Calixta realizes what Edna could not: sexual freedom. "The Storm" confirms Chopin's envisioning of the 'Cadian as an interstitial social character who could shift between white and black categories to question gender roles while veiling this purpose in regional disguise.

Before she wrote this particular story, Chopin introduced her 'Cadian Bobinôt and Calixta, his love interest, in "At the 'Cadian Ball." In this first story, Chopin firmly established the social divide between the 'Cadian people and the Creole aristocracy; thus, Calixta marries Bobinôt, and Clarisse, a Creole lady, marries Alcée. Calixta marries the 'Cadian, which allows her to shift into 'Cadian culture even as it enables her to remain flexible to question social norms regarding women.[38]

"At the 'Cadian Ball," first published in *Two Tales* (1892) and later placed in *Bayou Folk,* not only addresses strict social categorization as it existed in Louisiana at the time, but it also begins to reveal changes in the

Louisiana landscape that would dramatically affect Acadian culture in its dynamic process of becoming Cajun. Unlike "A Rude Awakening," which never names the characters as *Acadian, 'Cadian,* or *Cajun,* "At the 'Cadian Ball" names them as all three. Clarisse and Alcée refer to the balls as *'Cadian,* while Bruce, Alcée's servant, calls them *Cajun* ("AtCB" 183).[39] And, Chopin writes, "The glow of a sudden and overwhelming happiness shone out in the brown, rugged face of the young *Acadian*" (187, emphasis mine). Even as her other stories remain ambiguous about the ethnicity of these characters, this particular story touches on the ambiguity of how to label them in this time of rapid change, this between period that allows them to be labeled in reference to their Acadian-French heritage or by their developing American identification.

Chopin's 'Cadian code clearly marks Bobinôt as 'Cadian. His skin is "brown" and "rugged"; his personality is "good-natured"; his movement is "dull-looking and clumsy" ("AtCB" 184). The code extends to the women as well who glance at Alcée with "big, dark, soft" eyes "as those of the young heifers" (184). If compared to Clarisse's "slim, tall, graceful" figure, as "[d]ainty as a lily" (180), the division between Creoles and 'Cadians becomes clear. Furthermore, a dialect comparison solidifies this social boundary because the Creoles speak in a more elevated English dialect, still peppered with French, than the 'Cadians in the story. While Clarisse says, "The 'Cadian Ball. . . . Humph! *Par exemple!* Nice conduc' for a Laballière," demonstrating the loss of the "t" in English spoken by French speakers (183), Bobinôt's speech contains a more ignorant, and slangish, knowledge of English pronunciation: "*Bon Dieu!* You know that makes me crazy, w'at you sayin'. You mean that, Calixta? You ent goin' turn roun' agin?" (187). Both social and somewhat racial, this division dictates the two marriages that stem from "At the 'Cadian Ball," marriages Chopin would later question with her construction of an adulterous act.

Chopin's fiction also records a shift in Acadian identification as American because of the United States' advances into south Louisiana lands. In a telling passage, Chopin reveals the American threat to this once-isolated society:

> Any one who is white may go to a 'Cadian ball, but he must behave himself like a 'Cadian. . . . [Grosbœuf] had been giving them since he was a young man. . . . In that time he could recall but one disturbance, and that was caused by American railroaders, who were not in touch with their surroundings and had no business there. ("AtCB" 183)

This passage designates 'Cadians as white since only white people are invited to the ball. Furthermore, it comments on the American invasion of Acadian culture as not appreciated, in fact refused, by the 'Cadians. Later in the story, however, Chopin reveals the already blossoming influence of Americans in the speech of the French descendants: "They belonged to the younger generation, so preferred to speak English" (185). Alcée, Calixta, and Bobinôt, Creole and Acadian alike, feel the effects of American assimilation. With these eleven words, Chopin announces the ultimate shift taking place that would lead Acadians to accept and commonly use *Cajun* even as they continued to think of themselves as non-American, as evident by their refusal to allow the railroaders any future attendance at the balls. According to James Dormon, "[Cajuns] who remained in towns— those who became 'urbanized'—quickly acculturated to the norms necessary to their survival in that setting, learning to speak English, for example" (*The People* 65). This change occurred due to mechanization, which included the influx of railroad building throughout the South. In this story more than in her other work, Chopin records the initial stages of the Americanization of Acadians.

As an introduction to "The Storm," "At the 'Cadian Ball" also confirms Chopin's utilization of the interstitial 'Cadian who will play a larger role in her critique of social norms through a natural and sexual storm. Anna Shannon Elfenbein offers a reading of Calixta that places her in a similar sexual category as African American women in American literature. In "At the 'Cadian Ball," Calixta's description "suggests the stereotyped imagery frequently associated with racially and therefore sexually stigmatized women" because she is a "darker" character due to her Spanish blood (Elfenbein 121, 118): "Calixta's slender foot had never touched Cuban soil; but her mother's had, and the Spanish was in her blood all the same" ("AtCB" 179). Elfenbein's reading of Calixta arises from her study of the "tragic octoroon" as she appears in the fiction of George Washington Cable, Grace King, and Kate Chopin, all of whom "seized a stereotype and redefined its terms" (x).[40] Furthermore, "Chopin's attack on the 'moral conventionalities' about marriage, motherhood, and sex made her an exception in American literature at the turn of the century. But only in her treatments of women already stigmatized in the American racist's imagination is her treatment of sex unrestrained" (123). Chopin's most explicit, sexually realistic story confirms Elfenbein's statement since Calixta remains non-Anglo-Protestant and only ambiguously white. If this character's identity is read through Shaker's theory of Chopin's whitening Cajun characters, then Calixta's ethnic and sexual coding shifts with her marriage to Bobinôt, which makes her now identifiable as a 'Cadian wife. "The Storm" ends with every character in his or her proper social place, but it offers a critique of social norms by creating a space outside of marriage where desire can and does prevail. Calixta's 'Cadian identity through marriage allows her to move between racial and social categories. Chopin uses her character's social and racial ambiguity to create a space of desire for Calixta, which becomes Chopin's space of literary freedom. Like Lolotte, Calixta's nonblack color coding allows her to achieve her desires even as her not-quite-white coding protects her from serious repercussions, religious or otherwise.

"The Storm" continues the story of Alcée and Calixta's awaited consummation of their desire for each other. After five years of marriage to other people, both of these characters may have accepted their place in society, but they still refuse to obey social dictates. Although they do not plan the affair, a storm arises that "blows" them into each other's arms, as if Nature destined the sexual act between these two people. The explicit sexual scene located in this story pushes it past the adulterous silence found in *The Awakening*.[41] No wonder Chopin never attempted to publish this story. "Chopin portrays a woman's subjective experience of sex and a woman's active involvement and pleasure in lovemaking, in defiance of the genteel literary restrictions of her day" (Elfenbein 139), a portrayal made possible by Calixta's interstitial position arising from her 'Cadian marriage. Not only the sexual content, but also the concept of white female passion so openly described would have shocked the northeastern gentlemen publishers who distributed fiction fitting the standards of nineteenth-century American morality. If Chopin "discovered she could publish stories hinting at sexual matters. . . but only if she placed her characters in quaint locales, and if she veiled, through vague words, what they actually did," "The Storm" hides nothing behind veils or quaint locales (Toth 142). In fact, it writes of a dangerous threat to the family and refuses to claim it as such. The story ends with both marriages being more stable because of adultery. "The Storm" questions social constructs that create boundaries around the American family, and it does so through the one character capable of class and racial flexibility in terms of American identity: the Cajun.

Unaware of their spouses' infidelity at the end of the story, Clarisse and Bobinôt continue to live their lives without complaint, at least for the present. In fact, they are pleasantly rewarded by the affair in that Clarisse is granted a longer stay at her former home and Bobinôt and Bibi, his four-year-old son, return to a fulfilled Calixta. In the story's words, "[Clarisse] was charmed upon receiving her husband's letter. . . . And the first free breath since her marriage seemed to restore the pleasant liberty of her maiden days. Devoted as she was to her husband, their intimate conjugal life was something which she was more than willing to forego for a while" ("Storm" 286). And, on the other front, "Bobinôt's explanations and apologies which he had been composing all along the way, dried on his lips as Calixta felt him to see if he were dry, and seemed to express nothing but satisfaction at their safe return" (285). Thus, "the storm passed and every one was happy" (286). Everyone accepted his or her place in society; however, this acceptance has been compromised, or perhaps enabled, by the sexual act.

Through this story, Chopin seems to be arguing for human passion and desire, but not at the cost of marriage. After all, the two couples end where they began—happily married. Furthermore, Calixta's concern for Bobinôt's physical dryness and Clarisse's continued devotion to her husband prove the solidity of the marriages that are tested in this story. The story also includes vivid expression of the desire that rises between Calixta and Alcée for each other, and not for their spouses, indicating a possible space outside of marriage for desire. In many ways, "The Storm" is *The Awakening* awakened. What differs between the two is Chopin's final solution: a space of desire that rests beyond social constructs. So the passions spin through the storm, and everyone ends happy and satisfied.

One glaring racial issue in Chopin's story lives in the prevalence of a popular assumption of the higher classes regarding lower class white and black promiscuousness. Racial coding and its place in writing females' sexual desire led Sander Gilman to address the figure of the Hottentot in nineteenth-century America. His article, "Black Bodies, White Bodies: Toward an Iconography of Female Sexuality in Late Nineteenth-Century Art, Medicine, and Literature," argues that society, coded male, displaced female sexual desire onto the body of the African woman, visualized through the body of the Hottentot, by merging its "perception of the black" with "the perception of the prostitute" (248). This African body became the symbol for abnormal sexual drives, which were codified into scientific discourse made popular through nineteenth-century studies of physiology and physiognomy. He notes that during this period in history, "[t]he primitive is the black, and the qualities of blackness, or at least of the black female, are those of the prostitute" (248), which meant that all sexual disease and social abnormality were removed from the white body through "science." These studies and findings of African sexuality arose at a time when "the notion of a 'woman's sexual awakening' became, by definition, an impossibility," according to Cynthia Wolff, who explains that this impossibility stems from the belief that "men 'owned' their libido; women's libido was 'owned' by their prospective children" (383). According to popular belief, men experienced sexual desire while women felt only the desire to procreate. When combined, scientific and social beliefs formed the "[n]ineteenth-century understanding of female sexuality as pathological," pushing white female sexuality even more firmly onto the black female body (Gilman 235). In light of this insight into the nineteenth-century social mindset, how should one read the ambiguously racialized and sexually fulfilled Calixta?

Calixta is a woman who freely expresses her sexuality and is not punished for doing so because of her interstitial position between Louisiana racial and social categories. Birnbaum argues that because of the fetishization of whiteness in Chopin's fiction, Calixta becomes the colonized, thus saved, creature through sexual intercourse with Alcée (334). Her "hair, dishevelled by the wind and rain, kinked more stubbornly than ever" and her image in general evolves through the sexual act to a *whiteness* represented by her skin, "like a creamy lily" ("Storm" 284). Although Birnbaum reveals an enlightening reading of Chopin's story, other clues lie within the passage. For example, Calixta's hair is yellow, and her eyes are blue (282, 284); therefore, she is the model of *whiteness* to some degree. This model, however, also reminds the reader of the fair Ozème, whom Gaudet claims is a Creole of Color and not a Cajun because of his blue eyes. What becomes evident through Chopin's work is that Calixta, like her husband's Acadian people, is an interstitial character, capable of shifting between and questioning categories. As such, she opens the door between marriage and desire to include both within her life; her body creates the bridge to passion that exists outside social boundaries. Edna Pontellier could never realize this interstitial position because of her history and her marriage to a Creole; however, Calixta lives this reality because of her Acadianness through marriage.

Creating an interstitial position through the portrayal of 'Cadian characters, Chopin's work transforms Cajun representation in American fiction. Chopin not only categorizes her 'Cadians as simpleminded creatures, but she addresses the people's interstitial placement that lies between basic social structures by utilizing American confusion over how to read literary Cajuns. Longfellow's *Evangeline* introduces the Acadians to the nation in his attempt to formulate an American fiction; Cable's *Bonaventure* creates a story of Acadian Americanization through English education as a means of arguing for reunification following the Civil War and Reconstruction; and Chopin's fiction constructs a 'Cadian people who provide for her a space for literary freedom in the midst of a dynamic Americanization process. Chopin, in pursuit of her main goal—a more realistic depiction of female desire—moves the literary depictions of Cajuns forward by portraying their interstitial positioning between their Acadian past and their American future.

4. Our Cajun America

TWENTIETH-CENTURY REVISIONS OF CAJUN
REPRESENTATION

The representation of Cajuns in American literary works of the twentieth century reflects the ongoing Americanization of the people, leading
to their identity as Cajun Americans. While assimilation assumes a move
toward conformity, Cajun assimilation progresses along complicated
lines that lead to a hybrid identity as both Cajun and American by the
end of the twentieth century. For Cajuns, this Americanization process
contains several phases of becoming, including becoming Cajun and becoming American. During the first half of the twentieth century, much of
this process took place both in literature and in the actual lives of Cajuns.
Cajun literary representation developed along with Cajuns themselves as
the ethnic group moved from a position outside American norms, to an
American identification of self. Instead of Americanizing Acadians and
their descendants in literature, the process by which Longfellow, Cable,
and Chopin wrote of the Louisiana people, twentieth-century authors represent the actual assimilation process advancing within the Cajun communities of south Louisiana, causing tensions and conflict arising from
cultural changes.

Before they could become fully American, Cajuns were faced with the
national push to identify themselves as such. During the early twentieth
century, anxiety arose over notions of race and class structures as Americans felt threatened not only by the African American population following the Civil War and Reconstruction, but also by the increasing number of immigrants flooding across the nation's borders. In *Our America:
Nativism, Modernism, and Pluralism,* Walter Benn Michaels establishes
two literary phases that deal with immigration during the first half of the
twentieth century. At the turn of the century, Theodore Dreiser, Edith
Wharton, and Jack London wrote in the progressive vein, in which *American* meant a "set of social and economic conditions rather than a political

entity or cultural heritage" (68). In the most basic sense, being American meant being white, since "no law at the turn of the century could keep the vulgar from imposing themselves upon the genteel, but insofar as gentility could be effaced by whiteness and vulgarity by blackness, an entire social system could be erected on laws that kept blacks from imposing themselves on whites" (57). This system evolved by the 1920s into nativism, which argued that one must be born American because one could not become American. According to Michaels, Ernest Hemingway's *The Sun Also Rises* (1926) and F. Scott Fitzgerald's *The Great Gatsby* (1925) capture this new sense of national identity by disclaiming Jews and ambiguously defined nouveau riche as inherent parts of American identity (9). The ability to rise in class status and to become American through assimilation suddenly disappeared as national identity became an almost "inherited" trait (32).

Cajuns were inevitably affected by this national alteration in racial and cultural categorization. Both Ada Jack Carver and Elma Godchaux describe in literature the means by which Cajuns did become identifiable as American, a process based on conformity to specific laws and the American work ethic. Michaels argues that nondifference became an indicator of one's native identity by the 1920s (13–14), yet Cajuns remained different, and apart from mainstream American identification at this time. Perhaps for this reason, Louisiana state laws and more regional pressures proved that becoming American meant answering to codes of behavior and English usage that were not inherent in the Cajun way of life up to this point in history. Such laws demanded, at times, that Cajuns change their cultural ways, even as they began to choose among themselves to identify as American. With such shifts, the Cajun double bind arose as the people had to choose between their Acadian past, or what was left of it, and an American future, making conflict and tension basic components of being Cajun during the twentieth century.

Born and raised in Natchitoches, Louisiana, Ada Jack Carver used her personal history to examine Louisiana's cultural and ethnic tensions in a time of obligatory Americanization. In the foreword to her play, *The Cajun: A Drama in One Act* (1926), Carver writes about "the so-called Lost Peoples of the South, around whom romance and legend cling" (198). For her, *Cajun* referred to the "descendants of the unfortunate but worthy French farmers, who in 1755 fled from the English invasion to Louisiana" (198), establishing a romantic and misleading simplification of Cajun (and Acadian) history. She then goes on to relate the possible Cajun reaction to the

First Cousin Law of Louisiana, passed in 1900, which, in the play, greatly affects two Cajuns who reside in an isolated area with "no telephones nor telegraphs" (198).

As Carver explains in her stage directions, the Cajuns "were tragically caught in the net of circumstance" (199) when Louisiana decided to protect residents from the results of marriages between first cousins. To emphasize the consequences of such a marriage, Carver introduces Papite to the stage, a young man whose face is expressionless and who remains "only vaguely aware of what is happening about him" (200). In a symbolic touch, Carver binds this character with "a piece of string" that he plays with "a mournful strain that dies away on an unfinished note" (200), thus signifying the necessity for laws that could prevent such an incomplete existence. While the young couple mourns the loss of their ability to marry in the play, Papite remains on the stage as a reminder of more significant consequences of past traditions, even as Carver recalls for the audience more positive traditions in visual form.

Altars to Mary, pots of gumbo and coffee, and family bonds signify that this home indeed belongs to French Catholic Cajuns in south Louisiana. During one moment in the play, Armide, the mother, says, "I let the gumbo boil over! . . . Ah, such garlic! Such onion! . . . so divine" (206), juxtaposing the secular and sacred worlds of Cajuns. These religious reminders establish the ultimate reason the family members are convinced they must obey the law: the priest believes that they must do so. As Father Martel explains, "here where we live so long isolate. . . . It is like those two surging river, those river that flowed and joined . . . and wrought such havoc, such sorrow, and woe," which he parallels to the birth of Papite and other family members whose genetic defects signify such inner-family marriages (209). In response to these words, Armide replies, "Father Martel, he is priest" (209); her respect for the man and her obedience to the Catholic faith are more powerful than family traditions. Father Martel becomes not only the voice of religion in the play, but also the reminder of the Cajuns' place within Louisiana. Before he relates the information he has gained from doctors and a judge regarding first-cousin marriages, he emphatically exclaims, "surely you would not defy the law of your state!" (208). By interlocking the religious figure who remains the authority in the isolated community with the demands of the state, Carver's play emphasizes the degree to which the old traditions fade into more American notions of propriety. Complicating this in-between state, Julie, the young woman whose marriage plans have been halted, reveals in the end that it is already too late; she is expecting a child whose future remains uncertain and in danger, much like the older traditions of the Cajuns in Louisiana.

Such laws as the 1900 state law forbidding marriage between family relations required Cajuns to alter their concept of themselves as Americans at the turn of the century. Carver may focus solely on marriage laws,[1] but her play also reflects movements such as English-only usage on public grounds that were instituted through the 1921 Louisiana Constitution,[2] which again forced Cajuns to conform to American ways. The couple in the play reminds the audience of the complicated situation surrounding Cajuns as they continued to become American while also desperately holding on to their past traditions, French language, and Catholic beliefs.

The significance of this play stems from its examination of how new legal constructions affected the Cajun community. By 1866, the number of exogamous marriages involving Cajuns dominated, while Cajuns marrying within the Acadian community decreased, which Carl Brasseaux discusses as a point of assimilation for children either to or away from Cajun culture (*Acadian to Cajun* 106). Many of the "endogamous unions were often with cousins, particularly in the bayou regions, where social stratification was most pronounced" (107). By marrying within the community, Cajuns guaranteed the continuation of land ownership and of cultural ways within the family. If such marriage laws as the one Carver writes about had been passed earlier, they would have affected the "[a]pproximately 15 percent of the Acadian grooms in southwestern Louisiana during Reconstruction [who] carried the same surname as their brides" (107), demonstrating the existence, if not the prevalence, of such marriages among Cajuns. Carver's focus on such a marriage between relations proves a continued stereotype of Cajun backwardness. In reality, this practice was already fading, as Brasseaux's figures demonstrate, by the time an official state law was passed, although Carver argues in her stage directions that in "a few isolated communities" the traditions of such marriages "necessitate[ed] the passage of" the law (198). While Carver's play argues for Cajun difference, Brasseaux's figures prove that Cajun culture was already shifting.

Following the periods of Acadian history and change recorded in Cable's and Chopin's work, Acadians underwent an Americanization process, partly represented in Carver's play, that, according to Shane Bernard, "ranks as one of the most important events in the entire Cajun experience, along with the expulsion of their ancestors from Nova Scotia and south Louisiana's devastation during the Civil War" (*The Cajuns* xviii). By becoming more American, Cajuns became definitely white, but they remained outside of mainstream notions of American identity.[3]

"Chains," a 1936 short story by Elma Godchaux,[4] relates the changes occurring in the Cajun community due to assimilation, and one particular Cajun's rebellion against Americanization. This story also records how internal pressures to conform arose as Cajuns became more American. Godchaux describes her main character, Lurie Webre, as "one lazy Cajin" who refuses to drain the water from his land and plant sugarcane (784), reminding the reader of Sylveste Bordon in Chopin's "A Rude Awakening." Also like Chopin, Godchaux writes in dialect and captures the racial tensions that exist between Cajuns and African Americans. This story actually depicts such racial tensions in order to relate the connection Lurie experiences with an escaped African American convict at the end of the story and to parallel cultural conflict arising between Lurie and the other Cajuns who have already chosen to assimilate to American notions of progress. Although the community, especially John Boudreaux, attempts to force Lurie to plant his field, Lurie simply cannot do so because "he felt the iron chain of the swamp round his neck was unbreakable" (785). After Lurie discovers that he cannot clear his fields, whether or not he wants to, he chooses not to join the community's hunt for an escaped convict. Instead, the escaped convict runs into Lurie and teaches the Cajun the value of being free, of breaking the chains that limit him. While the rest of the community rests from its search, Lurie allows the convict to escape down the river, finally realizing that the river and surrounding swamp may be seen as bodies of freedom, instead of as chains that bind him. By freeing the convict, Lurie also escapes social expectations and assumptions regarding wealth and property value, American notions of success. This freedom can be interpreted as a metaphor for the Cajun situation at this time in American history. Much like Lurie, Cajuns realized they had to choose between progress and the past, a decision that could guarantee their identity as American.

While national identity became synonymous with nativism and Cajuns felt the push, both externally and internally, to become more American, south Louisiana began to promote the cult of Evangeline, based on an American projection of an idealized Acadian woman as the ancestor of Louisiana Cajuns. According to W. Fitzhugh Brundage, by 1920, national focus on Cajun culture took on new dimensions because of a top-down revitalization of Acadian culture, complete with pageantry and national tours. Susan Evangeline Walker Anding displayed her version of

Evangeline's costume at the Philadelphia Sesquicentennial Exposition in 1926; Dudley LeBlanc publicized his run for public office through his "Evangeline girls" tours, which traveled throughout Canada and New England; and Louise Olivier's work as a "professional cultural activist" aided in preserving what she considered "pure" folklore (Brundage 286–87). These three professionals greatly aided in the Acadian revival of the early twentieth century, a revival that allowed the elite population of south Louisiana, represented most prominently by the town of St. Martinville, to crusade for the preservation of Acadian culture through national marketing and tourism. Brundage considers this phase of cultural revival as much a result of Cajun Americanization as of native pride: "Almost certainly their exposure to and assimilation into 'American' life made them keenly aware of both the distance that separated them from their ancestors and the condescension of both Creoles and Anglos toward their heritage" (275). By claiming Longfellow's pastoral creation as their cultural image, these revivalists did not reclaim the Acadian past as much as an Americanized version of this past. Furthermore, "For all the distinctive local color of the Acadian 'revival,' it nevertheless displayed such quintessentially modern American traits as longing for folk tradition, discomfort with 'progress,' and zeal to commercialize culture and adapt it to contemporary tasks" (294). The reliance on Evangeline simply confirms Brundage's argument that what was saved was but "symbolic ethnicity" (293).[5]

This revival and the myths and poems that emerged to replace the lost memory of the dispersal reflected neither the lives of Cajuns nor the racial and social tensions that prevailed among south Louisianians. Fictional representations of Cajuns from the 1950s on focus heavily, however, on these topics and on the changes, both cultural and social, that were occurring within south Louisiana communities. As Cajuns became more American, the tourist industry attempted to freeze the image of Acadians in the form of Evangeline, while fictional representations of Cajuns evolved to illustrate this Americanization process, one complicated by the Cajuns' internal desire to be identified as American by outsiders.[6] This next phase in Cajun literary representation records the movement from maintaining difference to achieving an American identification and everything that such an identity could offer to the next generation of Cajun characters. While representing the degree to which Acadian memory in Louisiana had become symbolic, the Evangeline movement also emphasizes the distance from the Acadian past, one that would continue to increase as Cajuns chose American notions of identity.

By the 1950s, the Cajun situation altered as the people began to identify themselves as Americans, loosening Godchaux's fictional chains. Instead, they faced new conflicts that arose between generations as younger
Cajuns ventured beyond their homelands to discover the opportunities
afforded to them as Americans. Shirley Ann Grau and Ernest Gaines examine this alteration and the tensions arising from it. Both Louisiana
authors introduce Cajun characters who identify themselves as Cajuns,
while also desiring more than their Cajun families can provide socially
and economically. By leaving their homelands and experiencing life beyond Cajun country, such characters demonstrate the consequences, both
positive and negative, caused by such assimilation.

In *The Hard Blue Sky* (1955), Shirley Ann Grau captures this desire to
be American in the character of Annie, an islander in the 1930s. As a character, Annie becomes a powerful example of how modernity affected Cajuns.[7] Her vulnerability informs the reader of the interstitial position in
which Cajuns found themselves because of assimilation to American
norms. After her mother dies, Annie travels to New Orleans to attend a
convent school where she is exposed to life beyond her island home. She
returns to her isolated home only to discover that she no longer belongs
there. In a conversation with Cecile, a friend and neighbor on the island
who is married with children, Annie asks, "Didn't you ever think about
it. . . . Spend all you time cooking and feeding people and more people"
(Grau 105). Cecile responds, "That has come to me, sometimes . . . and I
have wondered about it" (105). Annie further admits she has "been thinking a lot" about "[a]ll sorts things. Like the way things are here and the
way they must be somewhere else" (108). Annie even imagines "what it's
like in California, and what it's like just over on the ocean side of Florida"
(108). She not only dreams of living away from her island home, but she
chooses to place such dreams in locations that are distant from any Cajun
way of life. Like the future heroines of Tim Gautreaux, Annie decides to
become American, which for her means leaving her isolated life and cultural ways far behind, a decision she begins to formulate at the end of the
novel when she chooses to return to New Orleans.

Grau's novel not only depicts Annie's conflict with her environment,
but she also represents the older generation of islanders who have never
thought of leaving either their cultural ways or their family homes.
Mamere Terrebone, the old, wise woman who will never and has never
wanted to leave her home, explains, "Annie, she leave. And before her
some more of them leave. And maybe they come back. And maybe not.

But me, I am always here" (386). Mamere captures in words the very shifts occurring throughout south Louisiana as such opportunities for change are offered to and desired by the younger generations of Cajuns. Annie represents a between point for Cajuns who find themselves longing for more, for a life outside what they view as cultural limitations.

The islands of which Grau writes are themselves caught between progress and the past, which the presence of certain objects proves. Isle Cochon, Terre Haute, and Isle aux Chiens, the three islands that make up the geographical location of the novel, include modern conveniences like a telephone (Grau 98), while still remaining isolated enough that the priest has to be shipped in on certain Sundays and the dentist is only sometimes available since "he goes fishing for days on end" (27). The islanders also happen to be an interethnic people[8] whose language reflects a mix of English and French. French phrases such as "Eh, lá-bas" are spoken along with such phrases as "talk at me," an example of Cajun Vernacular English (157, 328),[9] proving how much English is infiltrating the Cajun French of the people. With comments such as "Il vient d'poulailler," Grau allows the original language of the people to remain part of their characterization, as well as be a reminder to the reader of the French heritage and culture from which these islanders extend. By refusing to translate the phrases, Grau represents a people caught between past and present identities as English usage inevitably invades even the isolated community. Translation among the people themselves is already an integral part of their self-identification and an indicator of their interstitial position between their Acadian past and American present. Not only does the language reflect the intersection of American English and Cajun French, but the folkways also point to change. For example, the men continue to fish for a living, but now their boats are named such things as *Mickey Mouse* and they own Coca-Cola ice chests (54), demonstrating how far Disney and soft drink markets reach into even the most isolated parts of the nation. While children still hear about and believe in the *loup-garou* (325), their mothers admire the one washing machine on the island (256) and read old copies of *House and Garden* and *Ladies' Home Journal* (48).

In such a world, Americanization is already occurring, even if not to the same degree as in less isolated sections of the state. Annie's decision to leave the island simply demonstrates the next step away from such a lifestyle and toward an American identification of self. Any notion of independence or separation from American identification is shattered by the presence of Coke and Disney, two American products far removed from

Acadian and Cajun culture. Now, however, such products have become part of the culture, by choice. While such changes definitely cause conflict between generations, they have also become inevitable pieces of modern Cajun culture.

Like Grau, Ernest Gaines also realistically depicts the Americanization of Cajuns and the consequences of such changes, although he does so from an African American perspective that revises, once more, the literary Cajun. In "The World and the Jug," an essay in *Shadow and Act* (1953), Ralph Ellison writes, "The diversity of American life is often painful, frequently burdensome and always a source of conflict, but in it lies our fate and our hope" (127).[10] In Gaines's fiction, this conflict becomes twofold since he centers his novels around racial conflict while also addressing the painful reality of cultural conflict within communities as younger generations move away from their origins. By placing the Cajun–African American conflict at the center of the novels *Of Love and Dust* (1967) and *A Gathering of Old Men* (1983), Gaines emphasizes the interdependence of white and African American people in south Louisiana while simultaneously acknowledging how Americanization has affected both ethnic communities. In the end, the education of one Cajun leads to the defeat of Cajun–African American competition, the system stemming from American categorization, offering hope that arises through Cajun Americanization.

Before Cajuns could rebel against such an American system of classification, they answered to national notions of identification that labeled them as white and placed them above African Americans. In *The Autobiography of Miss Jane Pittman* (1971), Gaines dissects the very means by which Cajuns became white and American in opposition to their African American neighbors. Albert Cluveau, the Cajun who murders Ned, technically acts on others' orders. Before this murder takes place, Miss Jane introduces Cluveau as a "short bowlegged Cajun" who "used to fish right there side me" (107). Cluveau even pushes the relationship a step further as he "would follow [Miss Jane] up to the house and sit on [her] gallery and talk" (107). The Cajun would chop wood for Miss Jane as she requested or run errands for her at the plantation store (107–8). But everything between this Cajun man and this African American woman changes when her adopted son Ned returns to the quarters. While in the quarters, Ned promotes black pride and the battle for justice, which threaten the white power structure controlling the area. When the white community turns to Cluveau to destroy this threat, he attempts to persuade them away from this course of action because of his friendship, as fragile as it may be, with Miss Jane. When Miss Jane asks him, "Can you kill my boy?" Cluveau responds, "I must do what they tell me" (110). Whether or not he would rather stay out of this particular situation, Cluveau answers to those above him, and his failure to comply could be punishable by death. Too weak to refuse, the Cajun kills the African American man and is condemned by doing so. He "started hearing the Chariot of Hell even in his room" (128). Miss Jane's and Cluveau's acceptance of each other and then the disruption of this acceptance prefigures the relationship between Jim and Bonbon in *Of Love and Dust*, which once again acknowledges the reality of racism and the suppression of any friendship between the races.

As in the work of such writers as Grau, Gaines's fiction refutes the romantic image of the innocent Acadians promoted by earlier fiction and the early twentieth-century Louisiana revivalist efforts. Through Gaines's novels, a candid portrait of Cajun life emerges, which relies on his understanding of American social structure during the twentieth century that coded African Americans as inferior to and threatening to white American society.[11] Considering that lower-class laborers, white and black, worked the same jobs, the only means of establishing a white identity through labor was to compete and drive out those with whom one did not wish to be associated. Meanwhile, the white employers could and did maintain control over immigrants by employing them in the lowest of jobs. This power was so absolute that, as Karen Brodkin explains, the Irish "did not become white until those claims [of whiteness] were recognized by the political and economic elites" (65). In his study of the racial categorization of the Irish in America, Noel Ignatiev agrees: "To enter the white race was a strategy to secure an advantage in a competitive society" (2). Addressing industrial racism as a result of the Civil War, Ignatiev asserts, "The abolition of slavery called into question the existence of the white race as a social formation, for if the main underpinning of the distinction between the 'white' worker and the black worker were erased, what could remain to motivate poor 'whites' to hug to their breasts a class of landowners who had led them into one of the most terrible wars in history?" (164). Race became the one common denominator among "whites" who constructed their identity against an "invented and contrasting blackness as its evil . . . twin" (Brodkin 151).[12] Gaines's fiction questions and complicates this popular notion in his attempt to create stories of potential hope in the midst of stark reality and to explore a more accurate representation of what it means to be American.

Using his own experience in south Louisiana as his guide, Gaines captures the full humanity of both blacks and whites, free of all romantic lighting, as they search for personal and communal identity. His Cajun characters reflect Gaines's experience among the south Louisiana people, an experience that does not represent all Cajuns but does represent another version of the Cajun story. *Cajun* to Gaines simply meant "a white man who spoke French," with no sense of Acadian ancestry or a tragic past, offering a new sense of the word as defining a much broader portion of the south Louisiana population (Gaudet and Wooton, *Porch Talk* 84). As the more elite Acadian descendants relied on the myth of Evangeline to establish festivals and a tourist industry, the lower classes forgot origin narratives and simply lived in the present as Cajuns. Shane Bernard explains the evolution from Acadian to Cajun as a loosening of ties with Acadian ancestry and history, because in Louisiana "cross-cultural pollination transformed the region's white ethnic groups into a single new ethnic group, the Cajuns" (*The Cajuns* xix). In *A Gathering of Old Men,* Sully, a Louisiana State University student, explains, "There were Cajun people back here with names like Smith and Kelly, and they claimed to be Cajuns, too, their fathers' having married Cajun women" (131). Sully's statement proves that to be Cajun in Louisiana no longer signified Acadian descent.

Born in Oscar, Louisiana, in Point Coupée Parish, Gaines lived the first fifteen years of his life with his aunt Miss Augusteen Jefferson in the River Lake Plantation quarters where he witnessed the shifts between Cajun and black communities.[13] He finally left Louisiana because his mother and stepfather believed he could benefit from the stronger education system in California, where they were living. Gaines remained in California while he finished high school, college at San Francisco State, and graduate school at Stanford, beginning his literary career along the Pacific coast (Laney 280). In *Voices from the Quarters,* Mary Ellen Doyle details Gaines's development as a writer, beginning with his teenage years in the California public libraries.[14] His stories, however, are rooted in his memories of south Louisiana.

Although literary critics have discussed the establishment of social control through racial conflict, few have realized the significance of the Cajun role in this process in connection with their identification as white by the nation at large and by American literature in general, an identification whose vulnerability Gaines captures in his fiction. In an interview with Patricia Rickels, he admits that Cajun "whiteness" led to better conditions:

Well, you must understand that they *were* our major competitors. They *were* the share croppers, the people who were on the next field over from yours. The . . . Cajuns would have the forward land, which was the better land and the blacks would have the poorer land, because they were renting this same land from another white man. ("An Interview" 123)

Gaines continues to explain that Cajuns with the better land made more money, and then used the money to purchase machines that soon made black labor appear slow in comparison (123). As captured in several of Gaines's novels, the competition between Cajuns and black men for the plantation lands has led some critics to compare Gaines's Cajuns to Faulkner's Snopeses. Frank Shelton concludes that the Cajuns "are rapacious and Snopes-like in their attempt to possess all the land for themselves. In the life of pastoralism, it is suggestive that Gaines associates them with the tractor, which has become for him the 'machine in the garden'" ("Of Machines and Men" 21). Obviously, much had changed in Cajun culture, as demonstrated through Gaines's depictions of competition between the races in *Catherine Carmier* (1964), as well as in *A Gathering of Old Men*.

In Gaines's fiction, conflict refers as much to cultural change as it does to racial tensions. The introduction of American technology and convenience, as represented by the tractor, proves to what degree Cajuns moved away from their traditional farming methods as they became more American, unlike the African Americans who could not do so, perhaps simply because they could not afford to do so. While such technology pushes Cajuns from their former way of life, this American industry also forces even more distance and tension to exist between Cajuns and their African American neighbors, since such machines negate the work of the black people who once farmed the same lands.

Carefully constructing a realistic literary portrait of south Louisiana, Gaines offers a more complicated perspective of Cajun life. Fred Hobson emphasizes Gaines's achievement in depicting his "Cajun characters as sensitively as he portrays black ones, realizing that the hot-blooded Cajun who was shot and killed [in *A Gathering of Old Men*] suffered from a similar inferiority to the landowner whites of English descent who viewed both blacks and Cajuns as if they were 'a breed beyond you'" (*The Southern Writer* 96).[15] One might note also that Creole landowners acted superior to Cajuns and African Americans (96).[16] Indeed, in an interview with

Marcia Gaudet and Carl Wooton, Gaines makes a similar point when he states, "I've lived in that interracial, or ethnic, mixture of the Cajun, and the big house owned by the Creoles—not Cajuns, but Creoles—and the blacks" ("Talking" 228).[17] Mary Ellen Doyle recites a story of the present owner of River Lake Plantation, the place of Gaines's birth: "No one was very well off, not even the landowners, but status was distinct and codes were definite; the child Madeline [the current owner] could play with the blacks on the plantation but not with the local 'poor whites,' i.e., the Cajuns" (8).

Being a man, black or white, in Gaines's fiction means reversing racism in order to endorse humanity, thus challenging the racial and social system that allowed Cajuns to become white folks and American. As much as his African American males, his Cajun characters find themselves caught between progress and the past, racism and the future, making them necessary pieces of Gaines's history. Such tensions become central in *Of Love and Dust*,[18] which evolves around the story of Marcus Payne, a black convict leased out to Marshall Hebert's farm where Sidney Bonbon is the overseer.[19] This particular novel confirms the racial system that placed Cajuns precariously above African Americans as a means of guaranteeing the power position of the wealthy landowners. Aware of the tension between Marcus and Bonbon, Hebert pits the two men against each other in order to rid himself of both, proving that the wealthy white landowners maintained control over Cajuns and African Americans.

To appreciate Gaines's complex interrelationships among the characters in *Of Love and Dust,* one must first realize the already emerging pattern in his fiction: Cajuns and blacks are competitors because the aristocratic landowners force the two groups to battle for land, for rights, and for privileges in a white man's world, an American world. From Sidney Bonbon's superficial friendship with Jim Kelly, an African American worker, to his threat to Marshall Hebert, the entire plot revolves around a battle whose lines are drawn by neither of the main characters, Marcus or Bonbon. Marcus enters the plantation world under Hebert's bondage; Bonbon, no matter what he has on the plantation owner, still lives under the direction of Hebert and other white men in the area. In an earlier version of the novel, Marcus even confronts Hebert with the inferiority of Cajuns, insolently saying, "He ain't a solid White man, he's a Cajun. . . . You think he's the same kind of White man you is?" (Gaines, "*OL and D,*" Box 3-27, 277). While this statement proves Marcus's belief that Cajuns are inferior to the white landowners, and possibly to African Americans as well, Gaines removed it from the final draft of the novel, probably because it was too dangerous a line to be spoken by any African American to a white man in the 1940s South. Regardless of his ability to deny Bonbon's assumed superiority over him, Marcus cannot overcome either Hebert's powerful maintenance of social and racial boundaries or Bonbon's whiteness, which allows for the murder of Marcus without prosecution. Thus, the final action of the novel signifies another tragedy besides the death of one young black man. Society has dictated the actions of Marcus and Bonbon, as Gaines has explained: "As far as Bonbon goes. . . . I think I state in the story that Bonbon was determined by society and his environment" (O'Brien 34).

Regardless of the relationship between African Americans and Cajuns in *Of Love and Dust*, the novel is set in the 1940s when some rules always apply. Early in the novel, Jim explains that "The Cajuns had the front-est and the best land and the colored people (those who were still hanging on) had the middle and worst land" (*OL and D* 26). When they divided up their land to rent to sharecroppers, white landowners chose to bestow certain plots of land to each race. In doing so, they guaranteed a fierce competition between the Cajuns and the blacks even as they encouraged the work of both—from which they profited. *Of Love and Dust* further addresses segregation and the competition it endorsed by portraying the Jim Crow practice of "White Only" areas: "if you were a white man you could drink a beer in [the store], but if you were colored you had to go to a little side room—'the nigger room'" (43). Again, this enforced segregation policy promoted tension between Cajuns and their black neighbors because both were working on the plantation lands and drinking separately at the same store.

Jim understands that Bonbon realizes the corruption and manipulation of the blacks by society. Bonbon even tells him, "They had it rigged. There, they got me working that boy out there and they laughing at me behind my back. They make me the fool" (258). He also acknowledges that there is nothing either Marcus or Bonbon can do about it: "Me and you— what we is? We little people, Geam. They make us do what they want us to do, and they tell us nothing. We don't have nothing to say 'bout it, do we, Geam?" (258). This conversation develops from an earlier draft of the story in which Jim admits his sympathy for "Bon Bon," Gaines's original rendering of the Cajun's name: "Poor Bon Bon, ... he was the one I felt the most pity for, I really meant it" ("*OL and D*," Box 3-27, 328). Jim continues, "He had been told that ever since the day he was born. 'You

White, Sidney. . . . And no matter how you sink, you will always be above a nigger—because you White'" (329). Jim recognizes that the Cajun and wealthy white communities have forced certain racial beliefs onto Bonbon who must answer to society if he wants to remain white in the social stratification designed by those in power.

Marshall Hebert, the Creole or genteel Acadian landowner,[20] witnesses the tension between Marcus and Bonbon, and he decides to utilize this tension to benefit himself by attempting to force Marcus to kill Bonbon. By murdering for him years earlier, Bonbon gained leverage over Hebert. Hebert's position over Marcus allows him to bribe the prisoner with freedom if he kills Bonbon, demonstrating that Bonbon is disposable in the mind of the aristocratic landowner. Marcus, however, refuses to be "no hunting dog to go round killing people for nobody else" (*OL and D* 197). Jim fully comprehends the situation and thinks to himself, "Marshall was too big. If it was just Bonbon who wanted to hurt Marcus, you might be able to prevent that. Bonbon was nothing but a poor white man, and sometimes you could go to the rich white man for help. But where did you go when it was a rich white man?" (198). Bonbon's words to Jim about the "little people" who have "nothing to say 'bout it" also reflect the dangerous situation Hebert manipulates for Marcus and Bonbon (258). "Because Bonbon own people'll kill him if he don't" kill Marcus for trying to run away with his wife (224), Hebert realizes that setting the two men against each other would solve all of his problems. By orchestrating Marcus's murder at Bonbon's hand, Hebert neutralizes Bonbon's influence and cements his superiority. With the murder of Marcus, Bonbon now has a secret, too, and no longer holds any power over Hebert. For this reason, Jim reads the situation as a setup that only benefits Marshall Hebert. And so Bonbon kills Marcus and is forced to move away from Hebert's land. At the close of the novel, Hebert has worked out a plan to rid himself of all the witnesses to his crimes and finally to shake off the thieving Bonbon. Unfortunately, this solution comes with the death of Marcus and with the reinforcement of a racial and social system that allows Cajuns to be white at the expense of their African American neighbors.

Marcus's death does not fall within the traditional lynching ritual of the time, which would have been the typical reaction of a white community toward an African American male sleeping with a white woman.[21] By erasing lynching's place within such a story of interracial relationships, Gaines allows his characters, both Cajun and African American, to confront each other as individuals, thus somewhat denying the social system's domination over them. In 1940s south Louisiana, however, such rebellion was contained through the court system. Although Bonbon tells Jim that he did not want to kill Marcus, his place within white society, albeit marginal, frees him from any legal responsibility for Marcus's death. "There wasn't a trial, there was a hearing. Bonbon got off with justifiable homicide" (277). This injustice illustrates the Cajuns' place in white America and white America's rejection of equality for African Americans, both of which acknowledge Cajun Americanization in the midst of racial conflict.

Free to move as he pleases, Bonbon visits Jim to explain the situation and describe his realization that Hebert constructed the whole situation:

> He told me he didn't want to fight Marcus, he was hoping Marcus would run from him. If Marcus had made any attempt to run, he would have let him go, and there wouldn't have been a thing said about it. But when Marcus didn't run, he had to fight him. Not just fight him, but he had to kill him. If he didn't kill Marcus, he would have been killed himself. The Cajuns on the river would have done that. (277)

Instead of filtering Bonbon's words through Jim's narration, Gaines has Bonbon speak for himself, in an earlier version. In fact, in this version Bonbon even tells Jim, "You're my friend" ("*OL and D*," Box 3-9). By giving Jim the power to interpret the Cajun's words in the published story, Gaines allows Jim a more developed sense of self-pride and control. Jim responds with no pity or understanding, and "[Bonbon] saw this in [Jim's] face and [Jim] could see how it hurt him" (*OL and D* 278). Gaines has said that, "All [Jim] is trying to say is that there's got to be some kind of balance between these two people, because they won't ever come together unless there's somebody more in the middle to sort of bring them closer together" (Rickels, "An Interview" 127). *Of Love and Dust* admits the need for this balance but refuses to allow its existence at this time in southern history. And so Gaines concludes the novel with the crushed possibility of white and black friendship, due not to the men forming the bond but to the society that claims power over these men. In *A Gathering of Old Men*, Gaines provides the means for Cajuns to empower themselves against such social and environmental controls: American education. This empowerment occurs, however, thirty years too late for Marcus and Bonbon.

Sixteen years after publishing *Of Love and Dust*, Gaines discovered a way to address the necessity and potential for social change in south Louisiana. Such change, however, depended on the education and Americanization of a Cajun football player. Ironically, Gilbert Boutan's all-American desires create a path to racial cooperation, while simultaneously igniting a new conflict within the Cajun community. *A Gathering of Old Men,* a novel set in the 1970s, thus offers a new ending to the old racial tale of black oppression and a more evolved look at Cajun Americanization and its place within Louisiana racial conflict. Gaines's memory of his writing *A Gathering of Old Men* reveals the difficulty he had with working into his fiction the complexities of south Louisiana life. Once named *The Revenge of the Old Men, Gathering* began as a Cajun reporter's narration of the murder of a Cajun man by a black sharecropper.[22] Gaines himself explains this first draft in an interview with Patricia Rickels:

> [T]he book I am reading from tonight [*The Revenge of the Old Men,* ms. of novel in progress, read at Deep South Writers Conference, Nov. 22, 1978] has this same sort of thing in it, but the narrator of the story is a Cajun. He's going to be the hero of the book. . . . But he's the narrator. I'm going to have him say somewhere that he's a Cajun. He is the most *decent* person in the entire book, as of right now. ("An Interview" 123–24)

In the same interview, Gaines discusses the competition between Cajuns and blacks in the quarters and how the blacks blamed the Cajuns for their troubles because they were present to blame (123). This lengthy description of both the Cajun–African American situation and his latest work provides readers of Gaines's fiction with a more revelatory perspective on the situations he attempts to capture. Gaines fully realizes the interstitial position of Cajuns, between white and black social positions, in south Louisiana because he understands their lower class, thus inferior, place within the white community and their already evolving cultural ways.

Although *A Gathering of Old Men* begins with Beau Boutan's death, the novel focuses mostly on the story of transformation in south Louisiana that drastically affected ethnic communities. For this reason, Gaines interlaces several narratives of change together. One such story belongs to the African American men and their discovery of self-pride as they finally realize that "Now is their chance to stand" (*Gathering* 18). By choosing to stand alongside Mathu, the assumed killer in the story, the old men become proud, courageous black men willing to face certain death at the hands of the Cajun Boutan family. They realize that the death of the Cajun means Fix, Beau's father, will be "coming with his drove" (9), yet they are determined to stand.[23]

Meanwhile, another pivotal transformation that occurs in the novel involves the Boutan family and the son who chooses to be all-American, thus demonstrating how the Cajun family at the center of the novel also evolves as education and football, both signifying American identification, replace race as the central focus of the younger generation's lives. Gil even expresses sympathy for the old men when he confronts and denies his father: "Old men. Old black men, Papa. Who have been hurt. Who wait—not for you, Papa—what you're supposed to represent. . . . Tired old men trying hard to hold up their heads" (*Gathering* 137). This moment of understanding marks a pivotal transformation in both Cajun–African American relations and in the Cajun community itself, making such alteration instrumental to cultural loss and the social hope of which Gaines writes.

Gaines's novel acknowledges racial segregation and its consequences that have faced the African Americans in Bayonne[24] by having characters repeatedly remember that the murder of a white man by a black man guarantees a lynching. Early in the novel, we are told that Beau had a father who was infamous for his cruel actions against his black neighbors: "There's not a black family in this parish Fix and his crowd hasn't hurt sometime or other" (*Gathering* 18). At times in the novel, it is unclear whether Fix was responsible for the wrongdoings or not, but the people have long reconciled their memories to Fix's identity as evil.[25] At one point, Mapes, the local sheriff, even reminds a particular character that the crime he accuses Fix of committing was actually committed by a "Sicilian, not Cajun. She had nothing to do with Fix" (107). When asked about the blaming of Cajuns for black suffering in his own experience, Gaines explained, "You find a scapegoat. You've got to find a scapegoat. And in the case of the people where I come from, if the scapegoat was white, then he was a Cajun. That's all there is to it, whether he *was* a Cajun or not" (Rickels, "An Interview" 123). Although some of the men gathered around Mathu's porch were witnesses to Fix's numerous actions against blacks, Fix and his family become the scapegoat for all cruelties the blacks faced in this novel, demonstrating Cajuns' place between African Americans and white landowners and the containment of African Americans through this placement. Moreover, Fix and his family are similarly victims of social changes and mechanization that greatly affect the lives of the black men gathered on Mathu's porch. As Mapes states, "Then you blaming the wrong person. He's as much victim of these times as you are. That's why he's back on that bayou now, because they took that river from him, too" (108). Although

Cajuns once benefited and still benefit from social classification as white and from technological progress, Gaines emphasizes how they, as well as African Americans, are affected by such progress.

Although the Boutans are responsible for some, if not most, of the black suffering in Bayonne, Gaines carefully relates their story as well as the old men's histories. Unlike *Of Love and Dust,* the novel *A Gathering of Old Men* begins with the murder of a Cajun by an African American. Suddenly, the Cajun family has to confront the suffering, usually due to more violent actions, experienced by their black neighbors, often at the hands of the Cajuns. When Gilbert Boutan returns to Bayonne, he first encounters Candy, the niece of the current plantation owners, and the old men sitting around and on Mathu's porch. Lou Dimes, a Baton Rouge reporter and Candy's boyfriend, acts as the mediator between Gil and the others, reflecting the previous drafts of *The Revenge of the Old Men* and confirming Gaines's need to retain the objective reporter figure. Unfortunately, Lou cannot guide Gil to the truth about his brother's death, so Gil confronts Candy: "You never liked any of us. Looking at us as if we're a breed below you. But we're not, Candy. We're all made of the same bone, the same blood, the same skin. Your folks had a break, mine didn't, that's all" (*Gathering* 122). This statement captures the class stratification in Louisiana that supports the racial divisions running the Marshall plantation because it proves the placement of Cajuns between the Marshall family and their African American laborers who continue to make a profit for them. Earlier in the novel, Beatrice Marshall, the plantation mistress, admits, "I don't like [Fix]. I've never liked him. Why we ever let that kind on this land, I don't know" (*Gathering* 23). Miss Bea displays her own intolerance when she exclaims, "About time [Candy] shot one of them Cajuns, messing up the land with those tractors" (23). Such statements complicate, while explaining, racial categories by addressing upper-class, white superiority over Cajuns, which Gil denies when he confronts Candy with her prejudiced assumptions based on class structures.

By denying Candy any sense of superiority, regardless of her wealthy, white status, Gil begins to turn away from the social system that controls Cajuns by placing them between racial categories. In her reading of Gil's statement, Doyle asserts, "Gil is moved to turn on Candy and assert Cajun dignity *vis-à-vis* upper-class whites; in challenging her sense of superiority and condescension to his people, he seems to release his awareness of blacks as his equals, of Cajun injustice to them" (186). His words initiate the process that can potentially cause such racial structures to collapse,

allowing for understanding and sympathy across ethnic lines. Such a connection has already occurred on the football field, and it becomes even
more of a reality when Gil "told his daddy he needed Pepper and Pepper needed him" (171). Gil, perhaps more than any other character, realizes that to be American means allowing for cooperation. Admitting such
proves the degree to which this Cajun has already become all-American.

Gil's rebellion in the novel exemplifies the growing pains Cajuns were
experiencing at the time.[26] With education comes awareness of others,
drawing one away not only from racial oppression and ignorance, but also
from one's family, as is evident in Gil's case. In many ways, A Gathering
of Old Men relates the necessity of freedom and justice for both African
Americans and Cajuns and asserts the beginning of a new era. As Frank
Shelton writes, "The South has changed as a result of the very self-asser-
tion the black men manifest in the novel. Concurrently, however, something of great importance is being lost through the change, and the novel
becomes an elegy for a disappearing rural way of life that the old men are
trying to preserve in memory and that Gaines is trying to preserve in his
fiction" ("Of Machines and Men" 27). By taking their final stand, the old
men find pride in the midst of change, but what do the Cajuns find?

While Gaines acknowledges that change leads to mechanical progress
and industrialism, his work also testifies to positive changes that occur
through such Americanization. Gil becomes Gaines's vehicle not only
into the Cajun family narrative, but also to relating how his Cajun interstitial position makes him capable of racial conciliation.[27] His role in the
novel also addresses the divisions occurring in the Cajun household as
the younger generations receive higher educations and are exposed to a
broader worldview. For Gil, football rather than farming will be his future. As Daniel White points out, the people of the quarter unite as a family while the Cajuns find themselves loosening familial bonds (178). A star
football player, Gil relies on a black player to support his winning record,
making history for LSU: "It would be the first time this had ever happened, black and white in the same backfield—and in the Deep South, besides" (Gathering 112). Gilbert "Salt" Boutan and Calvin "Pepper" Harrison play their best only as partners, which Gil readily acknowledges. It is
not accidental on Gaines's part that the white player is a Cajun.[28]

Gil's stand against his father represents not only a change in racial politics in the South but also a change in Cajun family structure as Cajuns
rush to catch up with the modern world of college, fast food, and life away
from the farm. As far as lynching is concerned, Gil says, "Those days are

gone forever, I hope" (*Gathering* 143). Instead of appreciating this reading of history, Fix accuses Gil of dismissing family bonds and honor in
order to achieve all-American status along with his African American
teammate. In Fix's eyes, the blame rests on the education the family has
worked to give to Gil (145). Whether or not Fix truly realizes it, education is the reason for Gil's less than enthusiastic response to starting a
lynching party. Through his time at LSU, Gil has experienced desegrega-
tion to his benefit with his partnership with Calvin Harrison, and he has
moved away from the plantation lands and discovered a life beyond sugarcane fields. This particular story within the novel depicts the changing
world of Cajun Louisiana as education and modernization became more
accepted and the traditional culture was no longer protected by isolation
from the rest of the world. Gil's desire to become an All-American player
parallels his movement toward an all-American identification of himself
and realizes George Washington Cable's vision of Cajun Americanization
through education and its consequences.

In assessing the rapid Americanization process for Cajuns, Bernard
emphasizes the classroom's position as a powerful "medium for dissem-
inating Americanism" because the state "organized classroom programs
for instilling Americanism," such as celebrating "I am an American Day"
(*The Cajuns* 17). Gil's behavior represents the results of such programs that
affected Cajun children in the public school system. No longer tied to the
land, Gil still retains a strong sense of family ties, which Fix echoes when
he says, "There will be no split in this family. This is family" (*Gathering*
145). While this statement calls an end to any notion of lynching Mathu,
the assumed murderer, it does not mean forgiveness for Gil for evolving
away from the past ways. Fix punishes Gil by telling him, "Go run the ball.
Let it take the place of family" (146).

Although the reason for not retaliating in the old-fashioned way, with
a lynching, rests on football statistics, it still motivates the Boutans to reject their old ways and to accept the tragic death of their sibling and son.
Football accomplishes what was never possible between Jim and Bonbon
in *Of Love and Dust:* a true mutual dependency, no matter how fragile, between a Cajun and an African American that breaks through the previous
racialized system of American identification. Gil even admits to his father,
"I can't make it without Cal, Papa. . . . I depend on him, Papa, every moment I'm on that field" (*Gathering* 138). Fred Hobson addresses both the
revolutionary position Gil takes and its superficiality in face of the im-
mense injustice that came before as "more truthful than we might like to

think: it announces a South that has indeed changed but not always for the noblest of reasons" (*The Southern Writer* 100). Gil's small steps out of racial tension may be in the right direction, but he still has far to go before justice can be served. After all, Gil's ultimate reason for preventing the lynching is self-serving since he could not make All-American if he "was involved in something against the law" (*Gathering* 138), but this reason does move him further away from his family's sense of white superiority at the expense of their African American neighbors.

Even though his sense of justice comes at a price and is still somewhat affected by his upbringing, Gil stands as a hero to his Cajun people. As Russell, a deputy, asserts, "Sometimes you have to hurt something to help something. Sometimes you have to plow under one thing in order for something else to grow. You can help Tee Beau [Gil's nephew] tomorrow. You can help this country tomorrow" (*Gathering* 151). Russell explains that by playing football and winning the game the next day, Gil would be moving toward an equality never witnessed before on a southern field, an achievement worth more than any All-American title. Gil's friend Sully who drives him down to Bayonne says, "This was Cajun country. . . . This was Gil's country. . . . Gil loved *all* the people back here, and they *all* loved him, white and black. He would shake a black man's hand as soon as he would a white man's, and the blacks would beam with pride when he did" (*Gathering* 131–32, emphasis mine). Accepting his role as local star, Gil gladly plays to the masses, which offer him a more significant reason for refusing to retaliate, since he would lose at least half of his fans if he did. This act of self-preservation may condemn Gil to the ranks of the shallow souls, but it also raises him above his family history, building for his people a bridge out of its racially charged past, a bridge constructed out of American materials. Through his study of Cajun ethnicity, James Dormon confirms the possibility of the evolution Gaines imagines since "Cajun ethnicity has been essentially processual; . . . it has been in constant process of change, reshaping and reforming and assuming different dimensions of consequences and significance as it has responded to the shaping forces both within and without the group. Ethnicity has never been a static reality of Cajun existence" (90). By the 1970s, to be Cajun meant to be American, an ever-shifting and adapting identity.

Before closing the novel, Gaines reveals in a parenthetical aside that "LSU beat Ole Miss, twenty-one to thirteen. Both Gil and Cal had over a hundred yards each" (*Gathering* 212). While discussing the novel with Elsa Saeta and Izora Skinner, Gaines himself said, "the only ones who live in the present are Salt and Pepper. They're the ones living in the present and they're the ones who must make this America work. We've got to block for each other and do all kinds of things to get to the goal. The football players are a symbol for how we must do this together" (250). They are the all-American characters who symbolize hope that comes from the nation's diversity. By the end of the day, the Cajuns suffer without retaliation, and the union of Salt and Pepper and the acceptance of change present some hope to the torn community.

By creating Cajun characters and giving them voices, Ernest Gaines captures the world in which he grew up—and in so doing presents a new knowledge of Cajuns to an American audience. Neither simplistic nor angelic, the Cajuns of Gaines's fiction occupy a unique and complicated space in which actual Cajuns survived within south Louisiana. His fiction also addresses the role some Cajuns played in socially controlling African Americans, a history the 1920s revivalists wished to keep silent. According to Brundage, "In a real sense, the revivalists placed the Acadian saga outside the flow of southern and, indeed, American history," by telling themselves that the "Cajuns . . . were not really of the South" (272). Gaines erases all such facades as he strips away any notion of Cajun purity and innocence. He reveals another side of the Cajun past, full of flaws and graces, a people struggling to come to terms with their personal Americanization experience.

In addressing Cajuns as American, Gaines establishes their national status in literature. He also emphasizes his own identification as American, regardless of early twentieth-century notions, because of his experience in Louisiana:

> I think I'm more American than most people are. I know I have access to things white, and Cajun, and of course African. I can look at all those three bloods at times—I can put them all together, I can look at them individually, and see which one has taken over inside of me on certain days. I know that the blood of all those are in me. (Lowe 323)

He concludes, "I don't know any other culture but *American* culture" (324, emphasis mine), proving that what constituted being American continued to shift away from notions of whiteness. By publishing his novels, Gaines gives the world a clearer vision of a changing South and, consequently, a changing Cajun culture.

5. The Journey Home

JAMES LEE BURKE'S PARABLE OF CAJUN ASSIMILATION

"Change comes even to the bayou. But in our mind's eye, we still see New Iberia the way Dave Robicheaux does...."

—TUTWILER, "James Lee Burke's Acadiana: On the Trail of Detective Dave Robicheaux"

James Lee Burke has created a fictional character with international appeal who also reminds a regional people of a unique cultural past. Dave Robicheaux searches for resolution with his Cajun past in the corrupt world of south Louisiana where economic and industrial progress inevitably change what he considers a simpler Cajun way of life. What Dave must acknowledge and accept is that "[c]hange comes even to the bayou" (Tutwiler), but this fact remains Dave's greatest obstacle. In many ways, his detective work acts as a metaphor for Cajun cultural loss, and his violent behavior stems from his own need to reconcile his double identity, as both Cajun and American. Underlining Burke's detective series, a more provocative parable emerges: a revised version of the prodigal son story complete with a son who discovers that he simply cannot return to his father's figurative home, not because the father would not accept him but because such a "home," the past, no longer exists.

As is the case with most detective fiction, Dave's search for justice refers not only to his professional impulse to capture criminals, but also to his personal struggle to locate meaning in his fractured life, a need reflecting the postmodern world in which he lives. Samuel Coale asserts that mysteries remain popular because they "creat[e] a rational world amid an irrational or at the very least a non-rational world" (1). Such fiction clarifies, solves, and resolves cultural and communal problems that cause anxiety and fear to develop in the first place. Readers are thus comforted by easy and efficient resolutions. What began with Edgar Allan Poe and ratiocination has become a more complex handling of not only national concerns, but also ethnic insecurities and vulnerabilities because, as John Cawelti argues, "literary formulas assist in the process of assimilating changes in values to traditional and imaginative construct," because they "ease the transition between old and new ways of expressing things and thus contribute to cultural continuity" (36). Burke's Dave Robicheaux series depicts such changes and offers readers a more contemporary Cajun character to ease the transition between old and new ways.

In his hard-boiled detective series, Burke continues to create stories in which the detective discovers and contains threats to society, thus protecting the community from violence and harm. Dave Robicheaux is not, however, the typical tough guy; his motivation to resolve criminal activity in south Louisiana stems from an ethnic and regional perspective that creates complex relations between the detective and his search for justice. Instead of focusing on national anxieties, Burke directs his audience's attention to local geographical and political settings complete with fading ethnic traditions and cultural belief systems, thus placing the center of anxiety firmly within the ethnic community. Coale's interest in minority detective figures as a means of examining cultural differences pertains to the function of Cajun identity in Burke's work because "with all of these writers there remains the continuing problem of relating a marginal group . . . to the center and including them in mainstream popular fiction" (33). To be included in and recognized by the mainstream signifies an acceptance, a sense of belonging. Such belonging points to assimilation; after all, to become a popular author means that you must write to suit the needs of a national audience; however, this position can also be used as a point of power to distribute and perpetuate one's own image of one's ethnic community.[1] As for formulaic structures, the same principles apply: the writer can subvert tradition by claiming it as his own and revising the formula to suit his specific literary needs. Burke's Cajun detective series functions within this between position because it uses typical literary patterns to subvert the traditional meaning of such formula. Dave solves, often through violent means, the crimes that plague his hometown, but any complete sense of resolution is denied because Dave must continue battling personal crimes he has committed through assimilation.

Dave Robicheaux may be a detective, but he is, first and foremost, a twentieth-century Cajun who has assimilated to mainstream American culture, which causes him guilt and a sense of loss in terms of his relationship with his dead father. William Marling discusses detective fiction as it parallels the biblical story of the Prodigal Son: "The formula of these genres was to focus graphically, usually in the first person, on the temptations that led down the road to perdition, but to provide a moral ending with appropriately pious sentiments, making the narrative one of improvement" (6). Marling's "narrative of improvement" fits into the context within which Burke writes, but not always for the obvious reasons. Dave suffers from his disconnection from his father, but his "narrative of improvement" will never reconcile him with his father because the division extends from cultural, not personal, differences. For this reason, the prodigal son's return may never be re-enacted, since Dave's American assimilation has already occurred and changed him and has altered his connection with the past. While Dave successfully solves local crimes, he continues to contemplate larger issues, such as cultural loss, that simply have no resolution.

As evidence of such loss and change, Dave's Southwestern Louisiana Institute (later USL and now the University of Louisiana at Lafayette) degree makes him an example of the educated Cajun who quickly assimilated to an American, middle-class way of life via education. After attaining middle-class American status, Dave discovers that his education has helped to create a gap between himself and his father, which expands as Dave becomes more American while his father remains an illiterate Cajun fisherman and oil industry laborer. In *The Neon Rain* (1987), Dave explains that he and his brother "would change a lot when we went to college in Lafayette, and in many ways we would begin to leave our father's Cajun world behind us" (65). Such changes occurred in reality as well as in fiction, as Shane Bernard emphasizes repeatedly in his study of the Americanization of Cajuns. By the 1960s, Cajun "youths sensed not only a generation gap between themselves and their parents but also a cultural gap. They spoke English and, like young people across the nation, they listened to the Beatles, the Rolling Stones, and Bob Dylan" (Bernard, *The Cajuns* 61). Education and national changes made Cajun youths more American.

Dave Robicheaux's personal struggles can be read as a representation of the uncertainty facing Cajuns at the turn of the century. According to Bernard, by the end of the twentieth century *Cajun* "ceased to describe a mainly French-speaking, non-materialistic, impoverished people on the fringe of American society and instead referred to a largely English-speaking, consumer-oriented, middle-class community whose members closely resembled mainstream Americans" (*The Cajuns* 146). Cajuns became Americans who were more than capable of adapting their Cajun pasts to embrace modern American comforts.

Demonstrating this Americanization process and the futile attempt to return to the past, Dave's degree in English literature and his repeated allusions to literary works place him far from his father's illiterate Cajun French culture. In *Black Cherry Blues* (1989), Dave refers to literature to recall a rural and simpler Louisiana lifestyle that has long faded away. While in Montana to solve a murder, Dave carries "a paperback copy of Ernest Gaines's *Of Love and Dust*" in his pocket, which he reads in a local park: "I was already inside the novel, back on a hot sugarcane and sweet potato plantation in south Louisiana in the 1940s. No, that's not really true. I was back in New Iberia the summer after my second year in college" (188).[2] He recalls a moment in his own development away from Gaines's quarters and his father's Cajun life. Such literary moments force Dave to realize the chaos and violence that threaten his life, personally and culturally, which he also connects to his movement away from his father's home.

Burke purposefully exaggerates Cajun flaws in his detective fiction in order to address Cajun assimilation and change as inevitable while also discussing certain forces, such as the oil industry, that ushered in change at the request of the Cajun people, among others. In his quest to put an end to criminal activity, Dave not only realizes his own sinful nature, but also faces Cajuns' fall from grace, powerfully symbolized by their cultural loss. Through his construction of a fallen Louisiana, Burke portrays Cajun culpability in environmental destruction and injustice while also exposing tensions that arose within the Cajun community between the desire for progress and the need to maintain a Cajun identity.

The American genre of detective fiction, with its emphasis on violence and entertainment, provides Burke with a powerful, mass-marketed vehicle for his message of cultural assimilation and change because both the traditional detective formula and its more violent descendant, the hard-boiled detective story, address cultural and social anxieties. The hard-boiled detective story, in particular, began with the publication of *Black Mask,* a crime magazine published in the 1920s, a time when American authors such as F. Scott Fitzgerald, John O'Hara, and William Faulkner turned to a "dark style of narrative" (Marling ix). Cawelti argues that this interest in narrative tone may stem from a loss of traditional religious values and the development of scientific explanations of human behavior (56, 58), a loss that also threatens Cajuns at the end of the twentieth century. In a world of change and chaos, darkness threatens to overwhelm humanity. Burke may not follow all of the generic techniques, but his Dave Robicheaux series establishes the threat of darkness, especially in terms of fading cultural ways, and the necessity of dispelling this shadow from the hero's life. The hard-boiled detective "finds himself up against a corrupt and violent society that threatens to destroy him. He, too, is tempted, betrayed, and wounded, by that society to the point where he realizes that to preserve his integrity he must reject the public ideals and values of the society and seek to create his own personal code of ethics and his own set of values" (161). Dave faces real and cultural violence that threatens not only to destroy him, but also to desecrate the ethnic identity he holds sacred. Simultaneously he realizes that he has already become a part of this very darkness that threatens him, leading him to search for his "own personal code of ethics" and values. For Dave, such an ethical code and such a value system extend directly from his father, whose Cajun ways made him, in his son's eyes, the model for honest and sincere living. The question that haunts Dave, however, is whether or not he can live as his father lived.

Facing such darkness in his personal life as he finds himself disillusioned and betrayed by the New Orleans Police Department for which he has worked, Dave travels back to New Iberia in a passage of *The Neon Rain* that recalls the journey as a search for a past era, one of seeming naturalness:

> Annie [his second wife] and I rode the boat the last few miles into New Iberia, and we ate crawfish *etouffée*[3] on the deck and watched our wake slip up into the cypress and oak trees along the bank, watched yesterday steal upon us—. . . . It was the Louisiana I had grown up in, a place that never seemed to change, where it was never a treason to go with the cycle of things and let the season have its way. (281)

Dave interprets his boat ride back to New Iberia, his childhood community, as a journey back to "yesterday." Such details as *etouffée* and cypress and oak trees place Dave and the reader firmly within the Cajun environment, which is exactly what Dave wants. He wants to slip back to a past Louisiana of nature and culture. This passage ends with Dave's nostalgia: "It was the Louisiana I had grown up in, a place that never seemed to change" (281). *Heaven's Prisoners* (1988), which describes his adoption of his daughter and the murder of his second wife, forces Dave to face reality when crime comes crashing through Cajun Louisiana. Only about a year later, Dave realizes that no matter how well he remembers his childhood Louisiana, change inevitably comes to the bayou.

Both *Heaven's Prisoners* and *Black Cherry Blues* demonstrate Dave's inability to return to his father's home simply because symbolically it no longer exists. Although he successfully reinserts himself into the geographical place where his father lived, as he did as a child, Dave realizes that the Cajun world he craves has already been replaced by mainstream American culture and violence that sweeps him further away from the past to which he longs to return. Dave considers the Cajun bayou as a peaceful place, a safe haven inherited from Acadian forefathers and mothers: "If as a child, I had been asked to describe the world I lived in, I'm sure my response would have been in terms of images that in general left me with a sense of well-being about myself and my family. . . . I had a home—actually a world—on the bayou . . . a place that was ours and had belonged to our people and way of life since the Acadians came to Louisiana in 1755" (*HP* 45). Such bonds with his Acadian identity and past ways remind Dave that his Cajun identity cannot be taken away from him and that the land his family settled remains his. Murders, rapes, and other abuses invade this world on the bayou, however, and forever taint its place in Dave's memory. Through such passages, Dave struggles toward a personal consideration of and reconciliation toward change, which is doubly difficult because by acknowledging and allowing for change, he must loosen his ties to a past that he believes can bring him peace.

Dave's search for the past, and thus for resolution, frames his commitment to justice in the present. Throughout Burke's series, Dave relates, confronts, and addresses racial and ethnic crimes that are continuing to tear the nation from its roots. Whether in terms of a personal or social past, Dave realizes that to forget would be dangerous, and to deny even more so. Such novels as *Black Cherry Blues, Purple Cane Road* (2000), and *Burning Angel (1995),* among others, center around national policies that have attempted to erase differences and their consequences to modern day America.

Purple Cane Road opens by setting up the execution of Letty Labiche, a musician who along with her twin sister, Passion, was once the victim of sexual abuse. Letty and Passion, Creoles of Color, lived as children next to Vachel Carmouche who served as the electric chair engineer for the state. With his job as protection, Vachel continued to abuse the girls until he suddenly left south Louisiana. Letty and Passion lived in freedom until the day their tormentor returned with an African American girl. No one knows the truth about that day until Passion reveals the story toward the end of the novel. But Letty is set for execution because she was found washing her blood-soaked clothes behind her house as Vachel lay massacred in his home. The story of Letty and Passion is the pivotal plotline throughout the novel, complete with references to racial injustice based on the fact that a black woman killed her abuser who happens to be white, and thus she is facing certain death.

While Letty's story brings racial injustice to the forefront of Dave's detective work, *Burning Angel* best addresses racial conflict in south Louisiana and establishes Dave's need to right past racial wrongs, making it an interesting novel in relation to Ernest Gaines's specific focus on Cajun–African American relations. *Burning Angel* takes place about five years before *Purple Cane Road,* and it reveals past violence and white Louisianians' participation in and guilt over local injustices. As William and Charlene Clark note, Burke "loves his native land, and he refuses to dissociate himself from the tragedy and undeniable heroism of its past . . . at the same time, he refuses to rationalize away the horrors of slavery or the mutually demeaning system of racial injustice that eventually replaced it" (68–69). Burke's realistic vision of south Louisiana has led him to create the character Dave Robicheaux, who accepts the reality of racial crimes and attempts to address past wrongs because he realizes that if he ignores the past then he becomes part of such crimes.

Once again Dave finds himself in the middle of a complex plot to exploit the vulnerable when Bertha Fontenot, an old African American woman, requests his aid in protecting her from eviction from the plantation quarters where she has lived her entire life. Dave travels to the plantation to discuss the matter with Moleen Bertrand, the present owner. According to Bertha, Bertrand's "grandfather gave her family the land" (*BA* 21). Bertrand denies the claim and further argues, "The truth is we haven't charged her any rent. She's interpreted that to mean she owns the land" (21). In reality, she has worked the land in a way that makes it her own because she belongs to it. This passage recalls the nature of slavery and the southern tenant-farming system, both of which bond African Americans to the land without paying them fairly for their work.[4]

Unlike the house his father built on the land that still belongs to the family,[5] Dave realizes that the plantation lands of south Louisiana harbor memories of sin, guilt, and greed: "This piece of land was our original sin, except we had found no baptismal rite to expunge it from our lives" (279). Through this use of *our,* Dave acknowledges that his white American and Cajun identity, or just his identity as part of humankind, marks him as a participant in national crimes. The land forces him to acknowledge the reality of injustice and human violence, crimes that cannot and should not be forgotten.

The significance of the land increases when the people of the quarters cannot even claim the buried bodies of their ancestors. Dave describes the plantation graveyard and its fading identity as such because of neglect: "The graves were no more than faint depressions among the drifting leaves, the occasional wooden cross or board marker inscribed with crude lettering and numbers knocked down and cracked apart by tractors and cane wagons, except for one yawning pit whose broken stone tablet lay half buried with fallen dirt at the bottom" (*BA* 34). Like Gaines's old men, the Fontenot family has witnessed the desecration of their sacred and cultural space and of their way of life through the coming of the tractors that replaced them in the fields. Bertha refuses to lose her home, the only one she has known, to progress. This evil may be in a new form, but it is nothing new to south Louisiana where "slaves who worked the sawmills, cane fields, and the salt domes out in the wetlands would speak the language and use the names of their owners, and the day when a large sailing ship appeared innocuously on a river in western Africa . . . would become the stuff of oral legend, confused with biblical history and allegory, and finally forgotten" (102). According to Dave Robicheaux, what remains in twentieth-century south Louisiana is an African American people who now have biblical allusions and allegorical tales as a connection to a forgotten and lost past, much like Cajuns have used the myth of Evangeline, laced with biblical imagery and metaphor, to reconstruct their own past. In such a space that recalls slavery of all kinds, Bertha does not forget, however, her memories of a family who lived through such conditions and who died on the plantation, and this memory she is determined to preserve.

Burke not only consistently relates the racial tensions, injustices, and crimes that prevail in south Louisiana as reminders for the readers, but he also places Dave outside of the state borders in *Black Cherry Blues* to portray another ethnic stain on our nation's history as Dave confronts the murder of two Indians who belonged to the American Indian Movement and fought to retain the sacred ground on which their ancestors were buried. While searching for their bodies, Dave recalls "the Baker massacre of 1870. . . . a geographical monument to what was worst in us" (196). Earlier in the novel, he remembers that although the American government no longer massacred its natives, it still "starved them and gave them a rural slum to live in" (127). As part of the nation that has "taken from the Blackfeet," the tribe portrayed in the novel, Dave views his mission to uncover two missing bodies as an act of contrition for his nation's sins (127). This mission also becomes an act of contrition for his own sin of cultural loss. The American Indians die because of their dedication to preserving and protecting their identity as other than mainstream white American, an identity that Dave has accepted even as it meant division from his father's Cajun way of life.

By placing such racial and ethnic crimes at the center of his novels, Burke emphasizes Dave's movement away from his Cajun past as he has come to embrace and accept progress in his own life. Both the Fontenot family and the Native Americans of whom Burke writes are determined to deny complete assimilation into mainstream American culture by remembering and honoring their ancestors whose struggles mean survival in the present. By protecting the sacredness of burial grounds, they remind Dave that, even through death and change, cultural memory and ritual can remain alive within communities. While Dave strives to aid such communities, perhaps because of his own sense of loss, he also faces the personal crime of assimilation, which makes him guilty of such ethnic crimes both because he chose to move away from his Cajun past and because he chose to identify as an American, thus as a middle-class white man. In *Burning Angel,* Dave even goes so far as to parallel the crimes against African Americans with his own acceptance of American assimilation and its consequences in terms of his participation in the Vietnam Conflict. Through such an examination of conscience, Dave comes to terms with the horrors of his past and present:

> I believe Moleen Bertrand was like many of my generation with whom I grew up along Bayou Teche. We found ourselves caught inside a historical envelope that we never understood, borne along on wind currents that marked our ending, not our beginning, first as provincial remnants of a dying Acadian culture, later as part of that excoriated neo-colonial army who would go off to a war whose origins were as arcane to us as the economics of French poppy growers. (429)

No longer the victims of British imperialism, Acadian descendants are now participants in American imperialism, whether they realize it or not, and as such become enmeshed in the darkness that threatens their former way of life.

Ironically, Dave can and does return to his ancestor's land, something the African American and Native American characters cannot do without being threatened or even murdered. Such return is possible because of his assimilation to, thus nondifference from, American culture. Dave's return is marred, however, by the already developing distance between his past and his present way of life. Such victims as African Americans and Native Americans thus exist as both guides and accusers for Dave, whose own journey back home triggers questions about his notions of the sacred, remembered past in light of his Americanization.

Struggling to resolve such complications that extend from personal and social situations, Dave Robicheaux confronts the power of outside forces, represented by the oil industry and mainstream American culture, that have tempted him and other Cajuns by offering them possible economic advancement and that threaten Cajun culture by offering convenience. This infiltration of outside forces further distorted the traditional locus of culture because such advances broke down cultural traditions and re-shaped cultural ways. Louisianians, including Cajuns, welcomed indus-tries into the state because of their promise of jobs and money, but these companies also left environmental change and destruction in their wake. Carl Brasseaux writes of the oil industry, "Upon returning to Acadiana, [WWII] veterans discovered their homeland was being transformed . . . [into] an extension of the Anglo-American world" ("Acadian Education" 138). Glenn Conrad also notes that the "exploitation of these [oil] depos-its for a mechanizing America brought English-speaking geologists, tech-nicians, drillers, and roughnecks into Acadiana" (15) and irrevocably af-fected Cajun culture.

In *Black Cherry Blues,* Burke describes how the oil industry threatens south Louisiana lands and cultures, including Cajun culture. In Dave's life, the most significant and painful reminder of this destruction is his fa-ther's death, which was caused by industry negligence (*BCB* 51). Not only did men like Dave's father die because of a lack of safety measures, but the economy also felt the tragic consequences of industrial reliance when "the bottom had dropped out of the oil business," resulting in "the highest rate of unemployment in the country and the worst credit rating" (19). On a personal, cultural, regional, and state level, the oil industry irreparably changed Louisiana.

Facing this change, Dave recalls the time when the Lafayette Oil Cen-ter was being built:

And to accommodate the Oil Center traffic the city had widened Pin-hook Road, ... The oak and pecan trees along the road had been cut down, the rural acreage subdivided and filled with businesses and fast-food restaurants, the banks around the Vermilion Bridge paved with asphalt parking lots and dotted with more oil-related businesses whose cinder-block architecture had all the aesthetic design of a sewage-treatment works. (BCB 46)

As in the passage quoted above that describes him returning to his childhood home, here Dave seems to gravitate toward the natural beauty of the land, the oak and pecan trees. Unlike the earlier passage, however, this one explains how such nature can be removed to make way for progress that comes with an oil boom and fast-food restaurants, which make the roadway no longer one in Cajun country but any street in America. Asphalt replaces the geographical uniqueness of the land, making it anonymous as any other street in the country. The very land that calls to Dave and reminds him of his Cajun identity has no control over the desires of humans and the inevitability of change.[6]

Such human and environmental deaths act as reminders of the losses caused by the industrial changes that reshaped south Louisiana. By combining such physical signs of progress with personal moments of memory, Dave's story connects them to reveal a larger tale of cultural loss that heightens the prodigal theme evident in this detective series. Such passages depict the destruction of the home that Dave seeks. He will never have an actual moment of reconciliation with his father because his father is dead; he will never be able to return to a cultural space he considers his past because it has been replaced with asphalt slabs and office buildings. Whether crime enters the scene or not, Dave must realize that the changes that have already taken place make such a return an impossibility. What does remain as a bond with such a past and such people is memory, and it is memory that becomes Dave's beacon of hope as he battles not only to accept change in order to live peacefully in the present, but also to preserve difference in order to maintain his Cajun pride in the midst of a quickly homogenizing society.

Even as he holds fast to memories of his past, Dave must realize that memory can also change. As twentieth-century Cajuns became more American, their memory of an actual Acadian past faded. Simultaneously, Longfellow's *Evangeline* and its image of Acadian purity and patience began to gain popularity with the St. Martinville tourist industry around the 1920s, demonstrating W. Fitzhugh Brundage's argument that Evangeline and such Acadian images became both commodities and memories of Cajun identity. In many ways, *Evangeline* replaced actual Acadian folklore even among the Cajuns themselves as the story of the 1755 dispersal and consequent settlement in Louisiana.[7] Whether consciously or not, Burke's detective series rewrites *Evangeline*'s depiction of the Acadians by revising the story of Acadian innocence and, thus, reshaping the literary memory of Cajun life, one that addresses the tensions Cajuns face as they become more American and loosen their ties with their Acadian past. Burke sets his Cajun detective fiction in south Louisiana, specifically in New Iberia, just a stone's throw away from St. Martinville's Evangeline park and St. Martin of Tours Catholic Church, which harbor the Evangeline oak and statue. These cultural symbols constantly remind Dave and the reader that an actual past can be remade into a mythic one through the function of collective and cultural memory, which Dave constantly reconstructs through his reshaping of personal memory.

If Dave Robicheaux represents Cajuns who have risen in class and educational status through American assimilation made possible with the introduction of oil and other major industries to south Louisiana lands, his stories also represent how memory can become a means of holding on to the Cajun past while in the midst of rapid assimilation to American middle-class status. Dave may never be able to return to his father's "home" because such a space no longer exists in the violent and ever-changing world, but a bond with the past can be formed through memory.

Now, perhaps more than ever, cultural memory has become a means to maintain a sense of Cajun difference even as Cajuns identify as American because it remains a key to arguing differentiation in the midst of assimilation. Critical discussions of cultural and collective memory consistently question the factual nature of memory while also contemplating identity formation constructed by such re-presentations of the past. Maurice Halbwachs notes:

> We preserve memories of each epoch in our lives, and these are continually reproduced; through them . . . our sense of identity is perpetuated. But precisely because these memories are repetitions, because they are successively engaged in very different systems of notions, at different periods of our lives, they have lost the form and the appearance they once had. (47)

Memories change because we revise them as we associate them with new experiences and give them new meanings in our everyday lives. Although this process may seem to threaten our connection with the past, in truth it allows us to reform our relationships with our personal, cultural, and national histories in order to create narratives that speak to our present situations.

To further complicate the significance of the Cajun past as it is framed through memory, Dave adds his own meaning to his father's simpler way of life, thus changing the past to suit his present situation. Along with his sense of the past within present memory, David Lowenthal addresses the revising of the past in the shape of memory and its relation to communal identity when he claims, "To reshape is as vital as to preserve," because "[a]s a living force the past is ever remade. Heritage cannot be stored in a vault or an attic; the true steward adds his own stamp to his predecessors" (12). Through this constant evolution of memory, Dave searches for resolution because it is through memories that he confronts personal tensions regarding his interstitial place between an American present and an Acadian past. Dave demonstrates that Cajun culture is an in-between way of life, especially in terms of the late twentieth and early twenty-first centuries. In Burke's fiction, reshaping memory becomes a necessary and violent process through which cultural difference is threatened, and through which it can survive.

Detective fiction can become a means of affecting memory, whether intentional or not, because of its national and international appeal. While disparaging Burke for his exaggeration of violence in *Purple Cane Road* (269), Vaughan Baker emphasizes the connection between popular fiction and collective memory. Baker also lists such Louisiana mystery writers as Julie Smith and Barbara Hambly as participants in a popular media that falsely "shape our collective memory of our Louisiana culture" (263). She continues her argument by emphasizing that "contemporary detective fiction using Louisiana locales shows that it reinforces a gothic vision of the state as a dark, steamy, often violent place where uninhibited emotion reigns and the boundaries of civilized restraint are loose" (268).[8] Baker also calls for a new type of Louisiana fiction writer as a means of rewriting popular images of Louisiana life and people:

> To win the battle against the seductions of the popular media, Louisiana needs an army of writers dedicated to the task that properly belongs to the historian and has been appropriated by novelists—portraying an accurate cultural dynamic and resurrecting a vivid and meaningful experience of how real human beings lived their lives. Only these can accurately serve collective memory. (273)

This call to arms addresses fiction's power over collective memory and the extension of Louisiana detective fiction outside of the state and the nation. Such international popularity guarantees a wider audience for Louisiana writers, who then use this awareness of their work to share with readers a sense of that state's complicated racial past and rich cultural present.

Baker makes a significant point concerning the popularity and extensive distribution of Louisiana detective fiction. In truth, detective fiction has become a means of addressing national tensions and of educating cultural outsiders because of its national and international popularity. Baker specifically calls to task Burke, Smith, and Hambly, all of whom write about characters in search of personal meaning in a Louisiana that has changed and will continue to change, making the traditional path to solving crime a more extensive metaphor for the journey to cultural and communal identity in times of upheaval.[9] The very violence that Baker discourages reflects the disruptive power of change in terms of racial, ethnic, and personal discovery, and its exaggeration in detective fiction emphasizes the real consequences of alienation and confusion within the detective, the one person capable of solving crimes. In other words, Louisiana detective fiction has become a literary framework for ethnic and cultural conflict arising from the intersection of American mainstream culture and the fading ways of a unique Louisiana past.

While critics who have studied detective and mystery fiction readily admit that such works are "created for the purpose of enjoyment and pleasure" (Cawelti 2), Baker's essay frames detective fiction within a new context. Burke's fiction demonstrates to some degree Baker's claim that such fiction has an effect on collective memory, because his main character longs for the memories that Burke's audience shares through his writing. Through his use of a popular formula, Burke not only captures the real tensions located within ethnic communities that face complete American assimilation, but also the reality that such complete assimilation can be resisted with such fictional reminders of a history and heritage beyond fast food and shopping malls.

At the end of each novel, Dave Robicheaux realizes that he can always return to New Iberia, but he can never return to the past. As with Cajun culture, Dave learns to erase any notion of preserving, in full, events and people that have passed from his life. But memory remains part of him and a pivotal piece of his Cajun identity since, as Marita Sturken writes, cultural memory's "authenticity is derived not from its revelation of any original experience but from its role in providing continuity to a culture" (259). Dave's memories of his father and his childhood days provide him with a connection between the Cajun past and his present battle against evil. His continuing participation in *fais do-dos* (*HP* 116) and his memory of "Jolie Blonde" (100), although rare moments in his chaotic life, remind him and the reader of the past and seem to refute the notion that Cajun culture is dying, but such brief glimpses into Cajun traditions also emphasize the changes that have come to the bayou.

In *Purple Cane Road,* Burke actually conflates Dave's memory of his mother with his detective work, since he must uncover the truth regarding his mother's death not only to solve the crime, but also to resolve himself to his memory of her. Mae Guillory Robicheaux left Dave's family for another man, and Dave equates the loss of his mother with a Cajun past that has been tainted by the present world and its corruption. In a private moment of contemplation, he thinks, "But it was more than my mother's death that obsessed me. Long ago I had accepted the loss of my natal family and my childhood and the innocence of the Cajun world I had been born into" (*PCR* 178). By framing the desertion of his mother through his personal loss of innocence, and then using such loss as a metaphor for his cultural erosion, Dave establishes the double significance of his search for truth. In claiming his mother's innocence, he can, in a way, reclaim a piece of his own past, which he views as an innocent state of Cajun life. Throughout *Purple Cane Road,* he does not return to the past as much as he struggles to resolve his emotions about certain events. He proves successful in the end because he does revise his memory of his mother to claim her as the Cajun mother and wife, the prodigal woman who returns successfully to the fold through the uplift made possible through the work of her son. While searching through a scrapbook Mae created while still alive, Dave discovers newspaper articles relating his career in the New Orleans Police Department: "My mother had been virtually illiterate and was probably not sure of the content of many of the articles she had saved. . . . But I knew who my mother was. She had said it to her killers before she died. Her name was Mae Robicheaux. And I was her son" (341). The novel thus ends with a sense of resolution, even if the point of forgiveness and understanding exists in the space of memory. By rehabilitating his mother's reputation through his detective work, Dave can and does represent his memory of his mother in terms of her role in his life. Such moments in the Robicheaux series depict the spaces of hope Dave finds within the violently torn landscape of his regional, cultural, and psychological life.

This hope arises from his recognition of change, his detection of personal meaning within such change, and his resolution to these changes.

A couple of years after he reclaims his mother's memory, Dave romanticizes her along with his father in his mind, proving how time can alter memory. In *Crusader's Cross* (2005), he recalls both of his parents as "the most brave and resourceful people," even though they "were illiterate [and] barely spoke English" (68). That he includes his mother in this statement demonstrates how she has grown in his own estimation of her goodness and significance to his Cajun past. He even labels her, along with his father, as someone innocent of the outside world who found the strength to survive a difficult life: "They did all this with the innocence of people who had never been farther away from their Cajun world than their weekend honeymoon trip to New Orleans" (68). Murdered by the mafia because she witnessed a crime, Mae Guillory Robicheaux becomes another means for her son to construct memories of a simpler Cajun past, proving that Dave can and does revise his memory as a way to preserve hope in the present. In a poetic moment of mourning, he imagines that his mother's body "must have drifted southward into the salt water, and now I wanted to believe she and Big Al were together under the long, green roll of the Gulf, all their inadequacies washed away, their souls just beginning the journey they could not take together on earth" (*PCR* 283). He imagines the reconciliation and preservation of his family, both past and present, regardless of internal and external threats, and allows such images to reshape his memory of the past.

Dave constantly returns to his childhood memories in times of danger, as if they offer protection from the violent world that threatens him. Allen Pridgen notes that "[i]n search of an alternative to the dark present world he patrols, Dave at times retreats inward to memories of his childhood in post–World War II New Iberia" (70). Dave comes to terms with this retreat: "I try to remember the Louisiana of my youth and to convince myself that we can rehabilitate the land and ourselves and regain the past. It's a debate I seldom win" (*CC* 38). Although he can and does rehabilitate his personal memories of his mother, Dave realizes that he cannot do the same for the Cajun world surrounding him because it is impossible to return to the past, except through memory. And memory, as Barbara Bogue explains, may be a "cultural and nostalgic haven" for Dave, but it is also susceptible to changes because "[t]ime distorts memory and most often the good old days are not really so good" (130). For this reason, memory may be a space of hope for Dave, but it remains a faulty bridge to the past locked firmly in the present. Although his memories allow him to resolve himself to tragedies and losses, Dave's ultimate means of forgiveness, resolution, and survival is located in the present, in his own life as a Cajun in an ever-changing world.

One of the most telling signs of Dave's continual assimilation to mainstream American culture and its consequences becomes evident through his relationship with Alafair, his adopted daughter who is originally from El Salvador.[10] Attempting to aid her in finding a home in south Louisiana, Dave fills her life with pop cultural references and images, including "Disney films, Kool-Aid, *boudin*,[11] bluepoint crabs," which, he realizes, "were probably poor compensation for the losses she had known. But you offer what you have . . . and maybe somewhere down the line affection grows into faith and replaces memory" (*BCB* 42). Alafair quickly becomes an honorary Cajun as she adopts Dave's way of life, but her Cajun identity illustrates the degree to which Cajuns have assimilated to mainstream American culture. Dave continues to live with his memory even as he persists in helping Alafair dispose of her own, but the Cajun life he gives his daughter demonstrates a mix of Cajun and American cultural references. Dave and Alafair's relationship also represents the two-way process of cultural assimilation. Alafair can and does identify herself as a Cajun, regardless of her lack of Acadian heritage, even as Dave becomes more American and more divided from his father's way of life. Cajun culture has become part of American culture, complete with Hollywood references and English language usage.[12]

In Alafair, Cajun assimilation occurs simultaneously with Americanization, and she represents those who adopted Cajun ways, identifying themselves with their Cajun neighbors and spouses regardless of their lack of Acadian descent.[13] Even as "French names are now joining with the Smiths, Joneses, Schmidts, Garcias, Gallaghers et al." (Bernard, *The Cajuns* 39), the process by which Alafair becomes a Robicheaux creates an interesting example of this trend. Her becoming Cajun results from the Cajun trend to embrace outsiders and their cultural ways, which opens a two-way door: Cajuns became more American while introducing the nation to Cajun traditions. This relationship forces Dave to live firmly in the present following the murder of Annie, his wife, because Alafair requires his attention. Her Salvadoran heritage and her quick acceptance of her place within his home prove that one's past does not have to dominate one's present. Alafair's ability to adapt quickly to a Cajun American way of life after experiencing the tragic deaths of her parents acts as a reminder to Dave of his own inability to let go of the dead and the past in order to survive and find peace and happiness in the present. Interestingly enough, the little girl from El Salvador becomes a bridge between Dave and his Cajun present, allowing him to locate some sense of meaning and acceptance of the changes he has witnessed in Cajun life.

Alafair's experience of the Cajun past comes, ironically, from Batist, the "Cajun, Negro, and Chitimacha Indian" who works for Dave in New Iberia and who proves the interethnic reality of Cajuns and south Louisianians (*HP* 178); it does not come from Dave, who has already become too American to accept anything but standard English and proper grammatical constructions of language. The wise old man stands as the only physical retainer of Dave's father's way of life and Cajun French language, both of which are fading in a world of college education and upward mobility.[14] Dave has to instruct Alafair on standard language usage because she has learned certain English phrases from Batist. Noticing Batist's influence on Alafair's English, Dave thinks, "I was always amazed at the illusion of white supremacy in southern society, since more often than not our homes were dominated and run by people of color" (*BCB* 8). Such power extends from the respect Dave pays to Batist. In her study of Burke's Robicheaux series, Bogue argues that "Batist serves as a surrogate father in many regards, his loyalty and devotion unswerving and instrumental to Robicheaux's well being" (45). His position in Dave's life not only remains because of his loyalty, but also becomes significant because of his older ways that remind Dave of the Cajun past he so desperately seeks. Batist speaks in a mixed language complete with Cajun Vernacular English (CVE) and French phrases.[15] In one passage of *Black Cherry Blues*, Batist speaks in CVE: "You done got yourself in a mess here in Lou'sana. Don't make no mo' mess up there, no" (92). Later in the novel, he asks, "*Que ça veut dire*, Dave? What that needle mean, too?" (56). With such mixed language, mirroring his mixed heritage, Batist remains a physical connection to, a reminder of, and perhaps the strongest surviving bond with the Cajun past in Dave's life.[16]

By attempting to stop Batist's influence on Alafair's English, Dave, in essence, rejects his father's language of CVE. The very quality of speech that he disparages remains a powerful signifier of Cajun difference in a world where assimilation has become the dominant trend. Dave may honor his father's memory, but he describes him as a man "who couldn't read or write and spoke Cajun French and a form of English that was hardly a language" (*HP* 10), once again acknowledging and emphasizing how incapable he is of ever really returning to the past for which he so longs. Such moments prove Dave's ability to live in the present because he rejects the less than ideal aspects of the past, the aspects that he realizes will prevent Alafair from succeeding in contemporary America. These passages in the novels also represent Dave's realization that the solution, his personal sense of resolution, does not exist in the past, but in the present. Through such realizations that come to him because of his relationship with Alafair, Dave can begin to solve not only the violent crimes that dominate his life, but also his personal crime of assimilation. If he accepts change even as he continues to remember his Cajun identity, then both he and his Cajun identity can survive, although altered, even in the midst of Americanization. Alafair will speak standard English and learn within the four walls of the classroom; she will be a typical American child. She will also learn about Cajun foodways, music, and religious beliefs, which teach her that another way of life, of difference, once did and still can exist.

Throughout the Robicheaux series, Alafair continues to change as she matures into an adult who no longer relies on Dave's care. Eventually, she enters college and begins a life away from her father, reminding Dave once again that change is inevitable. Alafair's "Baby Orca T-shirt, red tennis shoes embossed with the words 'Left' and 'Right' on the appropriate shoe, a Donald Duck cap with a quacking bill, her Curious George and Baby Squanto Indian books," a mix of Americanized representations of American Indians and typical childhood interests, are all packed away inside a trunk Dave built for her (*PCR* 200). Her memories, as represented by these objects, are of life with Dave in America and not of El Salvadoran horrors. By re-creating Alafair's past in an image of typical American childhood, Dave re-makes her into an all-American girl with the independent spirit and free will that he has encouraged. Although he keeps her childhood locked in a trunk, Dave comes to terms with the futility of wanting to maintain his family situation, a realization made possible because of his relationship with Alafair. At the end of *Purple Cane Road,* he thinks, "I wanted . . . to keep Bootsie [his third wife] and Alafair there with me and let the rest of the world continue in its fashion" (338–39). No matter how much he may want to maintain his family's presence and his Cajun past, Dave must face the ever changing world. By choosing to face the obstacles of the outside world and battle against the forces that threaten harm to both his family and his community, Dave violently deals with demons to cleanse himself of past sins and to purify his memory of loved ones. Dave's past and present families signify a changing south Louisiana. They also represent hope for a Cajun future, one that extends from survival in the present.

Louisiana, like Cajun culture and memory, has changed and will continue to shift as time passes. The land reshapes itself year after year to accommodate larger forces, such as floods and manmade canals. Through its flexibility, the land survives. Dave contemplates his own "little piece of Cajun geography" and its "being consumed on the edges like an old photograph held to a flame" (*HP* 274) as a sign of loss. He also realizes that "the earth is still new, molten at the core and still forming, the black leaves in the winter forest will crawl with life in the spring" (274). Hope lives on, and with this hope "our story is ongoing and it is indeed a crime to allow the heart's energies to dissipate with the fading of light on the horizon" (274). Burke understands that Cajun identity, like memory, reshapes itself in order to survive in a world where meaning constantly changes. Hope extends from one's revisions of memory because it is through this process that memories remain meaningful for the present. Survival, personal and cultural, relies on such memories to remind Cajuns of their differences and to encourage pride in them. Survival and hope exist only if and when Cajuns realize, like Dave, that they cannot return to a Cajun past— such a place in time no longer exists except through memories distorted by the present. A resolution of the Cajun double bind becomes clear in Burke's fiction if read as an inverted parable: the answer is not in returning "home," but in making a home of one's own in the present. Like the geographical spaces of Louisiana that shift and change in order to survive, so must contemporary Cajuns, like Dave Robicheaux, learn to accept their American identities even as they endeavor to remember and to take pride in their Cajun difference in order to usher Cajun identity and culture, in its various forms, into the future.

6. Embracing Difference

CAJUNS TAKE THE NEXT STEP IN CAJUN REPRESENTATION

In "Notes About Political Theater," Tony Kushner claims that "[i]dentifying oneself . . . as Other . . . is an important political act. We take the right and the privilege of definition from the oppressor, we assume the power of naming ourselves" (26). He further argues for "the rapturous embrace of difference, the discovering self not in that which has rejected you but in that which makes you unlike, and disliked, and Other" (32). While Cajun literature may not seem to share much similarity with the purposefully flamboyant production of Theater of the Fabulous to which Kushner refers, the two areas of identity performance do overlap in the staging of difference as a mode of empowerment during the final decades of the twentieth century. Kushner's theory is that this significant embrace of difference, not as a point of oppression, but as a moment of self-pride and celebration, reveals how one can remain self-determinedly different. For Cajuns, this self-determined performance of difference can and does become a recognition of empowerment, but only after the realization of assimilation to an American majority since the determination of such difference occurs in conjunction with a recognition of dominant notions of American identity.

Contemporary Cajun authors construct details of Cajun culture as a means of remembering Cajun difference in the midst of realizing American identification, a process that has led to the formation of Cajun American culture. While Longfellow's *Evangeline* captures the geographical displacement of the Acadians in 1755, which led to the formation of Cajun ethnicity in Louisiana, this poem also begins the history of Cajun literary representation in American literature and its default English language, which the original Acadians did not speak. With the early twentieth-century push for English-only usage in America, the Cajuns experienced a linguistic displacement, which, like their earlier geographical dispersal, was successful. This success is double-sided, however, since Cajuns now use their knowledge of American literature and the English language to create their own portraits of Cajun life, complete with illustrations of the tensions that exist within Cajun communities because of such cultural displacements. Cajun use of translation thus becomes a reminder of assimilation even as it promotes the distribution of difference through the publication of self-representation in literature. In many ways, Tim Gautreaux and his fellow Cajun authors can and do capture Cajun culture in print and distribute these depictions across the nation because of their American identities, because of their English usage and literary backgrounds acquired through American education. Their work proves that Cajun literary representation exists in the space between Acadian and American identifications, just like Cajun identity, a space that allows for the celebration of difference following an assimilation process, both literal and literary, that dominated much of the twentieth century.

One such literary work that deconstructs the assimilation process in order to reinforce the inevitable difference of Cajuns is Chris Segura's "Dans le Royaume de la Lune," located in *Marshland Trinity* (1997). This particular story centers around the 1950s, the Korean War, and the American push for complete assimilation due to McCarthy scares regarding communism, illustrating the inevitable consequences of becoming American while continuing to identify oneself as Cajun. In this story of Bill, a six or seven-year-old Cajun boy who is growing up American in Jackson, Louisiana, English education becomes the tool for Americanization, as in George Washington Cable's *Bonaventure* and Ernest Gaines's *A Gathering of Old Men*. Segura relates the extent to which this younger generation, now forced to learn and speak standard English, has lost usage of Cajun French: "They knew nothing of French except the rudimentary grunts," a loss stemming from their mother, who "had forbidden them to learn it," because the parents "had been whipped and punished in school for speaking it" (389). She even claims that "[b]eing American meant speaking American" (390), echoing Bonaventure's "[I]n America you mus' be American!" (Cable 114). The children recognize Cajun French as a secret language used when adults do not want children to understand what is being discussed, emphasizing how much of the native language is already lost.

The concept of American identity in this story has further significance because of the era in which it takes place. Suddenly, in the 1950s being American meant not being communist, and anyone not identifying as fully American was considered an enemy. The McCarthy era established a necessity for the American identification of Cajun children because, as Shane Bernard explains, "the 1950s represented an era of patriotism and Americanism, and in south Louisiana this meant that many Cajun children continued to be punished for using French at school" (25). Cajuns had to disguise any difference, which they wanted to do in support of American unity against a common enemy.

"Dans le Royaume de la Lune" questions complete Cajun Americanization, however, when Sidney, Bill's brother and an American soldier who is captured in Korea, speaks out against American government policy, perhaps reflecting Korean brainwashing tactics. What he claims as fact is a more complicated account of American discrimination against those who seem other than pure Anglo-American. From the radio, Bill hears Sidney's voice telling "the story of the Cajun people, never once using the word 'Cadien. He told about the Great Upheaval. Sidney would never use words like 'cultural genocide' and 'economic oppression,' but what he said was true, beatings on school grounds for speaking French, the job discrimination that made it easier to work in Louisiana as a Texan than a 'Cadien, the horrible literacy and infant mortality statistics that persisted no matter how the per capita income grew" (476). Sidney's speech captures the realities of difference, and his recognition of such difference within the boundaries of America. In response, the American audience of the radio program calls Sidney and his speech "*Un-American*" (477). While the reader can choose to believe that Sidney's words arise as the consequence of brainwashing tactics, his words still provide a lens through which American and Cajun history can and should be viewed. Whether or not he intends to do so, he reclaims difference as he testifies to his people's history and defies any notion of a complete or nonantagonistic Americanization process.

At this juncture in the story, Bill's mother decides to take the boys back to Cajun country to protect them from the fallout caused by Sidney's words. Throughout the story, the mother chooses to raise her boys as Americans, to speak American English, and to live according to American standards. Even so, her father greets the boys with "*Comment ça va*" when they reach his truck, which will take them back to their Cajun home (496). Cajuns at midcentury were forced to choose between openly claiming their identity as different from a mainstream American, Anglo-Protestant image or accepting and readily assimilating to this standard. By returning with her sons to her father's home, the mother in this story reminds the boys from whence they came while also maintaining her instruction in English.

Segura's story captures the tensions that arose during the cold war era when "patriotism" became a requirement of being American and education systems became a tool for dispersing this patriotism.[1] The tale of continuing assimilation also depicts the use of translation as both a colonization of the Other and a possible tool for the empowerment of such Other for ethnic American writers. Martha Cutter emphasizes in *Lost and Found in Translation* that one of the goals of speaking in a double voice that extends from translation as trope is "to undermine the demarcation between the 'majority' discourse and the 'marginal' dialect" (16). Like Kushner's theory of celebrating difference, Cutter's thesis extends from within an already-enacted assimilation process from which ethnic authors speak in order to empower themselves, thus recognizing difference only after realizing assimilation. Sidney's speech demonstrates a similar process among Cajuns and symbolizes the literary production of contemporary Cajun authors in English. His use of English represents the Americanization process endorsed by schools and his own mother, while the words he speaks and the story he reveals in English make evident how such a tool for assimilation can be used to empower oneself and to recall difference. Contemporary Cajun authors have taken this one step further by using the English language to produce and distribute literary celebrations of difference.

During the 1960s and 1970s, both counterculture activists and their upper-class Cajun neighbors supported political agendas that endorsed the preservation of Cajun identity as a way to recall such difference following the demands of the McCarthy era. As a result of such efforts, the Louisiana parishes that harbored the majority of the Cajuns soon adopted the name *Acadiana*,[2] and the Louisiana government officially adopted the flag of Acadiana in 1974, creating ethnic symbols for the Cajun communities of south Louisiana. Around the same time, the state government also passed the Bilingual Education Act and the Ethnic Studies Act, while the Council for the Development of French in Louisiana (CODOFIL) was formed in 1968, recognizing the need to preserve an already fading linguistic heritage.[3] CODOFIL created divisions between more elitist Cajuns who chose to use the mythic portrait of Evangeline as a way to encourage national interest and those who chose to take a more grassroots stance toward cultural preservation (Bernard, *The Cajuns* 88).[4] Stemming from notions of standardization, CODOFIL supported instruction in standard French in Louisiana schools, which others took as an insult to Cajun French speakers and instructors. Part of the disagreement regarding which form of French to teach in the classroom extended from the theory that Cajun French was a spoken, not a written, language, to which several Cajun authors responded in literary form, proving that Cajun literature does not have to be in standard French or in English translation.

Stemming from this discussion, such poets as Zachary Richard and Jean Arceneaux, a pseudonym for folklorist Barry Jean Ancelet, decided to publish *Cris sur le bayou*, a collection of Cajun French poems (Bernard, *The Cajuns* 128). This collection modeled how Cajun French could be not only written, but also used to write creatively, inspiring other Cajun writers to follow suit, such as Antoine Bourque, a pseudonym for Cajun historian Carl Brasseaux, with his short story collection *Trois saisons* (1988), and Richard Guidry with *C'est p'us pareil* (1982). Cajun French literature focuses on American assimilation, loss of language, and a call for reclamation of heritage (131), and it does so from the perspective of loss. Cajun literature in English, which rose simultaneously with Cajun French work, centers around similar themes but does so from within the perspective of Americanization, complicating any depiction of Cajun identity. Instead of focusing on the loss of language and the need to reclaim cultural traditions, authors such as Tim Gautreaux write about the Americanization of Cajuns as a part of contemporary Cajun culture, emphasizing the continuing existence of difference within the process of assimilation. The English language not only places a work within the larger context of national Cajun literary representation, beginning with Longfellow, but it also reminds the reader of the interstitial space in which Cajun culture survives in the United States.

Proving the power of Cajun literature and culture in translation through his fiction, Tim Gautreaux captures not only the interstitial quality of Cajun culture, but also the empowerment of translation and difference within the Cajun community of the late twentieth century. If, as Marcia Gaudet claimed in 1989, "there has not yet been an accurate portrayal of the Cajun people or their culture by a major American literary figure" ("The Image" 77), then Gautreaux, in particular, and his depictions of Cajun culture answer Gaudet's call for an accurate, more complex depiction of Cajun life. Agreeing with Gaudet's statement that no major American literary figure has created an accurate portrayal of Cajun culture, Gautreaux set out in the 1990s to do so because, as he has said, "I found that if I didn't, nobody else would" (Hebert-Leiter 71–72). He admits that he wrote his first novel, *The Next Step in the Dance* (1998), to present a more accurate depiction of Cajuns while also illustrating that American culture is not homogenous and that ethnic identity cannot be swallowed up by the influx of fast-food restaurants and malls.

At a pivotal moment in the novel, Gautreaux places Paul and Colette Thibodeaux, a Cajun couple, in Los Angeles speaking Cajun French with each other, a reminder of difference within one of the most American of cities. They do not discuss world events or other pieces of news of tremendous purport. Instead, they express their feelings about ordinary Louisiana realities such as "the red bugs," "*écrevisses*," and "*Nelson Orville et son accordion*" (112). By allowing his characters to speak their native language within the English-speaking American city, Gautreaux reinforces their sense of difference and the reality that translation does not have to amount to complete assimilation away from and denial of one's linguistic and cultural origins. This bit of French remains a part of their identities even as they struggle to survive in Los Angeles and the world outside Acadiana. Their use of the language is fragmented, however, demonstrating how their sense of identity and language has already become Americanized regardless of their acknowledgment of a cultural past. Such pieces are reminders of difference, but such difference has already become part of and understood through an assimilation process, making translation significant to one's identity of cultural selfhood and always already understood in connection with an American identification of oneself.

While Gautreaux emphasizes how Cajuns can remain different within their American identification through literary depictions of everyday life, changes, and fragments of Cajun French, Ken Wells, another contemporary Cajun author, further parallels Kushner's theory of "the rapturous embrace of difference" by exaggerating this difference in his character Meely LaBauve (32), a descendant of Cajuns and American Indians who easily associates with his African American neighbors. Wells, a writer for the *Wall Street Journal* who grew up in Houma, Louisiana, uses his humorous style to place his Cajuns in the middle of more elaborate adventures, making his novels like Huck Finnish depictions of Cajun life.

Meely LaBauve (2000) begins his Cajun trilogy with the story of Meely, a Cajun boy, and his father Logan who find themselves in constant trouble with the law. In interesting ways, Meely's American Indian identity allows him to move in society as Chopin's and Gaines's Cajuns move between racial and class divisions. His cousin Iris Mary Parfait offers another in-

teresting illustration of interstitial positioning that arises from an eth-
nically diverse heritage. As an albino who may have African American
blood flowing through her veins, Iris Mary's total lack of color does not
change the prejudiced reaction of some in the community who automatically view her as black. Again, this partial Cajun is also partially non-
Cajun and Other in a way that allows her the freedom to move between,
thus questioning, social categories through her exaggerated performance
of difference.

As with all contemporary Cajun fiction, Wells also focuses on the issue
of translation in his work. While Gautreaux allows his Cajun characters
to use Cajun French and CVE without defining or translating either for
the reader to add authenticity to his fiction and to allow his characters to
speak for themselves (Hebert-Leiter 73), all of Ken Wells's novels contain a
glossary of Cajun terms, which include pronunciation keys for this Cajun
vocabulary. Wells obviously writes for non-Cajuns, as well as Cajuns, because he makes a point of explaining words, complete with phonetic spellings, that only cultural insiders can readily understand and pronounce.
In this way, he uses his fiction to instruct outsiders about Cajun culture,
again demonstrating how contemporary Cajun fiction has become a tool
for cultural pride and how translation can be employed as a means of
empowerment. Wells's lists also aid contemporary Cajuns who are forgetting or simply have never learned Cajun French, making such use of
translation an internal as well as an external guide. As in Gautreaux's fiction, the Cajun French terminology that survives in Wells's remains fragmented and in need of translation. The use of such vocabulary simultaneously demonstrates a marketing of Cajun fiction to a larger American and
English-speaking audience, again proving the paradoxical nature of such
translation.

In the midst of such translation and national recognition of cultural
difference, Gautreaux's work offers a more subtle and less exaggerated
hope for contemporary Cajuns who now realize that cultural change and
loss is inevitable. This hope stems from the history of Cajun identity as
something that has survived and will continue to survive Americanization, not because it will remain always the same but because the people
who call themselves Cajun are aware of their identity and its difference
within the nation. To establish this complex and sometimes paradoxical relationship between Cajun and American identification, Gautreaux's
fiction questions American-made images of Cajun culture while simultaneously focusing on Cajun assimilation into American mainstream

culture. His work also illustrates Cajuns' constant struggle between remaining Cajun and becoming more modern and mainstream American. In the end, his Cajun characters realize, as Segura's do, that no matter how American they have and will become, they are still inevitably Cajun, which creates the moment in which being Cajun American is realized as a celebration of difference in the midst of assimilation.

Like Ernest Gaines, whose stories are set in the fictional plantation quarters based on his actual childhood home in Point Coupée parish, Gautreaux also relies on his postage stamp of land, his home town of Morgan City, because he realizes that "a writer . . . owns a certain literary territory. It's the place of his birth, where he grew up, the language that he listened to, the values that were implied" (Hebert-Leiter 67).[5] While living in Morgan City, Gautreaux "didn't think about being Cajun" (70). It wasn't until he left Louisiana to earn his doctoral degree in English from the University of South Carolina at Columbia that he began to understand what it meant to be a Cajun: "When I moved to South Carolina, the food was totally different, and the religion was different. The politics was different. Everything was different. Attitudes were different. At that point it began to be clear to me . . . what being Cajun was" (70).[6] By the 1980s, the Cajun revival succeeded in making Cajuns realize the uniqueness of their cultural ways and in encouraging them to celebrate their difference. This success also illustrates the degree to which being Cajun has become a self-conscious signifier and not simply a way of life. With staged festivals and cultural commodification, Cajun culture has become, for some, a marketed memory. Not all Cajuns experience their ethnic and cultural identities through such productions, but the fact that such events and marketing exist is proof that Cajun culture is becoming more Americanized.

In a hilarious, yet poignant, passage of his first novel, *The Next Step in the Dance,* Gautreaux places Paul Thibodeaux, a Cajun living temporarily in Los Angeles, in the middle of a West Coast Cajun restaurant, allowing a Cajun to confront the commodification of his culture in a nation that attempts to contain difference by claiming knowledge of an Other. While Gautreaux experienced the lack of Cajun foodways in South Carolina, his character confronts the opposite situation: the marketing of difference. Paul immediately recognizes the false appropriation of his culture when he glances up at the decorative net that holds a few starfish, "animals he had seen only in pictures" (*Next Step* 80). Starfish are not commonly found along the Gulf coast and bayou banks of south Louisiana. Not only do the decorations imply a false place—one that does not exist anywhere, much less in Louisiana—but the waiter, "a healthy blond kid," also distorts the relationship between this representation of Cajun culture and the reality that remains hidden behind the narrative created by the restaurant: blond hair is not common among Cajuns. Paul remains where he is seated and examines the whole scene in more detail, finally asking, "What is all this stuff? I thought this was a Cajun place" (80).

Immediately after explaining that the restaurant provides "authentic dishes from the bayou state," the Californian states, "Today's special is blackened swordfish" (*Next Step* 80). Paul Prudhomme, a Cajun chef, created blackened fish when "he experimented with cooking a well-seasoned fish fillet on a superheated iron skillet" (Bernard, *The Cajuns* 116). He named the result "blackened redfish" (116). Swordfish, unlike redfish, is not native to Louisiana, making the California menu only partially authentic. Aside from the occasional great chef whose experiments become world-famous dishes, Cajun foodways do not diverge greatly from the past, making such dishes as *boudin, étouffée,* and *filé gumbo* a part of the contemporary Cajun diet.[7] With a native understanding of Cajun food based on these dishes, Paul's response clearly highlights the strangeness of the dish the waiter offers: "I never seen a swordfish in my whole life" (80).

After the waiter directs Paul's gaze to the dish another gentleman is eating, Paul cries out in protest, "It's all burned" (*Next Step* 81). The waiter explains, "Not burned, sir. Blackened" (81). Then he claims, "It's the most traditional way of cooking seafood among the Cajuns" (81). Actually, the most traditional way of cooking among Cajuns involves boiling seafood and meat, which Carl Brasseaux explains as a process "dictated not only by the toughness of locally produced meats, agricultural produce, and game but by extant cooling technology as well. Lacking funds for acquisition of Dutch ovens, the overwhelming majority of Acadian cooks prepared meals in kettles suspended above the hearth" (*Acadian to Cajun* 24). Along with boiling food, another tradition involves preparing a *roux* as the first step in many Cajun dishes.[8] Paul, in defense of his culture, asserts that the restaurant has it all wrong, and he says, "Someone's been pulling your leg, man" (*Next Step* 81).

Finally, Paul wades through "the descriptions of bayou lamb, Cajun barbecued liver, and escargot de Lafayette" until he finds "the word *gumbo* on the back page" (*Next Step* 81). Instead of exerting the energy needed to explain why the majority of the menu is ridiculous, Paul decides to eat what he can. His plan is foiled, however, when "his waiter brought a small cauldron of bitter juice so hot with Tabasco that after the third spoonful,

Paul broke into a sweat" (81). This occurrence demonstrates the prevalence of the myth that Cajuns enjoy their food "spicy hot," a misconception written, broadcast, and dispersed by those existing outside the geographic and cultural borders of Acadiana.[9] The waiter laughs as he says, "It takes time to develop a true Cajun palate," to which Paul replies, "Let me tell you, it sure don't take much time to ruin one" (81). Then he remembers the "medium-brown roux Colette made last winter as the base for a shrimp gumbo," making memory his bond with home, family, and his Cajun identity (81).

This particular scene in the novel addresses not only the selling of Cajun culture by outsiders and how this business aids in misrepresenting that culture, but also Cajun difference in response to this misrepresentation of cultural ways by outsiders. It does not, however, address how some of the blame for such cultural commercialism falls on the Cajuns who have become more mainstream American and have adopted and adapted the skill of marketing their culture to the nation and the world for financial gain, especially when it comes to foodways. Paul Prudhomme cooks and sells his dishes in New Orleans; John Folse, a Louisiana cook, was the "first American to open a restaurant in the Soviet Union" (Bernard, *The Cajuns* 116); and Al Copeland markets Popeye's Fried Chicken all over the world as spicy Cajun chicken (116–18). *River Road Recipes* and other Cajun cookbooks line the shelves of cooks across the nation. Gautreaux portrays a humorous exchange inside a restaurant to illustrate the exaggerations and inaccuracies dispersed by those outside of Cajun culture, but this scene also emphasizes the degree to which this culture has become a product to be sold and the cultural borders have been opened even by those who identify themselves as Cajuns, making Cajun culture American.

This humorous scene also proves how different Cajun culture remains within its Louisiana borders since the restaurant assumes that the product it is selling is accurate, as demonstrated by the waiter's presumption that Paul does not understand what *Cajun* implies. In truth, this episode characterizes the disconnection between popular notions of Cajun identity and the reality of Cajun traditions that are still strongly embraced today. Regardless of how American Cajuns have become, such passages remind us of how Other they remain by choice, and of the misunderstandings that occur because of false assumptions of knowledge of this Other. While literature has long assumed such knowledge, the breakthrough of Cajun foodways onto a national and international market in the late twentieth century further produced and distributed such images of American assumptions.

In the midst of such Americanization, Gautreaux's characters prove that regardless of chain stores and restaurants, difference remains a part of America's cultural landscape. "Floyd's Girl," a short story in *Same Place, Same Things* (1996), specifically argues that a Cajun can leave Louisiana but cannot forget his or her Cajun identity because this identity, although it originated within particular geographical borders, can travel beyond Louisiana. The story begins when Mary Lizette Bergeron is kidnapped by her mother's Texas boyfriend. With the help of the community, Floyd Bergeron rescues his daughter from the clutches of the Texan, a personal rescue that symbolizes a more significant metaphorical cultural rescue in the story.

Throughout the story, the characters remember Cajun culture through the framework of food, musical, and religious signifiers. Mrs. Boudreaux, a neighbor, worries that Lizette's religious faith will be neglected in Texas, while T-Jean's Grandmère, another neighbor, fears that her belly will miss the taste of Cajun food: "Can she get turtle sauce piquante[10] in Lubbock?" she wonders ("FG" 169). She thinks of "the gumbos Lizette would be missing, the okra soul, the crawfish body" (169). Along with these older women, Floyd also worries about what Lizette may lose if the Texan succeeds in driving her over the state border. His cultural markers recall family connections, linguistic patterns, and musical memories: "There was nothing wrong with West Texas, but there was something wrong with a child living there who doesn't belong, who will be haunted for the rest of her days by memories of the ample laps of aunts, . . . the musical rattle of French, her prayers, the head-squawking of her uncle's accordion, the scrape and complaint of her father's fiddle as he serenades the backyard on weekends" ("FG" 170). Floyd combines various particles of Cajun culture as a means of addressing why his daughter, a Cajun, belongs with him in south Louisiana. The "rattle" of Cajun French, the sounds of the accordion and fiddle, and the presence of family mark Cajuns as other than Texans and mainstream Americans.

Gautreaux depicts the saving of Lizette as a lesson to Cajuns and non-Cajuns who are all facing the disappearance of cultural differences as malls and chain restaurants erase unique characteristics by allowing for homogeneity. "For Floyd and his dedicated collaborators," argues Ed Piacentino, "the rescue of Lizette becomes a second chance to reenergize and reinforce the bonds of the Cajun community" (128). The story ends with Lizette's safe recovery. It also ends with Mrs. Boudreaux teaching the Texan that "if you woulda went off with her, all you woulda got was her little body. In her head, she'd never be where you took her to. Every day she'd feel okra in her mouth" ("FG" 180). No matter the threat the Texan presents to the community, Cajun identity remains strong and unique within America and American identification; it remains different.

This story stems from the Cajun diaspora that has expanded over the last several decades as Cajuns became more interested in the world beyond Acadiana, a world opened up by educational advances and better transportation methods.[11] World War II, new roads, and the oil boom all encouraged the rapid opening of the land and the quick assimilation of Cajuns into the bourgeois value system of the nation.[12] Lizette's mother represents the many Cajuns who were simply no longer fulfilled with life in south Louisiana. In "License to Steal," another story in *Same Place, Same Things*, Curtis Lado's wife left him because "she was tired of living in Louisiana with somebody didn't bring home no money. Said she wanted to move to the United States" (151). As Cajuns became more assimilated into mainstream America, they realized that their Cajun home and ways were different. The wave of Cajun dispersal following this realization illustrates a desire to become fully American and to suppress difference. Gautreaux has said that education and economic improvement lead one "to feel that your plainer beginnings are something you should leave behind, and I think that's sad" because "you begin to lose all sense of history and all sense of the past. And then you lose the sense of the importance of things" (Hebert-Leiter 69). Unwilling to lose his sense of the past, Gautreaux argues against this complete assimilation in his fiction by depicting Cajun differentiation as something in which to take pride.

In *The Next Step in the Dance*, Gautreaux carefully constructs the realization of pride through a journey motif as Colette, Paul's wife, repeats Curtis Lado's wife's sentiment regarding life in Cajun Louisiana. She "read *Cosmopolitan* and *Woman's World* and had begun to think that Tiger Island was a small, muddy pond" (*Next Step* 2), thus choosing to travel to Los Angeles, a city she thinks will provide her with more opportunities to make something of herself. By the end of the novel, Colette feels differently about her home town and the world beyond it only because she allows herself to experience the larger world. She illustrates Gautreaux's comment to Jennifer Levasseur and Kevin Rabalais that "sometimes you don't know how you fit into your community until you leave it" (31). Much like Annie in Shirley Ann Grau's *The Hard Blue Sky,* Colette finds herself unfulfilled and in need of something different.

Upon reaching Los Angeles, however, Colette discovers only a sense of isolation because she was born and raised in a place that emphasizes family bonds and spiritual connections with past generations, both of which are not obviously present in the lives of the Californians she meets. Her sense of loss stems from her inability to place her faith in a world structured only by the laws of science. As in "Floyd's Girl," Gautreaux frames Colette's crossing of cultural boundaries as a realization of difference that she cannot and does not necessarily want to overcome. After settling in the city, she realizes that "[s]he did not fit in with her fellow workers, who thought she talked funny. . . . The people she longed to be like . . . called her 'the swamp queen'" (75). In contrast to this dismissal of her ability to succeed, the people in Tiger Island consider her to be a beautiful woman worthy of the title "Miss America" (253). Due to the harassment she experiences in Los Angeles, Colette realizes that her home remains in Louisiana, since "[t]hings . . . make more sense" in her homeland (253). The distinction between "swamp queen" and "Miss America" points to views of difference and how these shift with place. Tiger Island Cajuns view Colette as an American, as a mainstream woman of beauty and talent, whereas Californians see her as an outsider who speaks with a strange accent. Colette has to choose between losing her Cajun distinctions to become recognizable as a typical American by her California co-workers or accepting this difference and taking pride in it, regardless of others' labels of it as strange and different.

Gautreaux does not construct this embrace of difference as simple, however, because he acknowledges the changes that have already occurred in south Louisiana that have significantly affected Cajun culture. As recognized by James Lee Burke, the oil industry is one such cultural infiltration with long-term consequences. Realizing such consequences, Glenn R. Conrad comments on the effects of the oil industry on South Louisiana in "The Acadians: Myths and Realities": "The exploitation of these [oil] deposits for a mechanizing America brought English-speaking geologists, technicians, drillers, and roughnecks into Acadiana" (12). When Paul and Colette finally return to Cajun country in Gautreaux's novel, they discover that "Tiger Island had changed for the worse" because of an economic depression brought on by the oil bust (*Next Step* 114). This reversal demonstrates their need to return to Cajun culture, but it also proves that such culture is always in flux and in danger of fading. Through her words, Colette binds the land and the people in such a way that the threat of cultural loss is realized not only by the ruined roadside but also by the reaction of the people to this depression. Because of the tremendous increase in revenues and jobs due to the oil explosion in the 1940s, the fallout from the end of the oil boom created a vacuum that destroyed the economic stability of the area, as previously portrayed in Burke's Robicheaux series and as Gautreaux also captures in fiction. Like Dave Robicheaux, Colette and Paul face the consequences of the oil boom and bust and of assimilation. Whereas Burke resorts to violent depictions of environmental and human deterioration, Gautreaux uses the oil bust to parallel the threat of cultural loss for the Thibodeauxs, forcing them to realize that they have to face even greater challenges before they can build a new home and life for themselves as Cajun Americans. Embracing difference becomes more challenging when such difference is threatened by such physical reminders of alterations that have occurred. Hope within such depression extends, however, from the very recognition of difference, of a reliance on an economy not based around such American industries.

The scene that greets Colette's gaze, as she travels down the roads of Tiger Island, is bleak: "Where the Big Gator [a dance hall] had stood was a freshly graded plain a quarter mile long. A bulldozer squatted where the dance floor had been. Farther down, where there had been other clubs, the roadside was bare" (114). Such images of economic depression become reminders of more significant change in cultural practices. According to Bernard, "Cajuns at first lamented the influx of insiders who came in search of oil," but "they soon became the backbone of the Gulf Coast oil industry" (*The Cajuns* 37). Proof of such involvement rests in the development of Lafayette, which grew from "a sleepy Cajun town into a modern American city" because of the "creation of the Oil Center office and shopping complex in 1952" (37), of which Burke writes in *Black Cherry Blues*. In the race to realize the success of the American dream, Cajuns chose to become the labor force in a machine that left its mark on the exhausted economy. Bitterly aware of this exploitation, "Colette's brother, Mark, . . . complained about the politicians and how they'd turned the state into a wasteland by courting only one industry for fifty years: big oil" (Gautreaux, *Next Step* 270).

While Colette interprets what she views through negative images of lack, Paul responds to the hope that remains in a devastated environment: "But at least everything was green and nothing was thorned. The rice fields were green, the fallow fields were roaring with willow, marsh alder, and honeysuckle, the sugarcane fields spread out as endless mesas of green, and even on truck-haunted Highway 90, a slender fuzz of grass stood up in cracks against the moving traffic" (*Next Step* 133). Sugarcane and rice fields, reminders of an earlier Cajun agricultural economy, remain even as the modern oil businesses collapse. Paul's hope stems from his connection with the culture that thrives in south Louisiana, one that existed long before oil became the dominant economic factor.[13] He hears "the reedy complaint of a diatonic accordion," which he considers "the sound of homeland," and thinks "of food and loss" (134). Connecting the economic depression with cultural memories and loss, Paul reminds the reader again of the dangers stemming from forgetting difference, from ignoring one's otherness, in the midst of assimilation.

While the first half of the novel records Paul and Colette's journey outside the boundaries of south Louisiana and their recognition of Cajun difference, the second half remembers a Cajun past and demonstrates the challenges facing Cajuns who now experience pride in a way of life that has faded as American mainstream culture and progress, as represented through the oil industry and mechanization, replaced traditional employment and linguistic patterns. Gautreaux's use of the oil bust in the 1980s frames a larger cultural battle for survival for the couple who must confront their own place within the assimilation process before they can reunite and fully embrace each other and their Cajun American identities as Other within the nation. Paul, the character who seems least divided from his Cajun origins, confronts the greatest threat to his actual survival while in the belly of one of the machines he repairs. His nemesis in his attempt to reclaim Colette, Bucky Tyler, an east Texan and a man determined to marry Colette, attempts to murder Paul by locking him into a boiler and turning on the steam. Paul's situation revels in its cultural implications since it is imitative of the traditional way of cooking Cajun dishes: "Now the fire would rage, and the remaining water would steam him like a crab" (*Next Step* 169). This entrapment in the boiler sheds light on Paul's emotional bond as a machinist with machinery since he begins "to cry great, slow machinist's tears, becoming angry because he was betrayed by one of his machines" (168). He remembers his family and friends and this empowers him to fight back. Paul's victory over the machine and the Texan contains within it other Cajun victories, such as the settlement in Louisiana and the struggle to maintain cultural traditions in the midst of American assimilation. Paul's time in the belly of the machine, a metaphor for the current challenges to Louisiana as it faces economic and cultural decline, forces him to realize his own position between American assimilation and Cajun differentiation and the inherent tension surrounding this position when his life is physically threatened.

His affair with his machines illustrates his own process of Americanization. Before climbing into the very machine that will entrap him, Paul admits to himself that "[s]omething about the rarity of what he was doing excited him, this getting into a machine, fitting inside the mechanism itself" (Gautreaux, *Next Step* 165). His adoration for old machinery links him to the past, but it is not the Acadian past because he repairs the machines that replaced Acadian hands with American metal. After his recovery from this tragedy, Paul is convinced by Colette to return to another traditional Cajun occupation, shrimping, which leads to another tragedy and Colette's personal realization of responsibility and difference.

Through the final chapters of *The Next Step in the Dance*, Gautreaux illustrates the importance of embracing Cajun difference and identification even as an American way of life continues to affect the traditional cultural values and traditions by introducing new technology that does not necessarily achieve any better results than old-fashioned understandings of geographical areas and cultural bonds. Now ready and willing to be a part of this Cajun community and to take pride in her participation within it, Colette actually manages a rescue mission when Paul and his crew are lost while on a shrimping expedition. Instead of accepting her place as an American by abandoning her heritage, Colette experiences an epiphany while floating in the Gulf that empowers her to embrace her identity as a Cajun. In a moment of private thought, she realizes that the "Coast Guard boys were not looking for friends or relatives, after all, just blips on radar or motes swimming in the vast, indifferent Gulf" (*Next Step* 295). Further into this thinking process, she concludes, "No one will look for you like someone who's known you all your life. Nothing fosters a rescue like ties in the blood" (295). In yet another passage, she realizes, "The searchers could do no better than they had done, and though they were professionals, they could operate only through science, not kinship," asserting her realization that Cajun difference may be something in which to take pride and to struggle to preserve (299). By asserting the inability of science to explain everything, Colette finally rejects her own belief in the inferiority of south Louisiana. This opens her to a whole new experience of the land, the water, and the people surrounding her. Her acceptance of being Other leads her to continue searching for that which outsiders have long given up on finding: the members of the Cajun community to which she now proudly belongs.

In the midst of the younger couple's struggle to discover themselves and their futures in Cajun America, Gautreaux introduces an older, wiser Cajun to remind his characters and his readers from whence Cajun difference extends and the significance of remembering such difference. While Colette desires an all-American life for herself and Paul lovingly maintains the very machines that altered a former way of Cajun life, *Grandpère* Abadie represents the older generation of Cajuns who spoke Cajun French and passed down family history orally long before the school system radically changed the language of the people. His English is clearly an example of the Cajun Vernacular English spoken by contemporary Cajuns who allow some Cajun French to influence the now dominant language. Nevertheless, his fluent Cajun French remains his most prominent connection with the past. His movement between CVE and Cajun French evidences the growing necessity of translation into English in the Cajun community because the younger generations are no longer fluent in Cajun French. As the oldest relative in the novel, Abadie preserves the language and folklore of the Cajuns. His "*Comment ça va?*" greets the younger generations, reminding them that the first language of the people was a dialect of French and that a time existed before translation became an integral part of Cajun American culture. Such connections with the past allow for the empowerment of translation because it is only with the realization of difference, of a time previous to one's acceptance of the linguistic majority, that empowerment can extend after assimilation has occurred.

Abadie's significance in the lives of the younger generation extends beyond his linguistic memories since he and the local priest preserve the genealogical records of the community, and some of his records are those printed in his personal memory of past lives, and not black marks on otherwise sterile, white paper or mythical or allegorical images. He not only recalls reading the church records regarding the tragic exile of the Acadians, but he also remembers the descendants of these original Acadians and the transportation to and survival of Acadian traditions in Louisiana, without having to rely on Longfellow: "Before Zefirin was Arsène, and before that was François, who was thrown out of Nova Scotia by those damned English. The what—the Spanish gave him some land that one time covered half of downtown" (*Next Step* 197). Father Clemmons finishes this history by relating the rest of the information recorded in the church documents: "Arsène made fiddles in the winter and fished in the summer. . . . The aristocratic priest kept notes on his congregation in Spanish, which I happen to read" (197). Although distorted by time, Abadie's memory of the past and of various cultural evolutions remains the most powerful tool in the attempt to represent the dynamism of Cajun culture because it is a physical reminder of the past and a container for cultural traditions that survive in the present amid assimilation to mainstream American values. His memory provides a connection to the past that realizes a reality outside of the literary representations of his people, beyond the American representations of Acadians and Cajuns, allowing a space for difference to remain intact.

Abadie becomes a central figure in the search for Paul because of his place within and meaning to cultural survival. Gautreaux captures the quickly changing coastline of Louisiana through the Cajun community's search for Paul and his crew. He describes the marshland as "a labyrinth of grassy rafts, sandbars that shifted with the seasons, peninsulas that disappeared with high tide, islands that built and waned" (*Next Step* 318). This shifting geography forces Colette to admit the difficulties involved in the search for Paul, even as it also imitates the reality of changing cultural memory and ways in the United States. It also parallels the rapid erosion that is occurring today, which constantly threatens the people and industries that rely on the southernmost areas of the state for survival. Mike Tidwell discusses this erosion and its connection to the cultural erosion occurring simultaneously in south Louisiana. He characterizes the geographic situation as "an unfolding calamity of fantastic magnitude, taking with it entire Cajun towns and an age-old way of life" (6).

Tidwell illustrates the extent of this erosion, both geographical and cultural, by relating the story of a fishing trip in which he was sure the boat was going to hit land. While watching the Global Positioning Satellite image guiding two Cajuns as they steer their boat, Tidwell sees the outline of a landmass on the system and prepares for a collision. "But even as we skid violently across tens of feet of land, the windshield doesn't shatter and I'm not thrown forward" (177). Over the seven years since the Cajun couple purchased the GPS system to aid in their fishing, much of the land has disappeared. The Cajuns have to combine their experience of the waterways and their witness of erosion with the GPS readings to maintain accurate bearings. Regardless of progress, old-fashioned experience remains a tool for maintaining safety and guaranteeing a certain degree of cultural and physical survival.

Abadie's experience and memory of the land demonstrates the value of cultural traditions in the midst of Americanization. He knows he must become a part of the search for Paul since he alone can feel the movement of the Gulf. Realizing it is not too late, he prepares for his own journey through the marshes surrounding the Gulf, which is one that will prove his necessary place within the culture of the people he has helped to raise. With only old maps that contain the names he remembers from his childhood, "a list of old friends," as a guide, he refuses to rely on scientific data or the newest technological equipment (*Next Step* 328), including GPS systems. Instead, he trusts "perhaps the map of feeling in his head" (329). The shifting and dangerous lands are nothing more than the lands of Abadie's mind, because he has lived to explore them. His wanderings through the various Gulf channels create, "In his mind . . . a lifetime of throbbing meanderings, and he daydreamed, memory and present becoming one" (329). At another moment of the search, he "looked for an opening in the shore of his memory" (330). This mental map emerges from a personal bond between memory and the land, distinguishing it from the maps created by outsiders to capture the land in print, much like Claude's maps in *Bonaventure*. Abadie's mind does not create an image that replaces the land as much as it creates a mental map that is coordinated to accommodate the natural changes of the coastlines. This feel for the meaning of the place opens Abadie to that which does not belong, that which is different, mainly the cries of Paul that echo "*A-ba-dieee*" through the blackness of the swamp air (334). In the end, the rescue of the men becomes possible because of Cajun reliance on community and memory, on their acceptance of difference, and not on American notions of progress. Colette and Abadie rely on their disparate understandings of meaning from mainstream American notions to save the men from certain death, proving once again that maintaining and embracing difference remains central to cultural survival in the midst of assimilation.

Cajuns realize that through assimilation they have become American and that, by embracing their Cajun differences from mainstream American culture, they can remain Cajun. For this reason Cajun identity and its ethnic and cultural implications may continue to change, but they will also continue to survive. So it is fitting that the novel ends in spring, the season of hope and regeneration. Louisiana has begun to recover from the oil bust, and this young couple finds success in the now healthy economy of their home town. At the end of the novel, Paul and Abadie sit under the oak and pass "the cup back and forth" (*Next Step* 340). Colette and Paul have weathered dangerous passages in their lives in order to realize that hope remains for the survival of Cajun identification, as Colette thinks at the end of the novel: "Then she looked down at the iron roofs of Tiger Island. Some were storm-worn and bent, some eroded and rusty, porous as a ruined soul, and some were scraped clean and gleaming with new silver paint" (340). Like Tiger Island, the Cajun population is made up of the old and the new, the young couples and the Abadies. In the end, Colette and Paul realize that they are Cajun Americans, finally recognizing that they are inevitably Cajun and taking pride in this identification, even as they realize they are American. By realizing this interstitial position of cultural significance, Paul and Colette become Cajun Americans, capable of celebrating what marks them as different in the midst of a continuing assimilation process.

Gautreaux may set his earlier work in 1980s Louisiana, a time of great change in the state, but he focuses on the past in his second novel, *The Clearing* (2003), which also illustrates a changing Cajun homeland in the 1920s and the consequences of these changes for Cajun culture. Unlike his previous work, this novel does not focus solely on Cajuns; the plot revolves around two northern brothers and their family conflict. *The Clearing* recalls the movement of northern companies and industries into south Louisiana following World War I, proving the already porous boundaries around Cajun Louisiana, which allow for the continuing Americanization of the people throughout the twentieth century. Although it focuses on the Aldridge family from Pittsburgh and their timber empire's expansion into Louisiana, the novel does address two generations of the Thibodeaux family. Merville Thibodeaux, much like Abadie, remembers dancing at *bals de maison*, eating *sauce picante*, and praying the Our Father in French (*Clearing* 63–64). At one point in the novel, "A window opened wide in his memory and Merville was afraid he might indeed be peering through it into death" (63). Merville does not make it to the end of the novel, and his death confirms the loss of his Cajun memory. Minos, his son, witnesses the baring of the land as the forests are cleared and the lumber sent out of the state, and he aides in this destruction by working as the engineer for the lumber company. Like Paul, Minos represents the twentieth-century Cajuns who embraced machines and progress as a means of earning a living. Meanwhile, Merville, like Abadie, remains a link to the past that is endangered by the influx of progress. Minos lives on as one of the next generation of Cajuns who will face continuous tension between their Cajun pasts and their American mainstream futures. Cajun fiction of the early twenty-first century thus continues to portray assimilation and loss. Gautreaux's work also, however, always reminds readers that in the middle of such change, difference remains, making Cajuns a unique American people.

The fiction of Segura, Wells, and Gautreaux not only celebrates and embraces difference, but it also proves that Cajuns have become respected American authors who will continue to capture their complex cultural dynamic for the entertainment and edification of Cajuns and non-Cajuns alike. Such fiction demonstrates their success in translating Cajun culture for a national audience, and in doing so capturing internal representations of ethnicity, empowering their claim as Other within American fiction. Their work remains one of the greatest hopes for Cajuns because it proves that they are more than capable of creating their own images of themselves to replace or to enhance the already popular public images of Cajun culture. It also captures the Cajun ability to adopt mainstream American ways in order to adapt them to fit Cajun values, another example of translation as empowerment. With its English language and American literature identification, Cajun fiction illustrates the tensions Cajuns continue to experience between their American and Cajun identities. As these authors prove, Cajuns can use their American identity to teach the nation about their cultural traditions, while also maintaining pride in what makes them Cajun Americans and different.

Conclusion: Local Pride, Global Connections

TWENTY-FIRST-CENTURY CAJUNS

A Boulder, Colorado, restaurant advertises its *Ragin' Cajun* burger; Southern Season, a Chapel Hill, North Carolina, shop, currently sells *Ragin' Cajun* snack mix; and B21, a pub in Williamsport, Pennsylvania, offers a *Rajun Cajun* turkey sandwich as part of its menu. While this moniker continues to refer to the University of Louisiana at Lafayette mascot, it now has also been appropriated by businesses outside of south Louisiana to label spicy foods. The Boulder restaurant, the Chapel Hill store, and the Williamsport pub prove how widespread national interest in everything Cajun has become since Henry Wadsworth Longfellow first published *Evangeline* in 1847. While the United States still demonstrates its fascination with Cajun culture through its proliferation of Cajun restaurants, movies,[1] and Cajun characters in popular fiction,[2] Cajun music has also gained an international audience through cultural appropriation. Australia, Holland, Germany, and Great Britain now advertise Cajun bands.[3] As Cajuns reconcile their Cajun and American identities as illustrated through their endeavors to embrace their difference through literary representation, the international community enacts an assimilation process because of its interest in this Cajun difference, mirroring the literary Americanization of Cajuns that began with Longfellow.

When Germans are listening to Cajun bands, it is clear that globalization has become a part of the story of Cajun representation in the twenty-first century, demonstrating how much Cajun culture has altered over the course of the last hundred years. In a world where the Internet links local products and populations to an international community, *Cajun,* along with numerous other ethnic signifiers, has become a recognized term on the global market even as it remains a regional label of pride among Cajuns themselves. In his study of the World Wide Web's effects on Cajun culture, Stephen Webre argues that the Internet can be employed as a tool for constructing identity since such a system offers "the opportunity for reconnection afforded to Cajuns in the new diaspora," a diaspora caused to some degree by the 1980s oil bust, which "sent educated and technically-trained Louisianians migrating out of state in search of economic opportunity" (444). In interesting ways, Webre's article, "Among the Cybercajuns: Constructing Identity in the Virtual Diaspora," frames its discussion of the Internet through a similar trajectory found in the study of Cajun literature by opening with references to Longfellow's *Evangeline* and closing with a discussion of how English, not Cajun French, is the dominant language of such Cajun sites. Webre explains this domination in reference to how "Cajuns have historically communicated with non-Cajuns in English, and communication with non-Cajuns about what it means to be Cajun, and about how the experience can be shared by those unfortunate enough not to have been born to it, is an implicit, and sometimes explicit, purpose of virtually all Cybercajun web sites" (454). Much like contemporary Cajun literature, Cajun Web sites are used to inform cultural outsiders and to share memories of cultural traditions, simultaneously providing a place for educating others and a space for reunion among the people themselves. Like literature, such sites do so through translation framed within an already accepted notion of American identification, which offers the possibility of embracing difference from within a process of assimilation.

The *Cajun* label may be a hot commodity today, but its origin is beyond popular marketing. As Cajuns become more educated, they choose to use this education to present an insider's view of Cajun culture to the general public, and no place is this more vibrant than in the publication of contemporary Cajun literature. While this inside look revises previous literary representations by illustrating the inaccuracies proliferated by these earlier works, as represented in the California restaurant scene in Tim Gautreaux's *The Next Step in the Dance*, it also demonstrates the degree to which such Americanization has to be acknowledged. Contemporary Cajun writing, including the work of Gautreaux, remains embedded in the Cajun past, usually in the period between 1920 and 1990.[4] Cajuns faced their greatest challenges in this period, including the oil boom and bust and the invasion of Wal-Marts and fast-food restaurants. This backward glance illustrates how Cajuns and their daily lives have shifted toward American mainstream culture, but it also allows Cajun authors to revise the literary record of Cajun Americanization to include their own perspectives on this process. As American as Cajuns have become, they retain a Cajun identity that remains a source of pride.

While Cajuns are a unique American ethnic group, their assimilation process and the consequences of assimilation echo various other ethnic experiences in this nation. Other minorities such as African Americans and American Indians have assimilated, usually by force, to more American notions of identity, leading to their use of English as a primary language and to their celebration of their differences through this dominant language. This use of English in ethnic literature of the United States is a major similarity among these works even as it remains a key to studying the paradox of such literature, since claiming an American identity always already signifies assimilation.

Much like Gaines whose African American perspective dominates his depiction of Louisiana racial relations and his own American identification, Louise Erdrich also emphasizes her multicultural roots as central to her novels about American Indian reservation life during the twentieth century. In her novels such as *Tracks* (1988) and *Love Medicine* (1994), Erdrich represents the interethnic reality of American Indian communities, placing her characters in the midst of situations that force them to confront the reality of their interstitial position between native traditions and American mainstream culture.

Like other twentieth-century ethnic writers, including Cajuns, Erdrich chooses to capture her tales of American Indian life through the English language. In a 1985 interview with Laura Coltelli, she argues that not all American Indian literature is the same, except in its use of English:

> One of the big mistakes that a lot of people make in coming to American Indian literature is thinking, oh, if it's Indian it's Indian. It's just like being in Europe and saying French literature is European literature. Well, of course, French, Italian, German, any culture, has its own literature, its own background, its own language, that springs from that culture. The thing that we have in common is that English is a language which has been imposed on Indian people through a whole series of concerted efforts. Almost all American Indian writers speak English as their main language, as their first language. (Coltelli 46–47)

This statement emphasizes the differences that remain within the larger framework of American Indian literature and stresses that the one definite similarity is the use of English. Studying ethnic writers' reliance on English, Martha Cutter argues that "[t]ranslation as trope transcodes ethnicity, but it also transcodes the meaning of the ethnic tongue so that it is no longer a disenfranchised dialect but rather part of the very texture of

American speech" (7). While this language has been forced on Cajuns and American Indians, such ethnic groups have subverted its control by using English to voice themselves in their literature.

The interest in and concern with language also dominates the study of African American literature. In *The Signifying Monkey*, Henry Louis Gates Jr. formulates an African American literary theory extending directly from African origins. His theory is founded on the existence of black vernacular and how this dialect remains different and unique as an American speech pattern. When such literature revises "texts in the Western tradition, they often seek to do so 'authentically,' with a black difference," and this difference is based on the use of black vernacular (xxii).

Ethnic American literature proves that language is central to representation but that language may reflect an assimilation or influence that has already occurred. Both Cutter and Gates provide theories that have allowed us to acknowledge both assimilation and the celebration of difference because gaining the use of the dominant language of English means being capable of remembering and perpetuating images of difference for the ethnic community and for the education of those outside of this community. This linguistic paradox reinforces, however, the loss that has already affected the ethnic populations, as Cajun literature demonstrates.

The study of Cajun literature provides additional insight into the double bind affecting ethnic American populations. From Longfellow through Chopin, the urge to write Acadians and their descendants as white and as potentially American departs from the relationship of white authors to other ethnic groups such as American Indians and African Americans. Cajun literature records the simultaneous processes of assimilation and difference as Cajuns realized that to prevent total cultural loss they must celebrate their differences in print. In his introduction to *The Invention of Ethnicity*, Werner Sollors deconstructs the process by which ethnic groups claim authenticity by addressing the invention of such identities and their mythologies. According to Sollors, "The focus is on the group's preservation and survival," thus "[a]ssimilation is the foe of ethnicity" (xiv). In response to this notion that permeates ethnic studies, Sollors argues that the formation of ethnicity is "not a thing but a process—and it requires constant detective work from readers, not a settling on a fixed encyclopedia of supposed cultural essentials" (xv). This particular study of Cajun literary representation proves that American ethnic identities are dynamic and rely to some degree on assimilation. Cajun history powerfully demonstrates how ethnicity can be a performance and a reality, a process of assimilation and of differentiation, a matter of change and of preservation for those who identify themselves as part of this group.

As contemporary Cajun literary representation illustrates, Cajuns, like other ethnic communities in the United States, have become American even as they continue to remain aware of their cultural differences. Cajuns continue to play the diatonic accordion, sing in Cajun French, and whip up a large pot of gumbo or jambalaya even as they speak in English, attend American public schools, and vote in national elections. Even if Cajun identity has become more self-conscious, and includes staged cultural festivals and prepackaged food, it is also a source of cultural pride that stems from the ability to survive the settlement in and development of a strange continent and a new nation. Contemporary Cajun authors write from this awareness; they do not write to criticize previous literary representations as much as to tell their own stories of being Cajun. If American fiction acts as a bridge between Cajuns and their American identification, then Cajun fiction also bridges this gap in order to remind Cajuns and teach Americans about traditional Cajun foodways, folk tales, music, and spirituality.

Although Wal-Mart and McDonald's have crossed Louisiana borders, they have not completely erased local ways. And although some form of gumbo is served across the nation, the real thing is still cooked in the homes of south Louisianians. Any Cajun who has chosen to leave his or her homeland and reside in another part of the United States has discovered how unique Acadiana remains. Like Gautreaux who moved to South Carolina for graduate school and realized how different his homeland was, contemporary Cajuns continue to experience this diversity. As Louisiana cultures change, it will be interesting to see if this experience continues to occur. Meanwhile, a shift in this experience will cause a variation in Cajun fiction. Will future Colettes and Pauls experience such pronounced difference in Los Angeles? Will literary Cajuns remain mostly rural? And if they do change in fiction, how will these stories unfold? Will they remain Cajun in outlook, or will their typical American accomplishments encourage them to forget Cajun traditions?

Regardless of how Cajun literature will continue to evolve, the study of it from Longfellow to Gautreaux proves that the story of Louisiana Cajuns is a survival story. In 2003, a historic event occurred that came with the bicentennial anniversary of the Louisiana Purchase and that placed Acadians and Cajuns on the front page of Louisiana newspapers and reminded Cajuns of such survival: Queen Elizabeth II apologized for the

British action taken against the Acadians in 1755. This royal proclamation stemmed from the lawsuit *Warren A. Perrin et al. v. Great Britain,* which was delivered to Margaret Thatcher and Queen Elizabeth in 1990. Perrin parallels his petition with the acts of his forefather Beausoleil Broussard in order to claim redemption for Cajuns and their culture: "Despite constant external pressures to assimilate, Acadians still maintain their separate cultural identity" (Perrin 119). This event is significant not because the apology will change where or how contemporary Acadians live, but because it encourages a sense of pride in the Cajun community of Louisiana. The Queen's apology was welcomed by Acadians across the world, but it reinforced the reality of Cajun formation since Cajuns exist today because of their settlement in Louisiana and their pride stems from their south Louisiana identity. This formal acknowledgment of the *Grand Dérangement* reminded Acadians and non-Acadians alike of the Acadian story as it is known through *Evangeline* and other literary representations of Acadian and Cajun history and culture. Perrin's victory has become another example of celebrating Cajun identity and its ability to survive, which he emphasizes by recalling the Acadian folk hero Beausoleil, and not the American-made Evangeline.

As the tourist industry and Cajun studies have gained momentum, Cajuns have experienced nostalgia for the past, even the mythical past of Longfellow and its reminder of the long-forgotten journey to Louisiana. While Perrin's lawsuit placed the battle for Cajun recognition within the framework of Acadian history and folklore, Longfellow's part in Cajun literary representation is pivotal and must be recognized as such because he created the means for contemporary Cajun authors to depict Cajun culture in print as different from a legendary past he created for the new nation. Whether or not contemporary readers are familiar with *Evangeline, Bonaventure,* Chopin's stories, Gaines's novels, Burke's Robicheaux series, or Gautreaux's work, the fictional representations in these works have made Cajuns international characters, and this global interest has encouraged contemporary authors to continue expressing their own Cajun identities and memories in fiction even as their cultural borders become more porous.

And so the paradoxes continue: assimilation because of differentiation, and differentiation in the midst of assimilation. *Cajun* no longer refers to a strictly Catholic, French people descended from Acadians, but it does still name a Louisiana ethnicity made up of distinct music, foodways, an English dialect influenced by Cajun French, and religious beliefs. The world watches for and recognizes pieces of Cajun culture while Cajuns are continuing to loosen their own recognition of themselves as Cajun or self-consciously to strengthen their unique identity through staged performances of difference. American children learn about Cajun culture from popular movies while Cajun children readily interact with others across the world over the Internet. But if it is through their dynamism that Cajuns have both come to exist and continue to survive as an ethnicity, then change is inevitable. Readers can only wait and see what becomes the next step in Cajun literary representation.

One thing is certain: Cajuns are far from disappearing, both in reality and in fiction. The historical formation and distribution of Cajun literary representation demonstrates the degree to which contemporary Cajuns take pride in their identity as other than Anglo-American, although still American. Cajun fiction preserves in print the process by which Acadians became Cajuns and Americans. As *Evangeline* became the memory of the dispersal for twentieth-century Cajuns, contemporary Cajun fiction has already become a memory of the Cajun past. And if *Evangeline* is the origin for Cajun literary representation in American fiction, then contemporary Cajun fiction is the revisioning of this representation, a retelling of the formation of Cajun Americans.

NOTES

INTRODUCTION

1. Longfellow was not the first author to write about the tragedy that led to the forma-tion of Louisiana's Acadiana, the name given to twenty-two Louisiana parishes inhabited by Cajuns. According to Mathé Allain's "They Don't Even Talk Like Us: Cajun Violence in Film and Fiction," "The earliest image of the Acadians is found in the *Philosophic and Polit-ical History of the Settlement and Commerce of Europeans in the Indies* (1794)," which Abbé Guillaume Thomas Raynal wrote as an "indictment of European colonization" (65).

2. According to Ancelet, Edwards, and Pitre, "The first *documented* arrival of Acadians occurred in New Orleans in April of 1764" (*Cajun Country* 12, emphasis mine). Although this may be the first documented arrival, it may not constitute the first arrival overall.

3. In *Naming the Other: Images of the Maori in New Zealand Film and Television,* Mar-tin Blythe argues that the "*word* blocks further thought. Moral: names set up an aesthetic that relies upon visual imagery for its force, whether this be romantic, horrific, comedic, or whatever" (4). The process of naming he discusses actually constitutes an example of a colonized people naming their colonizer. *Maori* is a native New Zealand term now used to identify the white population. The significance of this study to my work lies in Blythe's ex-planation of the Maori double bind. According to Blythe, Gregory Bateson and R. D. Laing popularized the term in the 1950s as "a theory of schizophrenia which suggested that ordi-nary family relationships in Western culture have a habit of tying people up in knots" (6). Cajun identity today represents this knotted situation since Cajuns are torn between their Cajun identification and their American identification, which causes tensions that are evi-dent in the writing of contemporary Cajuns.

4. *Evangeline,* the poem, and the various movies present Conrad's image of the good peasants with "simple virtue." *The Waterboy* (1998), an Adam Sandler movie, demonstrates the portrayal of Cajuns as "swamp dwellers, living in squalor" (Conrad 1).

CHAPTER 1

1. Lawrence Buell, Richard Brodhead, and Jane Tompkins provide evidence of the pop-ularity and success of these authors and their visions of America, as is documented in the course of this chapter.

2. Tompkins begins *Sensational Designs* with a study of why and how Hawthorne be-came established and remained in the American literary canon through literary and per-sonal connections. One of Hawthorne's supporters was Longfellow, a former classmate at

Bowdoin College, who praised *Twice-Told Tales* in his review of the collection in the *North American Review,* whose contributors made up "New England's cultural elite in the 1830s, 40s, and 50s" (Tompkins 10). By this time, "Longfellow was someone whose opinion carried weight in critical circles" (10), making his praise valuable to Hawthorne's reputation.

3. Demonstrating the success of the publishing world, American literature of the 1820s garnered a profit of 2.5 million dollars, as noted by Richard Brodhead. By the 1850s, the publishing business saw a ten-million-dollar increase in profits (44). Although Brodhead's numbers revolve around the publication and mass appeal of Harriet Beecher Stowe's *Uncle Tom's Cabin* (1852) and its domestically defined middle class readership (44), these figures also speak to Longfellow's place in American literature because of his own mass appeal at the time, which *Evangeline* increased.

4. In terms of Longfellow's use of European literary influences, George W. Arms explains, "we think of his use of European and American scene and legend, and we are apt to say that he avoided his own culture by using the first and then when he went to the second his method was to Europeanize native materials. . . . concerning his use of Europe we should not forget that pressure was greater in Longfellow's time than ours for native material. In going to Europe . . . he was moving against the literary currents of his day" (217). Cajun historian Carl Brasseaux also comments on Longfellow's use of European literary traditions to create an American literature: "he borrowed from oral epic tradition, incorporating in [*Evangeline*] well-known motifs from European folk literature. Emulating bards of old, Longfellow was self-consciously creating a usable past for Americans" (*In Search* 13).

5. *Evangeline*'s meter demonstrates one means Longfellow used to bond new Americans with ancient history and traditions to establish an American mythology worthy of international consideration. His class lessons aided in his creation of the classic hexameter in English poetry, an endeavor in which Longfellow was the first to succeed. At the time Longfellow wrote *Evangeline,* "No really successful English poem had yet been written in this form [hexameter]," notes Newton Arvin (109). Supposedly, the hexameter, six feet per line, did not translate from classical Greek and Latin to English because English "had only accent, and not time, for its syllables" (S. Longfellow, vol. 2, 71–72). For this reason, Lewis Semple writes, "the linking of verses together has much to do with oral reading" (*Evangeline,* Introduction xlix), which seems to imply that the poem's meter encourages oral reading over silent contemplation. The poem begins with such examples of its unique meter as "This is the forest primeval; but where are the hearts that beneath it / Leaped like the roe, when he hears in the woodland the voice of the huntsman?" (*Evangeline* 7–8), that beg to be read out loud in a sing-song voice. Longfellow perhaps meant for the work to be read aloud, mimicking ancient oral poems and their public performances by employing their meters for his native American work.

6. Simms's stories not only present tales of Native Americans but also include plantation fiction that focuses on slaves. By writing about the Acadian resettlement in Louisiana, Longfellow addresses a third ethnicity: Cajuns.

7. This romance tells the story of Abel and Manhattan, who represent "the primitive inhabitants and the first immigrants," who both claim the land. After the courts have decided who "owns" what, the two spend the pages of the novel walking around the island and claiming their pieces (Miller 141). For a further reading of this story and its publication history and for more on the formation of Young America and its effect on American literature, see Perry Miller's *The Raven and the Whale.*

8. As Tompkins explains, "[s]tereotypes are the instantly recognizable representatives of overlapping racial, sexual, national, ethnic, economic, social, political, and religious categories; they convey enormous amounts of cultural information in an extremely condensed form" (xvi).

9. Bauman quotes Schoolcraft's dedication to Longfellow in *The Myth of Hiawatha* (1856): "you have demonstrated, by this pleasing series of pictures of Indian life, sentiment, and invention, that the theme of the native lore reveals one of the true sources of our literary independence" (266).

10. In *Playing in the Dark,* Toni Morrison elaborates on this notion that white identity is defined as the opposite of the dark other.

11. As the South justified slavery, the North lectured by using the image of miscegenation's result. Through the mulatto character American authors addressed the complications and sins of slavery while also presenting a fact not as readily accepted by southern plantation owners, as Werner Sollors explains: "[I]t is possible to see the outline of a less visible counter-tradition in which the Mulatto actually appears as a most upsetting and subversive character who illuminates the paradoxes of 'race' in America, for the figure called 'Tragic Mulatto' may also have constituted a powerful critique of the southern plantation tradition's benevolent description of slavery" (*Neither Black* 234).

12. *Evangeline*'s prominent place in nineteenth-century literature has implications for racial issues beyond Cajun identity. In her study of Sidonie de la Houssaye's *Les Quarteronnes de la Nouvelle-Orléans* (1894–1895), Alice Parker emphasizes Evangeline's racial placement in order to compare and contrast the cult of Evangeline with portrayals of mulattoes of the time. She notes that Evangeline is "emblematic of the double diaspora" that led French peasants from France to Nova Scotia to Louisiana (75) but further argues that she "likewise symbolizes the values assigned to white females in the Francophone cultures of the New World" and that "Evangeline's darker sisters and cousins, through even more profound dislocations, experienced continuous exclusions from their geographical and cultural roots: there was no new home in the New World for African-American women" (75).

13. In a letter to Whittier written in 1844, Longfellow claims that he does "not belong to the Liberty Party. Though a strong anti-slavery man, I am not a member of any society, and fight under no single banner" (Seelye 41).

14. Longfellow never returned to the Acadian people in his later poems. He did, however, readdress Native Americans and other aspects of American history in later works. In all of these poems, the poet stands above the factual historian, preserving Longfellow's imagination more than any realistic portrait of the people represented. Similar to *Evangeline,* however, are the results of this creative rendering of the past, which seems at times to replace an actual past with the words of a poet. In *The Song of Hiawatha* (1855), "[t]he poet prevails; the anthropologist goes under" and "'Paul Revere's Ride' is not a trustworthy account. . . . It has merely supplanted what really happened in the public mind and memory" (Wagenknecht 132).

15. Jane Tompkins discusses this pattern further in chapters five and six of *Sensational Designs.*

16. Longfellow is referring to John F. Watson's *Annals of Philadelphia and Pennsylvania, in the olden time: being a collection of memoirs, anecdotes, and incidents of the city and its inhabitants, and of the earliest settlements of the inland part of Pennsylvania, from the days of the founders* (1830), Sherman Day's *Historical Collections of the State of Pennsylva-*

nia (1843), and William Darby's *Geographical Description of the State of Louisiana* (1816). In *Blue Collar Bayou: Louisiana Cajuns in the New Economy of Ethnicity*, Jacques Henry and Carl Bankston, two Louisiana sociologists, include a tremendously helpful table of English- and French-speaking writers of non-Acadian descent who wrote of Louisiana via fiction and history (table 1.2, 38). These two sociologists use the list to demonstrate which authors implemented which labels (French, Creole, Acadian, or Cajun) to describe the people of south Louisiana. Names of prominent American writers appear, including Longfellow, Cable, and Chopin. Also included are names of historians whose texts Longfellow relied on to broaden his knowledge of Louisiana: Darby and Flint. As for Darby, Henry and Bankston record his 1816 work, which Longfellow directly mentions in his journal, as using the three labels French, Creole, and Acadian, demonstrating his recognition of differences among the three labels (38).

17. Banvard began his work on the painting in 1840 when he traveled down the Mississippi for research. "When finished, the panorama covered about half a mile of canvas. . . . He afterward exhibited it in this country and abroad" ("John Banvard"). Banvard also wrote 1,700 poems, including "Descriptions of the Mississippi River."

18. In Longfellow's poem, the Acadians travel to the Mississippi River by land. Then they travel down the river to Louisiana:

> Far down the Beautiful River,
> Past the Ohio shore and past the mouth of the Wabash,
> Into the golden stream of the broad and swift Mississippi,
> Floated a cumbrous boat, that was rowed by Acadian boatmen. (*Evangeline* 741–44)

According to Brasseaux's study of Acadian migration patterns, the dispersed people would have considered an overland route too dangerous because of the colonial British troops attempting to contain the French Catholic people and the Native Americans whose dangerous presence was still felt in the western regions to the east of the Mississippi River. In actuality, groups of Acadians found their way to Louisiana by way of the Gulf of Mexico, on ships that carried them to the port of New Orleans where Spanish Governor Ulloa distributed land grants to them. Since critics have contrasted Longfellow's myth with history to insure the perpetuation of truth alongside fiction, there is little need to develop this history further here.

19. Longfellow's use of Philadelphia may allude to the signing of the *Declaration of Independence* as the founding of the nation. In reality, the Acadians shipped to the area following the 1755 dispersal did not receive warm welcomes from the British colony. Actually, the Acadians caught and spread diseases while onboard British vessels, and "[t]hese diseases posed a real threat to Philadelphia and spurred the provincial government into further negative actions," such as quarantine (Brasseaux, *Scattered* 19). Acadians who were shipped to Pennsylvania had continuous problems with the colonial government there "until the late 1760s, when they joined their relatives and friends . . . in a massive migration to Louisiana" (22). Pennsylvania may not have been the worst colony to which the dispersed Acadians were sent, but it was also not a place of independence for the French Catholic people.

20. *Creole* can have various definitions since its meaning has shifted over time. In this context, it refers to people of French or Spanish descent who were born in the New World and have risen to or were born into the Louisiana aristocracy. For more information on the complex history of *Creole* and its various meanings, refer to the introduction.

21. In their article "Tradition, Genuine or Spurious," Richard Handler and Jocelyn Linnekin refute earlier theories regarding tradition as a natural object that stands apart from our interpretations of it. Instead, they argue that tradition must "be understood as a wholly symbolic construction" and that it refers to "an interpretive process that embodies both continuity and discontinuity" (273). Tradition is not a natural object that is passed down from generation to generation as much as it is "a model of the past and is inseparable from the interpretation of tradition in the present" (276). In other words, it is not so much a preserved and contained object of the past as it is an ongoing and constantly reconstructed interpretation of the present. Thus, *Evangeline* and Voorhies's tale are both pieces of today's Cajun traditions because whether they are myth, *fakelore*, or folklore, they remain influential on contemporary interpretations of the Acadian dispersal and settlement in Louisiana.

22. Fifty years later, Amy Boudreau again told the story of the Acadian dispersal in her poem *The Story of the Acadians* (1955). Her rendering of the Acadian tragedy includes more than a retelling of the 1755 dispersal. Her version emphasizes the entire span of Acadian history from the 1604 settlement of what would become Acadia to the present. She even addresses her debt to Longfellow in the words of her poem:

> In later years a poet by pity moved,
> Wrote touchingly with beauty of their trials.
> *Evangeline,* Longfellow's poem, still lives,
> And with each reading *bridges* years and miles. (12, emphasis mine)

As she writes, *Evangeline* remains a bridge between Acadians and their American children, and between the actual Acadian past and our present memory of it. The end of the poem again emphasizes this concept of bridging the identity gap that 1950s Cajuns may have experienced as other than typical Americans, because she solidifies their place in the nation:

> . . . they grew up with America,
> This land of Red, White, and Blue,
> Wrote one of its first chapters,
> And one of its *finest,* too! (25)

She later claims, "Any portrait of 'America Today' / Bears imprint of Acadian life and charm" (27). Chris Segura will later tell a different story of Cajun assimilation and the difficulties faced during the 1950s, but Boudreau attempts to claim a space for cultural pride and hope for Cajun Americans during a time of national conformity and pride.

23. Instead of the saintlike Evangeline in convent garb wiping the brow of the dying Gabriel in a Philadelphia hospital, Voorhies has Emmeline finding Louis. Unfortunately, Louis has married another because he despaired of ever reuniting with his first love. Faced with a life in Louisiana without her fiancé, Emmeline falls to madness and dies. Both are eventually buried near Bayou Têche.

24. Among the various productions of the Evangeline story, this version is the most popular because of Dolores Del Rio's Evangeline statue: "Caught up in the enthusiasm of the moment, Dolores Del Rio . . . pledged money for the statue . . . and agreed that it be cast in her likeness" (Brasseaux, *In Search* 41). The statue was completed and placed by the church in September 1930 (41). Other movie versions include a 1913 black and white *Evangeline,* the only version filmed on authentic Canadian locations and the only one to begin the story of the two lovers in their childhood years; and a 1919 black and white version that

frames the narrative structure by having two modern lovers quarrel, which causes the girl's father to repeat the Evangeline tale to teach them about true love (Hal Erickson). The 1948 film *Louisiana Story* is another American film version of the Acadian dispersal (6).

25. Antonine Maillet, a Canadian Acadian, wrote "Évangéline Deusse," a 1975 play, about a prostitute searching for independence, an interesting variation on the name Evangeline since it completely turns from Longfellow's saintly heroine (Martin).

Maillet also wrote her own version of the Acadian dispersal and return to Canada to capture the oral history of her people in her 1979 Prix Goncourt winner *Pélagie-la Charette* (Martin). Maillet's career focusing on Canadian Acadian culture and literature makes her a fascinating contemporary of Cajun authors who began writing in the 1980s.

CHAPTER 2

1. Bonaventure obviously alludes to the *Declaration of Independence.*

2. Arguing against sectional division and identification at the expense of national progress and unity, Cable writes, "There is a newly-coined name that most agreeably tickles the ear of the young citizen in our Southern states, but which I would gladly see met with somewhat of disrelish: the New South. . . . What we want—what we ought to have in view—is the No South!" ("Literature" 44).

3. The prominent New Orleans historian Charles Gayarré went so far in his charge against Cable that he even "rented a hall to denounce Cable in public" (119), according to Christopher Benfey. Once a friend and supporter, the famous historian placed himself against Cable at a time when Cable's fame was rising while Gayarré's role as New Orleans's historian was fading.

4. Cable's criticism of his homeland came at a price. According to Fred Hobson, Cable "was the most reluctant of social critics, unqualified by temperament for his task, and he had taken ten years to bolster his courage to the point that he would speak out boldly. And when he finally did speak, he was in tone the most tactful and sympathetic of critics, proclaiming his own Southern heritage, confessing his own racial sins, and filling his essays with praise for the South—all in an attempt *not* to offend" (*Tell About the South* 117). But he did offend, and he offended to such a degree that he decided to move his family to Northampton, Massachusetts, for good in 1885. This move was not sudden, however, since Cable had settled his family in the Northeast during his reading tour "Twins of Genius" with Mark Twain, which lasted from November 1884 through February 1885.

5. Throughout this chapter, *Creole* is used to refer to the "white" population of New Orleans and south Louisiana for clarity. For more on the coding of *Creole* along the color line, refer to the introduction.

6. According the Carl Brasseaux, "Upwardly mobile Acadians who aspired to the planter caste embraced their wealthy neighbors' proclivity for conspicuous consumption" (*Acadian to Cajun* 4). Cable is making reference here to the poorer classes of Acadians. While he frames this reality in terms of their choice not to participate in the slave trade, in truth some may not have owned slaves simply because they could not afford to do so.

7. According to Paul Haspel, Cable had first experienced Acadian culture in 1866, when he was part of a surveying party searching for information around the Atchafalaya River (108). Demonstrating his interest in the area, he vacationed in Acadian country in 1869 (Turner 110). When Col. George E. Waring Jr. came to Louisiana to "collect social statistics

for publication with the Tenth Census of the United States" in 1880 (Turner 109), he asked Cable to be his local assistant, and Cable agreed. On November 12, 1880, Cable returned to Acadiana, lived among the families, participated in their culture and traditions, and recorded detailed notes on their wedding rituals, religious observances, foodways, and other folkways in his Acadian Notebook, an early set of field notes on Acadian culture. Although the material was never published as part of the census, Cable would not forget this people or his interest in them.

8. For more on this process, see chapter 1.

9. Such disparagement of linguistic Others actually began before the Civil War since there was a "social stigma associated with all things French [in Louisiana] by the early 1840s" (Brasseaux, *Acadian to Cajun* 95). The 1848 Irish potato famine and European Revolutions around the same time, both of which caused a greater influx of immigrants in the United States, did not help the situation (98–99). In 1916, Louisiana law demanded that all children under a certain age attend school. Then in 1921, the Louisiana Constitution included a new article requiring teachers and students to speak only English on public school property, making the education system the main means of enforcing English-only laws in the state. For more on this later development, which *Bonaventure* foreshadows, refer to Carl Blyth's "The Sociolinguistic Situation of Cajun French: The Effects of Language Shift and Language Loss."

10. In the 1990s, the English-only debate dominated American politics once again as Newt Gingrich, Speaker of the House, and Bob Dole, the Republican presidential candidate in 1995, argued for English-only laws, including the "English Language Empowerment Act" (Bernard, *The Cajuns* 143). Interestingly enough, Warren A. Perrin, a Cajun, argued fiercely against such acts and laws (143).

11. Acadian assimilation of which Cable writes did occur earlier among some Acadians in south Louisiana, but those who chose to assimilate did so for economic purposes not shared by the ethnic group as a whole. "This flight [by those who chose social advancement] across cultural lines would be undertaken in response to the vitriolic public denigration of their mother culture. The Acadian yeoman and laboring classes, however, lacked the cultural, linguistic, and educational wherewithal—*and evidently the inclination*—to join the cross-cultural migration" (*Acadian to Cajun* 99, emphasis mine), according to Brasseaux.

12. In Kate Chopin's representations of Cajuns in fiction, the term *Cajun* will reflect American disdain for the Acadian descendants by contrasting it to *'Cadian,* a word used to denote Acadian naming of self.

13. Enoch writes, "The only way to cleanse the Indian, claimed Carlisle, was through education," and the school took before and after pictures of new arrivals "that reflected the outward changes an education at Carlisle could produce" through shorn hair and western clothing (125). The word *cleanse* points to the belief that American Indians needed to be cleaned up and Americanized, made less savage.

14. Alexander Mouton was Louisiana Governor 1843–1846 and served as a U.S. Senator from 1837 to 1842.

15. Governor Mouton's family history is recorded in Cable's Acadian Notebook, located in Box 108 of The George W. Cable Papers. The ex-governor in the novel follows from this true story, as do other Cable characters. In "After-Thoughts of a Story-Teller," Cable writes about the models for some of his fictional characters: "In *Bonaventure* the hero and Tarbox are portraits—not photographs, I hope,—while the cure of Carancro, made with no model

either in sight or memory, turned out to be a surprising likeness . . . of a parish priest laboring within 15 miles of the place" ("After-Thoughts of a Story-Teller").

16. "Most lower-class Acadians and Creoles . . . were illiterate" during the decades leading up to the Civil War (Brasseaux, *Acadian to Cajuns* 95).

17. The correct spelling of this Louisiana town is Carencro. It is spelled as "Carancro" in this book whenever referring to the novel, and as "Carencro" when referring to the town itself.

18. Beausoleil remains a prominent folk hero for Acadians and Cajuns alike. The Acadian Memorial, located in St. Martinville, Louisiana, contains a mural depicting an Acadian arrival in Louisiana. Heading the group, in the center of the painting, stands Beausoleil, a reminder of the Acadian past and its history of survival. For more information on Beausoleil, refer to Brasseaux's *The Founding of New Acadia*, James Dormon's *The People Called Cajuns*, and Warren Perrin's *Acadian Redemption: From Beausoleil Broussard to the Queen's Royal Proclamation*.

19. According to Brasseaux, some Acadians opposed conscription, resenting being forced into military service against their wills (*Acadian to Cajun* 64). Although some Acadians were plantation and slave owners, others simply did not feel compelled to abandon their land to fight on either side of the Civil War. Moreover, their loyalties shifted when Texans began filtering in and ruling the western part of the state. Brasseaux demonstrates this fact by quoting the *Official Report Relative to the Conduct of the Federal Troops in Western Louisiana:* "While encamped at Vermillionville in October 1863, Union Brigadier General Charles P. Stone . . . reported that hundreds of residents in that overwhelming Acadian area had taken the oath of allegiance to the United States government and, having grown 'heartily tired of Texan rule,' wished to arm to protect the country from further inroads on the part of the rebel forces" (67). The Civil War from the Acadian perspective was thus a somewhat different war from the southern fight for slavery and states' rights.

20. The Acadian reaction to the conscription of 'Thanase follows from actual experience in the Civil War. Brasseaux writes, "Recruitment programs in southwest Louisiana were . . . directed by Anglo-Saxons, usually east Texans, who viewed the Acadians as social and cultural inferiors and treated them accordingly" (*Acadian to Cajun* 63). Moreover, "Unable to speak the invaders' language or read the confiscation orders [following Union victories in Acadian parishes], which the foraging party commanders delighted in waving under the noses of their hapless victims, the Acadian was powerless" (69). Cable writes of the Civil War as the occasion in which "many an Acadian volunteer and many a poor conscript fought and fell for a cause that was really none of theirs, simple, non-slaveholding peasants" (*Bonaventure* 9). According to Brasseaux, "Acadian apathy toward the war effort quickly degenerated into open hostility following the enactment of the initial Confederate Conscription Act in April 1862" (63). He also explains that desertion was a common problem because men realized that without them their crops would not be harvested (72).

21. In his Acadian Notebook, Cable records a culture little affected by outside influence and progress. His novel does the opposite: it records a changing culture influenced by American assimilation. His field notes testify to the need for Cajun assimilation, and his novel addresses how this assimilation must occur through the American education system.

22. Three governors to whom Cable may be referring are the following: Henry Schuyler Thibodeaux who settled the city of Thibodaux in 1801, governor for a month in 1824; Al-

exander Mouton, mentioned above; and Paul Octave Hébert, governor 1853–1856. All have Acadian surnames and an Acadian heritage.

23. It is worth noting that *Tarbox* is not a common Louisiana name and it carries no sense of French or Spanish descent. Cable may have chosen it simply to emphasize Tarbox's position outside of all Louisiana communities, a position he knew well from his own experience as the son of migrated northerners.

24. More on this topic is discussed in connection with the fiction of Ernest Gaines and James Lee Burke who record such shifts away from traditional Cajun work and ways of life. For further discussion of the Americanization of the Cajuns, refer to Shane Bernard's *The Cajuns: Americanization of a People.*

CHAPTER 3

1. For more on the various meanings of *Creole* and the history of the label in Louisiana, refer to the introduction. To distinguish between the complicated racial categories in south Louisiana, I use *Creole* to refer to those who claimed white identification and *Creole of Color* to refer to free persons of color of African and European descent in this chapter. Chopin uses "Nég Créol" as the title of one of her short stories, representing her own understanding of the various racial implications of the word *Creole* and the need to distinguish meaning in terms of race.

2. In order to emphasize the shift in Acadian culture as it evolves into Cajun culture, I use the term *'Cadian,* as Chopin does, to signify the transitional phase in this evolution. In this chapter, *Acadian* refers to the origins of the people and culture in south Louisiana, which links back to the 1755 dispersal. I also use this as the formal label of this people. I use *Cajun* to refer to the future state of this evolution, and the evolution of the term itself that led to the use of Cajun by the people themselves. During Chopin's literary career, *Cajun* held negative connotations, so I use the term only when assessing this negativity and in relation to today's critical readings of the works discussed. The overall use of *Cajun fiction* to address all of the works regarding Acadian and Cajun peoples simply allows for a continuous literary process that records the entire history of Acadian to Cajun identification through American literature.

3. As Frenchmen, the Cajuns found themselves in the same category as white Louisianians; as a poorer, more illiterate people, the Cajuns were labeled as "white trash" (Brasseaux, *Acadian to Cajun* 104). Thus, the term *Cajun* signifies a lower-class position that rests somewhere in between white landowning and poorer black communities, making Cajuns interstitial figures in both history and fiction. For more on my use of this term, refer to the introduction.

4. For further explanation of Louisiana's cultural and racial categories, refer to chapter 2.

5. Reading beyond Chopin's *Youth's Companion* stories, Sandra Gunning argues that Chopin's 'Cadian and Creole characters act as a means of writing these Louisiana ethnicities as "white" following emancipation, as exemplified in the short story "In Sabine," which, she claims, "also functions as a commentary on ethnic division among whites themselves, specifically Americans and Creoles in the context of increased anxiety over racial purity" (125).

6. They did so by claiming that *Creole* meant "white," versus the use of *creole* to refer

to those of nonwhite descent, as Barbara Ladd explains in *Nationalism and the Color Line*.

7. In *French, Cajun, Creole, Houma*, Carl Brasseaux explains that "upwardly mobile . . . Louisiana Acadians increasingly modeled their existence upon that of the white Creole planter class" (68).

8. In *Acadian to Cajun*, Brasseaux records *Cajen* as an earlier spelling of Cajun (102). As late as 1939, William Faulkner used the spelling *Cajin* to refer to Cajuns in *If I Forget Thee Jerusalem*, pointing to a confusion over not only how to categorize the ethnic community, but also how officially to spell the name.

9. Brasseaux frames his work, *Acadian to Cajun: Transformation of a People, 1803–1877*, around two significant events that forever changed both Acadian culture and American identification. He emphasizes the powerful forces of the Louisiana Purchase (1803) and the period of Reconstruction following the Civil War (ending in 1877) in Cajun identity formation. The Civil War and its result, Reconstruction and other attempts at national unity, greatly aided the Acadian shift to Cajun identification, a period and shift that Cable begins to describe in *Bonaventure* and on which Chopin's fiction focuses as the reason for possible racial and social instability in south Louisiana.

10. In his article "Natchitoches and Louisiana's Timeless Cane River," Robert DeBlieux describes Cane River, the area in which Chopin lived from 1879 to 1884, as viewed by eighteenth-century explorers: "In the late 18th century, travelers to the old Spanish-French settlement of Natchitoches frequently made note of the area's beauty and its genteel people. They were often astonished to find a place, so isolated from the rest of Louisiana, with opulent plantation homes" (15). DeBlieux even goes so far as to describe this piece of Louisiana as a "remote Eden" (15), echoing Longfellow's and Voorhies's portraits of the land as such in earlier works. This "Eden" with its "opulent plantation homes" was once the home of Kate Chopin and the backdrop for many of her Louisiana stories.

11. For more information on this period in Chopin's life, refer to chapter 6, "Cloutierville: The Talk of the Town," of Emily Toth's *Unveiling Kate Chopin*.

12. Ironically, Chopin's "first literary model was William Dean Howells," but she began reading Maupassant by the early 1890s (Toth 122–23).

13. In their introduction to *White Trash: Race and Class in America*, Annalee Newitz and Matt Wray discuss the significance of "whiteness" as a racial category. They argue that "In the minds of many scholars, writers, and activists working in this area [of color coding], whiteness is an oppressive ideological construct that promotes and maintains social inequalities," leading them to emphasize the need for "[m]aking whiteness visible to whites—exposing the discourses, the social and cultural practices, and the material conditions that cloak whiteness and hide its dominating effects" (3). Concerning Acadians as they shift in racial meaning throughout American literature, coloring them white is a movement (of which Chopin is a part) that attempts to make their differences invisible. Nevertheless, as is evident in Chopin's work, Acadian descendants remain different in the eyes of American readers, once again complicating and making ambiguous their place in American identification categories.

14. In typical Chopin fashion, the author never placed herself in any literary compartment. In fact, she "resented" the title of "local colorist," demonstrating her use of regional cultures for her own purposes (Taylor 139).

15. In "The Catalyst of Color and Women's Regional Writing: *At Fault, Pembroke*, and *The Awakening*," Pamela Glenn Menke argues in favor of Fetterley and Pryse and expands

on their introduction as she emphasizes the necessary influence of local color fiction on Chopin's first and final novels. Menke's article appears to conflate local color and women's regional writing in a way that confuses the argument established by Fetterley and Pryse; however, her point remains clear throughout the essay: Local Color was a definite influence, and a significant one, on Chopin's writings. She establishes this fact by stating that Chopin read Mary E. Wilkins Freeman's *Pembroke* in 1889, a year or so before she started writing professionally, and that Chopin wrote of her admiration for such authors as Grace King and Ruth McEnery Stuart (9), both New Orleans regional writers and contemporaries of Chopin. She elaborates on Chopin's regional influences in order to question critics' continual emphasis on Guy de Maupassant's dominant place in Chopin's work: "At least as important as Maupassant's achievement as a stimulus for Chopin's artistry in *The Awakening* is *Pembroke*, which Chopin read in 1894 and which she praised as 'the most profound piece of fiction of its kind that has ever come to the American press'" (9).

16. The Genteel Tradition stemmed from the notion of the "gentleman publisher," who published fiction that met moral standards. A publisher could rise in social status via the publishing world by means of his conduct, making "gentleman" signify conduct instead of blood relations or monetary wealth (Shaker, *Coloring Locals* 18).

17. *Scribner's Monthly Magazine* became *Century* in 1881 (Taylor 19).

18. From an 1890 letter from Chesnutt to George Washington Cable.

19. Donna Campbell relates the shift from feminine local color fiction, according to Howells, to more masculine naturalism in *Resisting Regionalism: Gender and Naturalism in American Fiction, 1885–1915*. She argues that local color fiction's simplistic, rural depictions could not withstand the onslaught of scientific thought that was voiced by Darwin, Spencer, and Huxley and that naturalist writers, such as Stephen Crane and Frank Norris, allowed to influence them to "a commitment to the accurate and detailed representation of ordinary human beings, a fascination with tracing the work ways of heredity, and a belief in the shaping power of the environment" (9).

20. Chopin's contemporary critics viewed her short story collections as local color works, perhaps because of their own confusion or ignorance about the stories' larger meanings: "Most of [the reviews] described Chopin's stories as local color tales from Louisiana—about which the reviewers were very muddled" (Toth 149). *A Night in Acadie* "was praised, blandly and unspecifically, for charm and sympathy; reviewers again blathered about bayous and quaintness" (195). Even as late as *The Awakening*, critics did not know quite what to make of the author's work. The August 1898 review of *The Awakening* in *The Nation* stated, "It is with high expectation that we open the volume, remembering the author's agreeable short stories, and with real disappointment that we close it" (Walker 165). Another reviewer wrote, "Miss Kate Chopin is another clever woman, but she has put her cleverness to a very bad use in writing 'The Awakening.'" (166).

21. Emily Toth writes that William Dean Howells "was simply not hospitable to [Chopin's] vision of women" and that he believed "No American . . . would write . . . novels about 'guilty love' (he would not say adultery)" (170).

22. By attributing the use of the term *local color* to "Théophile Gautier's school of writers in 1830s France" and emphasizing that "the term was later used by French realists—notably Flaubert and Maupassant—to refer to the essence of realism, the details and motifs characteristic of and appropriate to a particular setting," Helen Taylor explains how a seemingly typical American literary tradition is firmly entrenched in a European style of

writing (17). Taylor further documents the exchange of this tradition across the ocean and its resulting influence on American literature: "According to scholars of American local color, the term was used in postbellum America to describe three phases of fictional writing—especially the picturesque . . ., and less frequently the scientifically observant and the serious contemporary" (17). What is fascinating about this history, especially in regard to Chopin's fiction, is its placement of a traditional American genre within a European literary style. Chopin's utilization of the genre to relate more realistic portraits of female sexuality does not seem so far removed from the European concept of local color.

23. Some of the confusion may arise from a lack of understanding Creoles of Color and the residents of Isle Brevelle. After all, "Kate Chopin was the first writer to use the customs, traditions, and beliefs of the Cane River Creoles of Color in her fiction" (Gaudet, "Kate Chopin" 52).

24. Sandra Gunning identifies Ozème as "Cajun" in her work *Race, Rape, and Lynching: The Red Record of American Literature, 1890–1912* (117), and Marcia Gaudet uses Seyersted's identification of Ozème as "likely Cajun" to argue for a more comprehensive understanding of Louisiana Creoles of Color ("Kate Chopin" 50).

25. Another interesting passage that may have led critics astray begins the story: "Ozème often wondered why there was not a special dispensation of providence to do away with the necessity for work. . . . To sit and do nothing but breathe was a pleasure" (511). Some readers may view the concept of no work as coding this character as Cajun because of Chopin's earlier story, "A Rude Awakening," which identifies laziness as a possible Cajun characteristic located in Sylveste Bordon. Ozème does not, however, display any signs of laziness since "He worked faithfully on the plantation the whole year long, in a sort of methodical way" (511). This description may not coincide with popular views of Cajuns at this period in American history. Yet it does address, for today's readers, the similarities between Cajun and Creole of Color cultures, both of which prized good times while also acknowledging the necessity of work, a concept that separated them from the Anglo-Protestant work ethic.

26. Free people of color lived along Cane River. The settlement of Isle Brevelle originated with former slave Marie Thérèze Coincoin and her children after her white lover bought and freed them. Claude Thomas Pierre Metoyer, the white man who purchased their freedom, "gave her sixty-eight acres of land on the Côte Joyeuse section of Isle Brevelle and a modest allotment for their children" (Gaudet, "Kate Chopin" 46–47). Gaudet continues, "By the time of her death, Marie Thérèze and her children had an estate of almost 12,000 acres and at least 99 slaves" (47).

27. However, James Dormon writes that "many Cajuns owned slaves themselves, though normally not in large numbers (save for the plantation owners of Acadian descent, by definition not 'Cajun' [because of their upper-class status])" (*The People* 50).

28. Brasseaux explains the meaning of these balls for the community: "Numerous nineteenth-century observers noted that *bals de maison* were held every Saturday night. By all accounts, Acadians regarded these weekly house dances as a welcome respite from their difficult and monotonous existence" (*Acadian to Cajun* 28). By bringing the community together, these balls were also a means of preserving Acadian ties.

29. Dormon examines the consequences of Texan infiltration of Acadian lands in his work *The People Called Cajuns: An Introduction to an Ethnohistory*. "The rural/folk Cajun population was also thrown into increased contrast with other groups by virtue of the in-

migration of numbers of very different 'others;' others from the American Midwest and East Texas, who brought with them their own ethnocentric cultural baggage and their inevitable view of the Cajun-as-exotic" (66). This migration caused shifts in Cajun culture because the businesses that found their way to south Louisiana were controlled by outside forces, and "[i]t was in many ways a new world they made, and once again the Cajun population had to accommodate it or get out" (66). Chopin's story captures the East Texas movement into Louisiana and the antagonism felt between south Louisianians and the newcomers. Tim Gautreaux's fiction further records this conflict.

30. Brasseaux explains the corruption of the word 'Cadian to Cajun, which meant "white trash" (*Acadian to Cajun* 104). In their introduction to a collection of essays on "white trash," Annalee Newitz and Matt Wray argue that the term is as much a signifier of race as of class since it names poor whites as "Other." They argue: "The term white trash helps solidify the middle and upper classes' sense of cultural and intellectual superiority" (2). This superiority leads to a further theory about American class divisions: "white trash, since it is racialized (i.e. different from 'black trash' or 'Indian trash') and classed (trash is social waste and detritus), allows us to understand how tightly intertwined racial and class identities actually are in the United States" (4). Similar to nineteenth-century studies of female sexuality (discussed later in this chapter), class studies were also placed within scientific discourse to argue for legitimization. Newitz and Wray record the U. S. Eugenics Records Office reports between 1880 and 1920 to further address the relationship between popular race and class divisions as biological at the time (2). In relation to the use of *Cajun* by the end of the nineteenth century, Acadian descendants can be viewed through similar class studies because of their own racial and class ambiguity, which threatens the "white" Creoles who were claiming pure whiteness following Reconstruction in New Orleans.

31. With this usage of *Cajun,* those of Acadian descent who were wealthy landowners divided themselves from their poor brethren. According to Dormon, "The 'Genteel Acadians,' of course, provided the success story for which the United States has been at least mythically renowned; the process whereby poor immigrants, by dint of hard work, frugality and a little luck, rise to positions of wealth, power, and prestige" (*The People* 31). Dormon contributes the term *Genteel Acadians* to folklorist Patricia Rickels who coined the term in her own study of class division within Acadian culture (*The People* 30). In the end, "Those who achieved [economic] success . . . ultimately came to join the dominant planter/bourgeois class," intentionally separating themselves from the common Cajuns (33). Chopin's fiction captures the lower-class population of Acadian descendants and not the "Genteel Acadian" people.

32. Cable uses the word as the name outsiders give to Acadians, but he does not seem to mirror the negative use of the term.

33. This story was published posthumously.

34. In October 1893, a hurricane hit Grand Isle and destroyed the resort, killing 2,000 people (Toth 79). This tragedy inspired Chopin to resurrect her own memories of her island summers in "At Chênière Caminada" and *The Awakening.* Grace King captured the resort in her short story "At Chênière Caminada." Lafcadio Hearn similarly captured the tragic destruction of Last Island by an 1856 hurricane in his novel *Chita: A Memory of Last Island* (1889). This literary fascination with the Gulf islands led Helen Taylor to write the following: "from New Orleans south toward the Baratarian Islands is used by . . . Cable, Hearn, King, and Chopin to suggest a shift from the mundane and real into a sphere of heightened

existence, poetic intensity, and legendary richness" (177). Continuing the history of danger along the Gulf coast, a hurricane hit Galveston on September 8, 1900, killing 6,000 people. Then, on August 29, 2005, Katrina devastated southern Louisiana from Grand Isle upward through New Orleans. Although Katrina's death toll may not be as high as the 1900 storm that ravaged Galveston, the consequent flooding of the area has led to a similar rebuilding of the city. On September 13, 2008, Hurricane Ike made U. S. landfall in Galveston, Texas. As with previous deadly storms, these destructive events triggered survivors' stories that continue an interest in the coast as a place of intense experience.

35. This peninsula is located off Grand Isle in the Gulf of Mexico.

36. In "*The Awakening's* Signifying 'Mexicanist' Presence," Phillip Barrish offers a similar argument in regard to Mariequita and her ability as a Mexican, thus lustful, woman to represent a space beyond social norms of behavior, thus offering a means for Robert Lebrun to identify as masculine and Edna to discover her sexual desires and to realize her lack of desire to adapt to the social norms of Creole New Orleans.

37. Seyersted found the story in Chopin's diary that Chopin's grandson Robert Hattersley loaned to him (Toth 243).

38. Brasseaux addresses the significance of crosscultural marriages in the shift from Acadian to Cajun culture: "The cultural interchanges born from these unions transformed the Cajun community producing, in the process, a new people. This new community would create a cultural synthesis based on traditional Acadian values but including numerous cultural, culinary, linguistic, and musical elements of the group's adopted members" (*Acadian to Cajun* xiv). He writes, "Once absorbed into Acadian society through intermarriage, rival cultures could not survive" (44). Thus, Calixta's identity as a 'Cadian wife alters her Cuban identification.

39. What is interesting is that the African American servant codes Acadians as *Cajuns*, which has already been established as a negative term. This code seems to reflect either a popular pronunciation of 'Cadian that Bruce overheard and placed within his own dialect or his notion of 'Cadians as his equals or inferiors, as exemplified in the African American characters discussed above.

40. "Desirée's Baby" and "La Belle Zoraïde" are both examples of Chopin's use of the tragic mulatto motif in her fiction.

41. Emily Toth points out Chopin's lack of sexual realism in *The Awakening* and her silence regarding the sexual act even as Edna participates in it. She calls these moments in the text "white space" (213).

CHAPTER 4

1. The play addresses the reason for such marriage laws, in particular the safety and health of the children. Cajun communities face the threat of such genetic diseases as Friedreich's Ataxia, Usher's Syndrome, and Tay-Sachs today because of such interfamilial marriage over the past generations. In an article for the Lafayette *Daily Advertiser,* Judy Stanford quotes Dr. Michael Wilensky as arguing, "We have a high incidence of the genetic disorders here [in south Louisiana]. Part of the reason is because of intermarriage among Cajuns during the early years. It enhances a recessive gene" (Stanford).

2. According to James Dormon, "in the Louisiana constitution of 1921 public schools were denied an option previously open to them: The option of offering instruction in French

as well as English" (*The People* 70). Furthermore, "Governor Long's efforts to build an effective educational system in the state initiated an all-out assault on illiteracy, but it was clear that 'literacy' was to be defined as *English* literacy" (70). Cajun children soon learned that speaking French on school grounds would result in punishment and shame, including being called names such as "swamp-rat" and being "made to kneel in corners on kernels of corn, or [being] slapped . . . with rulers" (Bernard, *The Cajuns* 18). By 1944, Act 239 of the state legislature instituted even tougher state compulsory attendance laws to further guarantee Cajun school attendance, which made English education a dominant factor in the transformation of Cajun culture throughout the twentieth century (33).

3. The different spellings of *Cajun* that were popular during this time, including *Cajin* and *Cajan*, demonstrate America's continuing difficulty defining and categorizing this particular people and their place in the nation.

4. William Faulkner's "Lion," published in *Harper's*, also won an O. Henry Prize that year.

5. This revival also inspired the movement to study the folklore of south Louisiana. Such work as Lyle Saxon's *Gumbo Ya-Ya* (1945) testifies to continued national fascination with south Louisiana and its unique cultural communities, but this work also demonstrates how folklore from such communities was becoming a matter of collection and examination. Following Alcée Fortier's lead, students began examining folklore for various reasons, including the study of both folktales and Louisiana French dialects (Ancelet, "Cajun and Creole"). Corinne Saucier examined folktales from Avoyelles Parish for her 1923 thesis and her 1949 dissertation, written in French; Calvin Claudel received his Ph.D. from UNC after completing his dissertation on Louisiana French folktales in 1947; and Elizabeth Brandon studied the songs, tales, and social history of Vermillion Parish for a 1955 collection ("Cajun and Creole"). Whatever the reason for its existence, such work remains significant. Barry Jean Ancelet explains that "[t]hough these studies are lacking in serious folklore scholarship, they nevertheless provide a veritable mine of information and transcribed texts" ("Cajun and Creole").

6. Evangeline developed into the national and regional symbol for Louisiana Cajuns in part because Louisianians, including Acadian descendants, realized her value to tourism. Her name and her story were nationally famous by the time south Louisiana began to promote Cajun tourism in the early twentieth century. Evangeline's loyalty, purity, and "white" identification made her a perfect face for the tourist market. Meanwhile, her popularity outside Louisiana established a bridge between the lower-class Cajuns and the rest of the nation. In many ways, she became a significant link that allowed for the double bind Cajuns experience today as both Acadian descendants and Americans.

7. In an interview with John Canfield, Grau describes Annie and her neighbors' lives as in constant conflict with the environment (42), a tension that Annie cannot resolve and that perfectly describes her situation in life and her impulse to leave her home behind her forever.

8. In a statement that responds directly to the racial situation in Louisiana and how it differed from the national mindset, Grau argues, "If you look at, say, the English colonies in Africa in the nineteenth century and the French, the French blended in very nicely and settled down and were part of it. The English did their darnedest to stay separate" (Canfield 45). This quote speaks directly to the situation portrayed in *The Hard Blue Sky* that tells the story of an interethnic people, "a mixture of French and Spanish mostly, though an oc-

casional very dark child shows Indian or Negro blood" (Grau 9–10), a "short dark [people] with a wide round face" (179). According to Grau, "all of the people in *The Hard Blue Sky* are probably of mixed blood. They certainly should be, if I didn't make them" (Canfield 45).

9. For more information on CVE history and form, see *Cajun Vernacular English: Informal English in French Louisiana*, a special issue of a journal edited by Ann Martin Scott. CVE is a dialect maintaining certain sentence structures and borrowings from Cajun French spoken by Cajuns throughout the twentieth century as they were forced to speak English on public grounds. Some characteristics of this dialect include the lack of the "th" sound, making it a "t" or "d" sound, and the extra "you" or "no" at the end of sentences.

10. This essay was written as a response to Irving Howe's essay, "Native Sons and Black Boys," in which Howe praises the work of Wright and argues that Ellison's and Baldwin's works were made possible through Wright's expression of African American anger. Ellison disagrees in his response.

11. In *The Invention of the White Race*, Theodore W. Allen studies the formation of race as it pertains to the United States. He elaborates on the definition of white Americans by addressing the economic and social structures built to maintain this whiteness and by claiming that the formation of the white race was not only genetic, but also political (22). As such, the concept was invented "only when the bourgeoisie could not form its social control apparatus without the inclusion of propertyless European-Americans" (19). Through this system, such poor whites as Irish and Cajuns could and did rise socially, and sometimes economically, while their black counterparts remained firmly on the lowest rungs of society, a system portrayed in Gaines's fiction. Displaying his personal realization of the means by which class structure allowed for and promoted racial conflict by positioning the lower-class Cajun against the laboring African American, Gaines captures a more complete picture of how class and race enforce social control in south Louisiana, the same type of social control that gained for the Irish and the Cajuns white identification on the backs of their less fortunate, and perhaps darker, neighbors.

12. Toni Morrison makes a similar point in *Playing in the Dark: Whiteness and the Literary Imagination*. Her main thesis is that "For the most part, the literature of the United States has taken as its concern the architecture of a *new white man*" (14–15), and that this architectural structure has been built on a base made out of a black presence: "Africanism is the vehicle by which the American self knows itself as not enslaved, but free; not repulsive, but desirable; not helpless, but licensed and powerful; not history-less but historical; not damned, but innocent; not a blind accident of evolution, but a progressive fulfillment of destiny" (52). To realize freedom, to realize whiteness, Americans had to create the opposite: the enslavement of Africans. Morrison's text further discusses specific white texts and how they demonstrate her argument. Such African American writers as Gaines demonstrate how they refute this white construction of blackness by emphasizing the full humanity of African Americans.

13. According to Bernard, Pointe Coupée parish was roughly 54 percent black in 1960, but still controlled by white leaders and landowners (*The Cajuns* 54).

14. In *Native Sons in No Man's Land: Revisiting Afro-American Manhood in the Novels of Baldwin, Walker, Wideman, and Gaines*, Philip Auger begins his argument regarding African American rewriting of the negative depictions of black manhood with a discussion of the importance of discourse to this rewriting process: "Each of these writers approaches self-definition and, more specifically, the writing of oneself as a 'man' as contingent on con-

trolling discourse—having some power over language—and thus having the power to define the self" (2). From the *Narrative of the Life of Frederick Douglass* (1845) through the African American novels of today, education and literacy are "validation[s] of manhood" because through them one can write one's self (3). Ernest Gaines's move to California and his path to the local public library increased his own literary knowledge, allowing him to further write himself and his people.

15. Gaines further examines the complicated social structures of south Louisiana through Paul Bonin, the white jailer in *A Lesson Before Dying* (1993). Although Bonin does not get directly involved in the action of the novel, he acts as a conduit between the white and black populations by handing Jefferson's journal to Grant, thus guaranteeing that Jefferson's voice is heard. Gaines has admitted that he wishes to be remembered "as one who 'tried to write as well as he could and tried to be fair. Fair toward my characters and fair to other people'" (Doyle 24). As they are presented in Gaines's novels, Cajun characters and their own complicated cultural erosion make up a significant part of Louisiana change along with the evolution of the black laborers.

16. Gaines identifies Creole landowners as white. He defines *Creoles of Color* as the "group of fair-skinned racially mixed people" who view themselves as a separate ethnicity, and who also present an interesting reading of the interstitial positioning of certain Louisiana races and ethnicities (Gaudet and Wooton, "Talking" 229).

17. In the opening chapter of her book *Voices from the Quarters,* Mary Ellen Doyle presents a comprehensive guide to reading Louisiana architecture. As she states, one could tell the social placement of the people by their homes. For more on the divisions between the Big House, the quarters, and the Cajun cabins, refer to pages 6 and 7 of Doyle's book.

18. The original draft of the story ended with Marcus and Louise's escape from south Louisiana, a happily ever after that simply was not possible or realistic in 1940s Louisiana. White society would not allow a Cajun woman and an African American man, regardless of their sincere feelings for each other, to escape the political and racial implications of their love. In an interview with Gaudet and Wooton, Gaines explains that he changed the ending based on E. L. Doctorow's advice. Doctorow was his "editor-in-chief at Dial at that particular time before he became a famous writer" ("An Interview" 214), and he simply commented, "Ernie, I really like the first part of that novel, and I really like the last part of the novel, but the first part of that novel and the last part of that novel have nothing to do with each other" (214). Whereas the first part followed a tragic literary pattern, the last part was more comic in structure and tone. Gaines followed his editor's advice and rewrote the end of the novel.

19. "Three Men," one of the five stories included in *Bloodline* (1963), contains a similar story line with the exception that it captures the fate of the convict before he is leased out to the plantation owner. Unlike Marcus who agrees to work for Hebert because he views this release from jail as a chance for escape, Proctor Lewis, the protagonist of the story, realizes that he must go to Angola and "sweat it": "I didn't want have to pull cover over my head every time a white man did something to a black boy—I wanted to stand" (152). At the end of the story, Proctor does not have complete confidence in his ability to refuse the opportunity to work off his prison term in the fields, but he has still learned what it takes to be a man, a lesson Jim also learns in *Of Love and Dust.*

20. Although Gaines's Hebert definitely belongs to the wealthy, land-owning class, this particular surname is a popular one within Cajun communities. It can be, and usually is, an

Acadian surname in south Louisiana, but it can also define one as French or Creole but not of Acadian descent. Furthermore, as *Cajun* became a signifier of poor whites of French descent in south Louisiana, wealthy Acadians distanced themselves from these poorer brethren by assimilating to socially higher Creole ways. Those who remained connected with their Acadian roots still chose to remain divided from Cajuns, leading to the coinage of *genteel Acadians* to refer to this upper-class community of Acadian descendants in Louisiana. Regardless of ethnic identification, Hebert represents the class divide between wealthy landowners and lower-class Cajun laborers.

21. In *Exorcising Blackness: Historical and Literary Lynching and Burning Rituals,* Trudier Harris lists the parts of a lynching ritual: "There is mutilation and torture of the burned man, relic or trophy hunters, and the initiation of children" (8), all of which are missing from Gaines's final version of the murder of Marcus. In an earlier version of the story, Jim realizes the inevitability of lynching. He even dreams of Bonbon and the Cajuns riding unhooded into the quarters and "putting the ropes 'round our necks" ("*OL and D,*" Box 3-27, 291). Gaines replaced this more traditional version of the lynching ritual with one less violent, if not less unjust. Indeed, even the "communal spirit [that] defines lynching and burning" is missing as Bonbon faces the task of shooting Marcus (Harris 10).

22. This early version of the text also changes in other ways to become the novel that was finally published. The story becomes a more Faulknerian text: the fatalism of Jack as the reluctant and guilt-ridden alcoholic plantation master instead of a white supremacist, the multiple narrators, and the strength and paternalism of Candy are not part of the original text ("*Gathering,*" Box 9-9, 9-36). Moreover, James Joyce's influence on Gaines is evident in the published version's format of the story in a day (Gaudet and Wooton, *Porch Talk* 16). Matthew Spangler discusses the place descriptions as another area in which Joyce's writing influenced Gaines. He argues that "these descriptions are located in such close temporal proximity to the mental attitudes of certain characters that they are largely shaped by the specific points of view and proclivities of those characters" (113). He also points out that both Joyce and Gaines create characters who have a "desire for escape" that "reflects specific historical conditions," such as British rule or racial oppression (114). Although Joyce may be a powerful influence on Gaines's work, most significant is Gaines's continual message of "survival with dignity," to which he credits Ernest Hemingway's "grace under pressure" theme (Gaudet and Wooton, *Porch Talk* 166).

23. In his discussion of black manhood as represented in Frederick Douglass's 1845 *Narrative of the Life of Frederick Douglass* and Ellison's *Invisible Man* (1952), William Andrews argues, "Like Frederick Douglass, Ellison's protagonist understands that freedom and fulfillment for a Black man in America depend on the recovery of his cultural antecedents and the assertion of his individual identity against those forces that would deny him either one" (67). Gaines's *A Gathering of Old Men* demonstrates this point through the memories and actions of old African American men who finally realize that to be "men" means to recover their cultural memories and to take a stand against "those forces that would deny" them dignity, individual identity, and pride.

24. Bayonne, like Faulkner's Yoknapatawpha County, is Gaines's fictional little postage stamp of land based on his own home in south Louisiana. Bayonne may also allude to Hemingway's *The Sun Also Rises,* as it is the town where Jake fishes before continuing on to the bullfights.

25. In the novel *In My Father's House,* Gaines wrote of a similar group of old men standing up against and finally protesting earlier evils performed by a white man. In this earlier novel, the men discuss their previous shame and their present willingness to fight with the only weapons they have left—their bodies (125–26).

26. Along with the increase of tourists due to the popularity of the character Evangeline, Louisiana also opened its borders to the oil industry, which greatly affected Cajuns. Shane Bernard relates the story of Lennis Hebert to demonstrate "how the oil industry served as an Americanizing influence" (*The Cajuns* 38). From a potato digger making five dollars a day, Lennis "rose to division manager of an oil-field supply company, acquiring all the trappings of success offered by mainstream society: cars, television, a new home" (39). The full effects of the oil industry are portrayed in James Lee Burke's Dave Robicheaux series and in contemporary Cajun literature written by Cajuns.

27. In regard to racism during the Cajun Americanization process, Shane Bernard writes, "Cajun culture by its nature fostered attitudes more laissez-faire than found elsewhere in the South, and Anglo-Protestant enmity toward both Cajuns and blacks created at least a modicum of compassion between the two minorities" (*The Cajuns* 56). Although this explains why and how Gaines portrays Cajuns in a particular light, it does not erase the fact that racism continued to exist in Cajun country. In a later chapter, Bernard argues, "This antipathy [of African Americans] toward Cajuns extended back to the nineteenth-century, when blacks tended to regard the ethnic group" as "'poor whites'" (66). Furthermore, "In Pointe Coupée, St. Landry, and Evangeline Parishes, white parents formed private schools [during desegregation], called segregation academics, attracting a substantial number of students who had formerly attended all-white public schools" (65). All of these feelings and actions maintained racial tension, a tension Gaines tries to explain and resolve in his novels.

28. *The Revenge of the Old Men* also included Gil, but he was a politician running for office in the original story. His political career forced him to visit his family with his PR man tagging along behind him, making the possible damage to his image still the motivating factor for not getting involved in any anarchical retaliation against Mathu and his crew ("*Gathering*," Box 9-36). Gil's evolution into a football hero who wins fame because of his relationship with his black teammate better addresses Americanization and its effect on Cajun culture.

CHAPTER 5

1. Popular fiction both revises the past and replaces folklore and memory with written and published texts, much as *Evangeline* replaced Acadian dispersal lore in south Louisiana. In *The Southern Writer in the Postmodern World,* Fred Hobson discusses the relationship between popular culture and fiction regarding Bobbie Ann Mason's *In Country* (1985) and Lee Smith's *Oral History* (1983), both of which were written around the time Burke began his Robicheaux series. With the media making its way into even low-income homes, the nation loses its regional identifications as the Midwest accent of news anchors replaces local dialects. Mason's *In Country* reveals that "the past is no guide to the present" (Hobson, *The Southern Writer* 15). Even more significant, Smith's *Oral History* portrays the melting of folk into popular culture and the result: "the indigenous folk culture turns into a cheap im-

itation of itself for the sake of commercial mass culture" (30). By creating a Cajun detective who has become a popular figure in the national imagination, Burke has aided in making contemporary Cajun figures part of commercial mass culture. He does not reduce his portrayals of Cajuns to cheap imitations as much as he uses them to address larger issues, including changing Cajun culture and fading spirituality as the consequences of sin and violence in late twentieth-century America.

2. Continuing with such references to Ernest Gaines and his Louisiana fiction, Burke writes in later novels that Alafair, Dave's adopted daughter, becomes an author. Aiding in this pursuit is none other than Gaines himself. In *The Tin Roof Blowdown* (2007), Alafair is threatened by Ronald Bledsoe who indirectly attacks her by destroying her manuscript. After this incident, Alafair explains to Dave that she "send[s] one [copy of her work] to Ernest Gaines," so all is not lost (216).

3. *Étouffée*, "smothered," is a rich gravy that is served over white rice. Crawfish or shrimp is usually added.

4. Several critics have studied the doomed interracial relationship between Ruthie Jean Fontenot and Bertrand in *Burning Angel*, including Samuel Coale who discusses this particular relationship in regard to Burke's southern influences in *The Mystery of Mysteries* (153).

5. In *Burning Angel*, Burke writes of Dave, "[o]ur house had been built of cypress and oak by my father, a trapper and derrick man, during the Depression" (30).

6. According to Mike Tidwell, the oil industry caused cultural and environmental destruction through the construction of multiple canals used to transport oil from wells to barges. These canals cause massive erosion that increases exponentially: "Scientists at Louisiana State University estimate that no less than a third of the total coastal-zone degradation can be traced directly to canals, and note that, once dug, these canals tend to *double their width every fourteen years*" (118), a tragedy that has not only physical, but also cultural, consequences.

7. As Carl Brasseaux notes, "as a result of the interaction of popular culture and capitalism, the 'true' story of the Acadians emerged, by mid-twentieth century, as the only viable tradition of the Grand Dérangement in Louisiana" (*In Search* 48).

8. More than the written depictions of Louisiana life, Louisiana critics most readily denounce *The Big Easy*, a 1987 film that also places a Cajun cop in the crime-ridden city of New Orleans. This particular film circulates multiple New Orleans and Cajun stereotypes to a national and international audience, much like the texts Baker disparages. Suddenly the entertainment afforded to such fiction evolves into forces of distortion as stereotypes become the image of Louisianians for the rest of the nation and the world. Charles Stivale studies the music and dance scenes of this particular movie on pages 75–88 of *Disenchanting Les Bons Temps: Identity and Authenticity in Cajun Music and Dance*. He states that his study of the dance sequences in this movie focuses on the "purported tendency to undermine the dominant culture by adapting it" (78). Nevertheless, "the fervent desire, expressed by various spokespersons on Cajun culture, to hold on to what they construe as traditional and authentic while simultaneously employing the media and technological means that at once weaken this hold and fail to translate these very values," remains the paradox underlying Cajun representation by Cajuns on a national and international level (77).

9. While Smith's Skip Langdon is a reluctant debutante whose large body and liberal

ways automatically distance her from the Uptown New Orleans lifestyle into which her parents are desperate to fit, Hambly's Benjamin January (or Janvier depending on who names him) finds himself even more at a loss to locate a safe place for his dark visage within 1830s New Orleans, a time of great upheaval and identity crisis because of the American movement into and settlement of the city. Both Langdon and January clearly do not fit neatly into the traditional image of the detective in American fiction, and their identity as other than typical, both in literary formula and cultural terms, makes them marginal characters who must solve the crimes at hand. Throughout Hambly's series, she emphasizes January's talent for disguise in language and clothing by pointing out the need for such subterfuge: the American invasion of the city, which changed laws and customs pertaining to racial differences and rights. At a moment of crisis in which American and Creole are battling for supremacy, a free man of color steps up as the rational being more than capable, if not always willing, to discover the truth.

10. Burke named the character after his youngest daughter who is named for Burke's grandmother Alafair Benbow (Carter 44). Alafair Burke has followed her father into the crime genre.

11. *Boudin,* "blood sausage," is a popular dish among Cajuns. It is seasoned pork and rice served in a sausage casing.

12. While Cajuns became more American because of their exposure to mainstream national culture, Americans became more familiar with Cajun cultural ways because of this exposure. Burke has ties to both Texas and Louisiana communities through his family. Although he was born in Houston in 1936, he admitted to R. Reese Fuller that "I've always considered this area [south Louisiana] my home. My family has lived in New Iberia since 1836" ("The Man Behind Dave Robicheaux"). In an earlier interview with Dale Carter, Burke claimed West Montana and Louisiana as his two homes (50). His Dave Robicheaux series illustrates the interest he takes in south Louisiana and the social justice and cultural issues that he has witnessed there. Burke may come from Texans, but his personal identification of himself reaches back to his family's south Louisiana roots. He proves that the assimilation of Cajuns worked and continues to function as a two-way process.

13. In *Henderson, Louisiana,* Marjorie Esman discusses the transformation of Acadians into Cajuns and its effects on Cajun identification: "This occurred by virtue of cultural adaptations and the influx of new immigrants, most of whom were quickly assimilated by the older Acadian residents. . . . Today probably fewer than 5 percent of the Cajun population is of pure Acadian ancestry, and many who swear that they are 'pure Cajun' have non-Acadian surnames," such as Hayes, McGee, and Schexnayder (7–8).

14. According to C. Vann Woodward, "there is no one more quintessentially Southern than the Southern Negro" (6). Batist demonstrates the power of this statement in terms of Cajun, as well as southern, culture.

15. For more information on CVE history and form, see chapter 4.

16. In a discussion of Gaines's work, Fred Hobson writes of Gaines and Fred Chappell, "It is perhaps no accident that both come from rich repositories of southern folk culture . . . and neither has shown much interest in the contemporary world of television and shopping malls as most of their contemporaries" (*The Southern Writer* 82). Like Gaines and his disinterest in pop culture, Batist also retains his bond to Louisiana folk culture because of his distance from mainstream culture. In many ways, he is Dave's opposite, which makes him necessary to the formation of Dave's memory.

CHAPTER 6

1. Shane Bernard discusses education's place in the Americanization of Cajuns in *The Cajuns: The Americanization of a People*. He addresses the denigration of Cajuns in the state geography textbook, *The People of Louisiana* (1951), that described Cajuns as "an un-sophisticated agrarian people . . . slow in adopting 'American' ways" (32), which empha-sized the need to educate Cajuns away from their traditional ways, especially their linguis-tic background. In this study, Bernard records several stories of punishments received for speaking Cajun French in schools during the 1940s and 1950s (33–34). As a consequence, the "percentage [of French speakers among Cajuns] would plummet to 21 percent for those born between 1956 and 1960, a woeful decline from the 83 percent for Cajuns born at the dawn of the century" (34). By taking these actions within the classroom, "educators across the country molded baby boomer children into good Americans," which resulted in dras-tic changes for Cajuns in the United States and for the need for translation between genera-tions (34).

2. The name given to the twenty-two south Louisiana parishes that make up Cajun country, which "in 1971 the Louisiana state legislature officially recognized for its unique Cajun and Acadian heritage (per House Concurrent Resolution No. 496)" (Bernard and Bernard, "Acadiana").

3. The French movement in Louisiana is exemplified by the creation of the Council for the Development of French in Louisiana (CODOFIL), a movement supported by Jimmy Do-mengeaux. This movement arose from the realization that French usage, Cajun and Creole, was on the decline in south Louisiana. In fact, "Cajun French ha[d] virtually ceased to exist among the younger generations," making English the now primary language among French Louisiana descendants (Bernard, *The Cajuns* 127). CODOFIL worked to preserve what was left of French usage in Louisiana, but it favored standard French over Cajun French (125). According to Bernard, Domengeaux even "despised Cajun French" (126), although he would become a proponent of the dialect later in life. Some of this argument against Cajun French stemmed from the concept of the dialect as oral only. To refute this notion, James Donald Faulk published *Cajun French I* in 1979. Unfortunately, this text translated Cajun French terms to phonetically written English (126). Although Faulk's work had its faults, it made the concept of written Cajun French possible, as demonstrated by Project Louisiane, a project spearheaded by three Canadian universities, and the various Cajun French dic-tionaries that have since been written. Today, Louisiana universities offer courses in Cajun French, which testifies to the power of the Cajun French movement and to the loss of the language among Cajuns; it is now a course of study and not necessarily a way of life.

4. In response to the Evangeline myth, Albert Belisle Davis, a contemporary writer of Cajun fiction and a Nicholls State University professor, published the poem "*Song of Evan-geline*: The Modern Psychiatric Hospital" in his collection *What They Wrote on the Bath-house Walls: Yen's Marina, Chinese Bayou, Louisiana* (1988). Davis frames this collection as the *petites lunettes* of a blind netman he first wrote about in his novel *Leechtime* (1986), which relates the story of the Cajun Adrian and his discovery of his wife's infidelity. All of the poems speak of Cajun life on the bayous, but "Song of Evangeline" stands out as a fem-inist critique of Longfellow's depiction of an Acadian woman. A female patient in the psy-chiatric hospital deals with her rape by escaping her actual identity and imagining that she

becomes strong women of history, including Joan of Arc and Catherine the Great. When asked if she imagines herself as Evangeline, she replies, *"Never"* (47). Before she refuses this identity, her Evangelinesque behavior is revealed:

> What of the man you waited for?
> *Gabriel?*
> Yes. The one you loved . . . .
> Why do you laugh?
> *At me.*
> *At a woman's waiting*
> *the shadow of that wall.* (46)

For this traumatized woman, Evangeline symbolizes feminine weakness and naivete, so she claims instead the great and powerful women of history who led countries and fought for their beliefs through action, and not through patient waiting. Whereas the 1960s celebrations of Cajun culture, like the Acadian Bicentennial Celebration, accepted and endorsed the mythical Evangeline and her story of patience, contemporary Cajun authors, such as Davis, not only question this mythical façade, but also create strong female characters who represent the complexities of contemporary Cajun culture.

5. Gautreaux also learned "how important it is to listen to the people around you and to remember as accurately as you can how people spoke when you were younger" from Gaines (Hebert-Leiter 67). When he heard Gaines read his writing out loud, he realized that Gaines "was working with cadences and the grammar of individual speakers" that can only be learned from listening (66). Another great influence on Gautreaux's writing is Walker Percy, whose class Gautreaux took at Loyola University New Orleans in 1977. Percy taught his students to ask themselves why they wrote (67). And Gautreaux also mentions Flannery O'Connor as a great influence because "she was *very* expert in the way she assembled her story structure" (68).

6. Darrell Bourque is another such contemporary Cajun author whose poetry also addresses such topics as memory, change, and difference. In "My Mother's Memory, Portrait," he recalls meals that included "gumbos and jambalayas," while also remembering rituals such as visiting graves (Bourque 52). The poem's message is a simple one that pertains to all Cajuns: "Remembering that a life cut away from past life is illusion" (52). Bourque acknowledges the work of other Cajun artists when he dedicates "Louisiana Maples in Late Winter" to Tim Gautreaux (67). The final line of the poem compares the dramatic coloring of the changing maple leaves to poetry, a fitting connection between Bourque's creation and the earlier work of Gautreaux, who began his creative writing career as a poet. This dedication demonstrates Cajun artists' awareness of each other as they strive together to achieve a more realistic depiction of Cajun life in poetry and fiction.

7. Gumbo, part stew and part soup, is a popular recipe in south Louisiana. The word *gumbo* comes from the African word for okra, proving the blend of cultures that created this famous meal (*Louisiana Legacy* 46).

8. At the beginning of such recipes as jambalaya, shrimp stew, shrimp Creole, and gumbo, one is always instructed to "make a roux," a combination of flour and oil used "as a thickening agent for bisques, gumbos, soups, gravies, and stews" (*Louisiana Legacy* 36).

9. As part of their definition of "Cajun Foodways," Kara Tobin Bernard and Shane Ber-

nard suggest that this is a "misconception fueled by the media and purveyors of *faux* Cajun cuisine." More information on the traditional Cajun foodways can be found on the *Encyclopedia of Cajun Culture* website.

10. A highly seasoned stew that is spicy and a little sweet and served over rice, it can be made with a variety of meat, including chicken, turtle, or alligator.

11. According to Bernard, Cajuns "[a]lthough a traditionally antimaterialistic people whose Acadian ancestors hailed from precapitalistic France and whose recent forebears had been subsistence laborers, . . . found it increasingly difficult to resist tantalizing goods offered by mainstream America. Many embraced its consumer ethos: they wanted good jobs so they could acquire luxury items and participate in the American Dream," much like Colette Thibodeaux (*The Cajuns* 34).

12. Carl Brasseaux explains that although visitors to south Louisiana were welcomed by the Cajuns, "their materialistic values, strange customs, competitiveness, and preoccupation with business were not, at least among the lower classes" (*Acadian to Cajun* 21). Dormon also asserts that the main reason for the success of misrepresentation of Cajun culture by cultural outsiders stems from different values and ethics: "The catalogue of their ascriptive vices, it should be noted, tends to feature those qualities alien to the emerging Anglo-Bourgeois value system, by terms of which New England Puritanism would represent *Summum Bonnum* of the human value system. Indeed, the evidence is overwhelming that the British never really understood the Acadians, a situation that was to have a shattering impact on the Acadian population of 1755 and the years that followed" (*The People* 13). While this history remains central to Cajun difference, Cajuns began to want to be more American in the second half of the twentieth century, as demonstrated by Bernard in his study of Cajun Americanization.

13. One Cajun has said, "When I was growing up on the farm, money didn't mean much to us, but oil's changed us. Now, everyone's trying to keep up with the Joneses" (Bernard, *The Cajuns* 39).

CONCLUSION

1. Two such movies include *Scooby-Doo on Zombie Island* (1998), a feature-length cartoon complete with references to spicy food and voodoo magic, and Adam Sandler's *The Waterboy* (1998), which relates the story of a Cajun with a talent for football.

2. In *Midnight Bayou* (2001), Nora Roberts creates a mystery/romance plot around a Cajun woman and her ancestor's tragic death. Sandra Hill, another romance writer, has also chosen to write a Cajun trilogy, which includes *Tall, Dark, and Cajun* (2003), *The Cajun Cowboy* (2004), and *The Red-Hot Cajun* (2005), proving national recognition of the word *Cajun* and the stereotypical connotations of the label outside of south Louisiana. These are just a few examples of popular fiction that includes Cajun characters.

3. A search for Cajun bands on the web turns up links to bands all over the world. Such Cajun bands as Allez-Gator and Cahoots: Cajun Down Under have been formed in Australia, not in south Louisiana. Cajun Pioneer and Colinda are located in Germany. And Cochon Bleu was formed north of Holland. What is most ironic is that even Great Britain, the former enemy of the Cajuns because of the 1755 deportation, has not only accepted but also become part of this international Cajun craze, as demonstrated by the UK band, The Hack-

ney Ramblers, and the opening of The Cajun Barn, a bar that celebrates Cajun music in South East London (www.louisianacajun.com/subcategory.asp?idmma.).

4. In both *The Clearing* and the novel on which he is currently working about travel along the Mississippi River during the 1920s (Hebert-Leiter 74), Tim Gautreaux chooses to portray a past when Cajuns had to realize their double bond with both American and Cajun cultures.

BIBLIOGRAPHY

Adams, David Wallace. *Education for Extinction: American Indians and the Boarding School Experience 1875–1928*. Lawrence: UP of Kansas, 1995.

Allain, Mathé. "They Don't Even Talk Like Us: Cajun Violence in Film and Fiction." *Journal of Popular Culture* 23.1 (1989): 65–75.

———. "Twentieth-Century Cajuns." *The Cajuns: Essays on Their History and Culture*. Lafayette: Center for Louisiana Studies, 1978.

Allen, Theodore W. *The Invention of the White Race: Racial Oppression and Social Control*. 1994. New York: Verso, 2002.

Ancelet, Barry Jean. "Cajun and Creole French Music Association on Louisiana French Folklore and Folklife." Cajun and Creole French Music Association. *Cajun Network*. 1999. 25 Jan. 2005. www.cajunnetwork.com/ccfma/Ancelet.htm.

———. "Elements of Folklore, History, and Literature in Longfellow's *Evangeline*." *Revue de Louisiane* 11:2 (1982): 118–26.

Ancelet, Barry Jean, Jay Edwards, and Glen Pitre. *Cajun Country*. Jackson: UP of Mississippi, 1991.

Anderson, Benedict. *Imagined Communities*. Rev. ed. 1991. New York: Verso, 1999.

Andrews, William L. "The Black Male in American Literature." *The American Black Male: His Present Status and His Future*. Ed. Richard G. Majors and Jacob U. Gordon. Chicago: Nelson-Hall Publishers, 1994. 59–68.

Angers, Trent. *The Truth about the Cajuns*. Lafayette: Acadian House, 1989.

Appelo, Tim. "Cajun Crime King." Amazon.com. 6 July 2004. www.amazon.com/exec/obidos/ts/features/5636/104-5567174-0994326.

Arms, George W. *The Fields Were Green: A New View of Bryant, Whittier, Holmes, Lowell, and Longfellow*. Palo Alto: Stanford UP, 1953.

Arvin, Newton. *Longfellow: His Life and Work*. Boston: Little, Brown, 1962.

Assman, Jan. "Collective Memory and Cultural Identity." *New German Critique* 65 (1995): 125–34.

Auger, Philip. *Native Sons in No Man's Land: Rewriting Afro-American Manhood in the Novels of Baldwin, Walker, Wideman, and Gaines*. New York: Garland Publishing, Inc., 2000.

Babb, Valerie Melissa. *Ernest Gaines.* Boston: Twayne Publishers, 1991.

Baker, Houston A., Jr. *Blues, Ideology, and Afro-American Literature: A Vernacular Theory.* Chicago: U of Chicago P, 1984.

Baker, Vaughan B. "Mad, Bad, and Dangerous: Conceptions and Misconceptions of Louisiana's History and Heritage." *Louisiana History* 42.3 (2001): 261–75.

Baldwin, James. "Everybody's Protest Novel." *The Norton Anthology of African American Literature.* Ed. Henry Louis Gates Jr. and Nellie Y. McKay. New York: W. W. Norton, 1997. 1699–1705.

Bankston, Carl L., and Jacques M. Henry. *Blue Collar Bayou: Louisiana Cajuns in the New Economy of Ethnicity.* Westport: Praeger, 2003.

Barrish, Phillip. "The *Awakening*'s Signifying 'Mexicanist' Presence." *Studies in American Fiction* 28.1 (Spring 2000): 65–76. *MLA International Bibliography.* EBSCOHost. Lycoming College, Williamsport, Snowden Lib. 4 Sept. 2008. www.galenet.galegroup.com.

Bauman, Richard. "The Nationalization and Internationalization of Folklore: The Case of Schoolcraft's 'Gitshee Gauzinee.'" *Western Folklore* 52 (1993): 247–69.

Beer, Janet. *Kate Chopin, Edith Wharton, and Charlotte Perkins Gilman: Studies in Short Fiction.* New York: St. Martin's Press, 1997.

Belizaire the Cajun. Dir. Glen Pitre. Madacy Entertainment, 1986.

Benfey, Christopher. *Degas in New Orleans: Encounters in the Creole World of Kate Chopin and George Washington Cable.* 1997. Berkeley: U of California P, 1999.

Bernard, Karen Tobin, and Shane Bernard. "Acadiana." *Encyclopedia of Cajun Culture.* February 2004. 20 April 2004. www.cajunculture.com/Other/creole.htm.

———. "Cajun." *Encyclopedia of Cajun Culture.* February 2004. 20 April 2004. www.cajunculture.com/Other/creole.htm.

———. "Creole." *Encyclopedia of Cajun Culture.* February 2004. 20 April 2004. www.cajunculture.com/Other/creole.htm.

Bernard, Shane. *The Cajuns: Americanization of a People.* Jackson: UP of Mississippi, 2003.

Bhabha, Homi K. *The Location of Culture.* New York: Routledge, 1994.

———. Introduction. *Nation and Narration.* Ed. Homi K. Bhabha. New York: Routledge, 1990. 1–7.

The Big Easy. Dir. Jim McBride. Vidmark, 1987.

Bikle, Lucy Cable. *George W. Cable: His Life and Letters.* New York: Charles Scribner's Sons, 1928.

Birnbaum, Michele A. "'Alien Hands': Kate Chopin and the Colonization of Race." *Subjects and Citizens: Nation, Race, and Gender from* Oroonoko *to* Anita Hill. Ed. Michael Moon and Cynthia N. Davidson. Durham: Duke UP, 1995. 319–41.

Blyth, Carl. "The Sociolinguistic Situation of Cajun French: The Effects of Language Shift and Language Loss." *French and Creole in Louisiana*. Ed. Albert Valdman. New York: Plenum Press, 1997. 30–32.

Blyth, Martin. *Naming the Other: Images of the Maori in New Zealand Film and Television*. Metuchen, NJ: The Scarecrow Press, 1994.

Bogue, Barbara. *James Lee Burke and the Soul of Dave Robicheaux*. Jefferson, NC: McFarland, 2006.

Boudreau, Amy. *The Story of the Acadians*. 1955. Gretna, LA: Pelican Publishing, 1997.

Bourque, Antoine. *Trois saisons*. Lafayette: Center for Louisiana Studies, 1988.

Bourque, Darrell. "Louisiana Maples in Late Winter." *The Blue Boat*. Lafayette: Center for Louisiana Studies, 2004. 67.

———. "My Mother's Memory, Portrait." *The Blue Boat*. Lafayette: Center for Louisiana Studies, 2004. 52.

Brainard, Dulcy. "James Lee Burke." *Publisher's Weekly* (20 April 1992): 33–34.

Brasseaux, Carl. *Acadian to Cajun: Transformation of a People, 1803–1877*. Jackson: UP of Mississippi, 1992.

———. "Acadian Education: From Cultural Isolation to Mainstream America." *The Cajuns: Essays on Their History and Culture*. Ed. Glenn R. Conrad. Lafayette: Center for Louisiana Studies, 1978.

———. *The Founding of New Acadia: The Beginning of Acadian Life in Louisiana*. Baton Rouge: Louisiana State UP, 1987.

———. *French, Cajun, Creole, Houma: A Primer on Francophone Louisiana*. Baton Rouge: Louisiana State UP, 2005.

———. *In Search of* Evangeline: *Birth and Evolution of the Evangeline Myth*. Thibodaux: Blue Heron Press, 1988.

———. *"Scattered to the Wind": Dispersal and Wanderings of the Acadians, 1755–1809*. Lafayette: Center for Louisiana Studies, 1991.

Bridges, Tyler. *Bad Bet on the Bayou: The Rise of Gambling and the Fall of Governor Edwin Edwards*. New York: Farrar, Straus and Giroux, 2001.

Brodhead, Richard H. *Cultures of Letters: Scenes of Reading and Writing in Nineteenth-Century America*. Chicago: U of Chicago P, 1993.

Brodkin, Karen. *How Jews Became White Folks and What That Says about Race in America*. New Brunswick: Rutgers UP, 1998.

Brundage, W. Fitzhugh. "Le Reveil de la Louisiane: Memory and Acadian Identity, 1920–1960." *Where These Memories Grow: History, Memory, and Southern Identity*. Ed. W. Fitzhugh Brundage. Chapel Hill: U of North Carolina P, 2000. 271–98.

Buell, Lawrence. Introduction. *Henry Wadsworth Longfellow: Selected Poems*. New York: Penguin Books, 1988. vii–xxxii.

———. *New England Literary Culture: From Revolution through Renaissance*. Cambridge: Cambridge UP, 1986.

Bukoski, Anthony. "The Burden of Home: Shirley Ann Grau's Fiction." *Critique: Studies in Contemporary Fiction* 28.4 (1987): 181–93.

Burke, James Lee. *Black Cherry Blues*. 1989. New York: Avon Books, 1990.

———. *Burning Angel*. New York: Hyperion, 1995.

———. *Crusader's Cross*. New York: Simon and Schuster, 2005.

———. *Heaven's Prisoners*. 1988. New York: Simon and Schuster Pocket Books, 1989.

———. *The Neon Rain*. 1987. New York: Simon and Schuster Pocket Books, 1988.

———. *Purple Cane Road*. New York: Doubleday, 2000.

———. *The Tin Roof Blowdown*. New York: Simon and Schuster, 2007.

Bush, Robert. *Grace King: A Southern Destiny*. Baton Rouge: Louisiana State UP, 1983.

Byerman, Keith E. *Fingering the Jagged Grain: Tradition and Form in Recent Black Fiction*. Athens: U of Georgia P, 1985.

Cable, George Washington. Acadian Notebook. Box 108. The George W. Cable Papers, Manuscripts Collection 2, Manuscripts Department, Tulane University, New Orleans, Louisiana.

———. "After-Thoughts of a Story-Teller." Box 97, Folder 3. The George W. Cable Papers, Manuscripts Collection 2, Manuscripts Department, Tulane University, New Orleans, Louisiana.

———. *Bonaventure: A Prose Pastoral of Acadian Louisiana*. 1888. New York: Braunworth, Munn & Barber, 1901.

———. Box 97, Folder 1. The George W. Cable Papers, Manuscripts Collection 2, Manuscripts Department, Tulane University, New Orleans, Louisiana.

———. "Literature in the Southern States." *The Negro Question*. Ed. Arlin Turner. New York: Doubleday, 1958. 37–46.

Calhoun, Charles C. *Longfellow: A Rediscovered Life*. Boston: Beacon Press, 2004.

Campbell, Donna M. *Resisting Regionalism: Gender and Naturalism in American Fiction, 1885–1915*. Athens: Ohio UP, 1997.

Canfield, John. "A Conversation with Shirley Ann Grau." *The Southern Quarterly* 25.2 (Winter 1987): 39–52.

Carney, Rob. "Clete Purcel to the Rampaging Rescue: Looking for the Hard-Boiled Tradition in James Lee Burke's *Dixie City Jam*." *The Southern Quarterly* 34.4 (1996): 121–30.

Carter, Dale. "Trouble in the Big Easy: An Interview with Edgar-award Winning Author James Lee Burke." *Armchair Detective* 25.1 (1992): 40–50.

Carver, Ada Jack. "The Cajuns." *The Collected Works of Ada Jack Carver*. Ed. Mary Dell Fletcher. Natchitoches, LA: Northwestern State UP, 1980. 198–210.

Cawelti, John C. *Adventure, Mystery, and Romance: Formula Stories as Art and Popular Culture*. 1976. Chicago: U of Chicago P, 1977.

Chateaubriand, Francois-René. *Atala*. 1801. Trans. Irving Putter. Berkeley: U of California P, 1980.

Cheyfitz, Eric. *The Poetics of Imperialism: Translation and Colonization from The Tempest to Tarzan*. Philadelphia: U of Pennsylvania P, 1997.

Chopin, Kate. *The Awakening*. New York: Dover, 1993.

———. "At the 'Cadian Ball." *Bayou Folk* and *A Night in Acadie*. New York: Penguin Press, 1999. 142–51.

———. "A Gentleman of Bayou Têche." *Bayou Folk* and *A Night in Acadie*. New York: Penguin Press, 1999. 158–64.

———. "Ozème's Holiday." *Bayou Folk* and *A Night in Acadie*. New York: Penguin Press, 1999. 349–55.

———. "A Rude Awakening." *Bayou Folk* and *A Night in Acadie*. New York: Penguin Press, 1999. 70–78.

———. "In Sabine." *Bayou Folk* and *A Night in Acadie*. New York: Penguin Press, 1999. 44–54.

———. "The Storm." *The Awakening*. Ed. Sandra Gilbert. New York: Penguin Press, 1983. 281–86.

———. "A Visit to Uncle Tom's Cabin." *At Fault*. Ed. David Caudle and Suzanne Disheroon Green. Knoxville: U of Tennessee P, 2001. 186–91.

Clark, Keith. *Black Manhood in James Baldwin, Ernest J. Gaines, and August Wilson*. 2002. Urbana: U of Illinois P, 2004.

Clark, William Bedford, and Charlene Kerne Clark. "James Lee Burke: ' . . . Always the First Inning.'" *Southern Writers at Century's End*. Ed. Jeffrey Folks and James Perkins. Lexington: UP of Kentucky, 1997. 60–69.

Coale, Samuel. *The Mystery of Mysteries: Cultural Differences and Designs*. Bowling Green, KY: Bowling Green State UP, 2000.

Coltelli, Laura. *Winged Words: American Indian Writers Speak*. Lincoln: U of Nebraska P, 1992.

Conrad, Glenn R. "The Acadians: Myths and Realities." *The Cajuns: Essays on Their History and Culture*. 3rd ed. Ed. Glen R. Conrad. Lafayette: Center for Louisiana Studies, 1978. 1–18.

Cutter, Martha. *Lost and Found in Translation: Contemporary Ethnic American Writing and the Politics of Language Diversity*. Chapel Hill: U of North Carolina P, 2005.

Davis, Albert Belisle. *Leechtime*. 1986. Baton Rouge: Louisiana State UP, 1989.

———. *Marquis at Bay*. Baton Rouge: Louisiana State UP, 1992.

———. "*Song of Evangeline*: The Mondebon Psychiatric Hospital." *What They Wrote on the Bathhouse Walls: Yen's Marina, Chinese Bayou, Louisiana*. Louisiana: Portier Gorman Publications, 1988. 44–48.

De la Houssaye, Sidonie. *Pouponne et Balthazar*. 1888. Lafayette: Center for Louisiana Studies, 1983.

DeBlieux, Robert. "Natchitoches and Louisiana's Timeless Cane River." *Louisiana Cultural Vistas* 13.2 (2002): 12–25.

Dirty Rice. Dir. Pat Mire. Pat Mire Films, 1998.

Domínguez, Virginia R. *White by Definition: Social Classification in Creole Louisiana.* New Brunswick, NJ: Rutgers UP, 1986.

Dormon, James, ed. *Creoles of Color of the Gulf South.* Knoxville: U of Tennessee P, 1996.

———. *The People Called Cajuns: An Introduction to an Ethnohistory.* Lafayette: Center for Louisiana Studies, 1983.

Doucet, Clive. *Notes from Exile: On Being Acadian.* Toronto: McClelland and Stewart Inc., 1999.

Doyle, Mary Ellen. *Voices from the Quarters: The Fiction of Ernest J. Gaines.* Baton Rouge: Louisiana State UP, 2002.

DuBois, W. E. B. *The Souls of Black Folk.* 1903. New York: Penguin Books, 1989.

Dubus, André. *Selected Stories.* New York: Vintage, 1995.

———. *The Times Are Never So Bad: A Novella and Eight Short Stories.* Boston: David R. Godine, 1983.

Dubus, Elizabeth. *Cajun: A Novel.* 1983. Baton Rouge: Levee Press, 1994.

———. *To Love and to Dream.* New York: G. P. Putnam's Sons, 1986.

———. *Where Love Rules.* 1985. New York: Charter Books, 1987.

Duet, Tiffany. "Cajun Literature." *The Companion to Southern Literature: Themes, Genres, Places, Movements, and Motifs.* Ed. Joseph M. Flora and Lucinda MacKethan. Baton Rouge: Louisiana State UP, 2002. 122–25.

Ekstrom, Kjell. *George Washington Cable: A Study of His Early Life and Work.* Cambridge: Harvard UP, 1950.

Elfenbein, Anna Shannon. *Women on the Color Line: Evolving Stereotypes and the Writings of George Washington Cable, Grace King, and Kate Chopin.* Charlottesville: UP of Virginia, 1989.

Ellison, Ralph. "The World and the Jug," *Shadow and Act.* 1953. New York: Vintage International, 1995. 107–43.

Emerson, Ralph Waldo. "The American Scholar." 1837. *The American Tradition in Literature.* 10th ed. Ed. George Perkins and Barbara Perkins. Boston: McGraw-Hill, 2002. 361–73.

Enoch, Jessica. "Resisting the Script of Indian Education: Zitkala Ša and the Carlisle Indian School." *College English* 65.2 (Nov. 2002): 117–41.

Erickson, Hal. "Evangeline." *All Movie Guide.* 1 Oct. 2003. www.allmovie.com.

Esman, Marjorie. *Henderson, Louisiana: Cultural Adaptation in a Cajun Community.* New York: Holt, Rinehart and Winston, 1985.

Estes, David. "Introduction." *Critical Reflections on the Fiction of Ernest J. Gaines.* Ed. David Estes. Athens: U of Georgia P, 1994. 1–11.

Ewell, Barbara C. "Introduction: Re-Viewing the Tradition of Louisiana Women

Writers." *Louisiana Women Writers*. Ed. Dorothy H. Brown and Barbara C. Ewell. Baton Rouge: Louisiana State UP, 1992. 3–15.

Faragher, John Mack. *A Great and Nobel Scheme: The Tragic Story of the Expulsion of the French Acadians from their American Homeland*. New York: W. W. Norton, 2005.

Faulk, James Donald. *Cajun French I: The First Written Record and Definitive Study of the Cajun Language as Spoken by the People in Vermilion and Surrounding Parishes*. Abbeville: Cajun Press, 1977.

Faulkner, William. *If I Forget Thee, Jerusalem*. 1939. New York: Vintage Books, 1995.

Fetterley, Judith. *The Resisting Reader: A Feminist Approach to American Fiction*. Bloomington: Indiana UP, 1978.

Fetterley, Judith, and Marjorie Pryse, eds. *American Women Regionalists, 1850–1910*. New York: Norton Press, 1992.

Fuller, R. Reese. "The Man Behind Dave Robicheaux." *The Times of Acadiana*. Lafayette, LA. 5 June 2002. 28 March 2003. www.timesofacadiana.com.

Gaines, Ernest J. *The Autobiography of Miss Jane Pittman*. 1971. New York: Bantam Books, 1972.

———. "Black Writers Should Get Off the Soapbox." *Los Angeles Times,* February 9, 1975. Box 11, Folder 36. Ernest Gaines Collection, Collection 115, Special Collections, Dupré Library, University of Louisiana at Lafayette, Lafayette, Louisiana.

———. *Catherine Carmier*. 1964. New York: Vintage Books, 1993.

———. *A Gathering of Old Men*. 1983. New York: Vintage Books, 1992.

———. "*Gathering of Old Men*." Box 9. Ernest Gaines Collection, Collection 115, Special Collections, Dupré Library, University of Louisiana at Lafayette, Lafayette, Louisiana.

———. *A Lesson Before Dying*. 1993. New York: Vintage Books, 1994.

———. *Of Love and Dust*. 1967. New York: Vintage Books, 1994.

———. "*Of Love and Dust*." Box 3. Ernest Gaines Collection, Collection 115, Special Collections, Dupré Library, University of Louisiana at Lafayette, Lafayette, Louisiana.

———. *In My Father's House*. 1978. New York: Vintage Books, 1992.

———. "Three Men." *Bloodline*. 1963. New York: Vintage Books, 1997. 121–55.

Gates, Henry Louis, Jr. *The Signifying Monkey: A Theory of African-American Literary Criticism*. New York: Oxford UP, 1988.

Gaudet, Marcia. "The Image of the Cajun in Literature." *Journal of Popular Culture* 23.1 (1989–90): 77–89.

———. "Kate Chopin and the Lore of Cane River's Creoles of Color." *Xavier Review* 6:1 (1986): 45–52.

Gaudet, Marcia, and Carl Wooton. "An Interview with Ernest J. Gaines." *Con-*

versations with Ernest Gaines. Ed. John Lowe. Jackson: UP of Mississippi, 1995. 200–216.

——. *Porch Talk with Ernest Gaines: Conversations on the Writer's Craft*. Baton Rouge: Louisiana State UP, 1990.

——. "Talking with Ernest Gaines." *Conversations with Ernest Gaines*. Ed. John Lowe. Jackson: UP of Mississippi, 1995. 221–40.

Gautreaux, Tim. *The Clearing*. New York: Alfred A. Knopf, 2003.

——. *The Next Step in the Dance*. 1998. New York: Picador, 1999.

——. *Same Place, Same Things*. 1996. New York: Picador, 1997.

——. *Welding with Children*. New York: Picador, 2000.

Gayarré, Charles. *A History of Louisiana*. 4 vols. 1866. New Orleans: James A. Gresham, 1879.

——. *Louisiana: Its Colonial History and Romance*. New York: Harper and Bros., 1851–1852.

——. *Romance of the History of Louisiana*. New York: D. Appleton, 1848.

Gilbert, Sandra. "The Second Coming of Aphrodite." *The Awakening*. Ed. Sandra Gilbert. New York: Penguin Press, 1983. 7–33.

Gilman, Sander. "Black Bodies, White Bodies: Toward an Iconography of Female Sexuality in Late Nineteenth-Century Art, Medicine, and Literature." *"Race," Writing, and Difference*. Ed. Henry Louis Gates. Chicago: U of Chicago P, 1985. 223–61.

Godchaux, Elma. "Chains." *The Southern Review* 1 (1935–1936): 782–98.

Grau, Shirley Ann. *The Hard Blue Sky*. 1955. Greenwich: Fawcett Crest Books, 1958.

Greene, J. Lee. *Blacks in Eden: The African American Novel's First Century*. Charlottesville: U of Virginia P, 1996.

Griffin, Joseph. "Creole and Singaleese: Disruptive Caste in *Catherine Carmier* and *A Gathering of Old Men*." *Critical Reflections on the Fiction of Ernest J. Gaines*. Ed. David Estes. Athens: U of Georgia P, 1994. 30–45.

Gunning, Sandra. *Race, Rape, and Lynching: The Red Record of American Literature, 1890–1912*. New York: Oxford UP, 1996.

Halbwachs, Maurice. *On Collective Memory*. Trans. Lewis A. Coser. Chicago: U of Chicago P, 1992.

Hallowell, Christopher. *People of the Bayou: Cajun Life in Lost America*. New York: Dutton, 1979.

Handler, Richard, and Jocelyn Linnekin. "Tradition, Genuine or Spurious." *Journal of American Folklore* 97 (1984): 273–90.

Harris, Trudier. *Exorcising Blackness: Historical and Literary Lynching and Burning Rituals*. Bloomington: Indiana UP, 1984.

——. *The Power of the Porch: The Storyteller's Craft in Zora Neale Hurston, Gloria Naylor, and Randall Kenan*. Athens: U of Georgia P, 1996.

Haspel, Paul. "George Washington Cable and Bonaventure: A New Orleans Author's Literary Sojourn into Acadiana." *The Southern Literary Journal* 35.1 (Fall 2002): 108–22.

Hebert-Leiter, Maria. "An Interview with Tim Gautreaux." *The Carolina Quarterly* 57.2 (Summer 2005): 66–74.

Hobson, Fred. *But Now I See: The White Southern Racial Conversion Narrative.* Baton Rouge: Louisiana State UP, 1999.

———. *The Southern Writer in the Postmodern World.* Athens: U of Georgia P, 1991.

———. *Tell about the South: The Southern Rage to Explain.* Baton Rouge: Louisiana State UP, 1983.

Ignatiev, Noel. *How the Irish Became White.* New York: Routledge, 1995.

"John Banvard." *Museum of History: Hall of North and South Americans.* 2000. Famous Americans. 20 Oct. 2003. www.famousmaericans.net/johnbanvard.

Jones, Anne Goodwyn. *Tomorrow Is Another Day: The Woman Writer in the South, 1859–1936.* Baton Rouge: Louisiana State UP, 1981.

Kammen, Michael. *Mystic Chords of Memory: The Transformation of Tradition in American Culture.* 1991. New York: Vintage Books, 1993.

Kaplan, Amy. *The Social Construction of American Realism.* Chicago: U of Chicago P, 1988.

King, Edward. *The Great South.* Ed. W. Magruder Drake and Robert R. Jones. Baton Rouge: Louisiana State UP, 1972.

King, Grace. *Memories of a Southern Woman of Letters.* New York: Macmillan, 1932.

———. *Monsieur Motte.* New York: A. C. Armstrong and Son, 1888. Online. Documenting the American South. 2004. 14 Feb. 2005. docsouth.unc.edu/southlit/kingmons/menu.html.

———. "The Story of a Day." *Balcony Stories.* New Orleans: L. Graham, 1914. Online. Documenting the American South. 2004. 14 Feb. 2005. www.docsouth.unc.edu/southlit/kingbalc/king.html.

Kushner, Tony. "Notes about Political Theater." *Kenyon Review* 19.3/4 (Summer/Fall 1997): 19–34.

Ladd, Barbara. *Nationalism and the Color Line in George W. Cable, Mark Twain, and William Faulkner.* Baton Rouge: Louisiana State UP, 1996.

Laney, Ruth. "Bard from the Bayou." *Conversations with Ernest Gaines.* Ed. John Lowe. Jackson: UP of Mississippi, 1995. 276–81.

Levasseur, Jennifer, and Kevin Rabelais. "Interview with Tim Gautreaux." *Mississippi Review* 27.3 (1999): 19–40.

Locke, John. *Two Treatises on Civil Government.* 1690. Intro. W. S. Carpenter. New York: E. P. Dutton, 1960.

Long, Huey. "Huey Long Campaigns for Governor in St. Martinsville, LA." 1927. *Great American Speeches*. 23 Feb. 2005. www.pbs.org/greatspeeches/timeline/#1920.

Longfellow, Henry Wadsworth. *Evangeline*. 1847. Ed. Lewis B. Semple. Gretna, LA: Pelican Publishing, 1999.

———. *Henry Wadsworth Longfellow: Selected Poems*. Intro. Lawrence Buell. New York: Penguin Books, 1988.

Longfellow, Samuel. *Life of Henry Wadsworth Longfellow*. 2 vols. Boston: Ticknor, 1886.

Louisiana Legacy: A Rich Tradition of Artistry with Food and Joy in Life. Thibodaux Service League. New Orleans: Celestial Publishing, 1989.

Lowe, John. "An Interview with Ernest Gaines." *Conversations with Ernest Gaines*. Jackson: UP of Mississippi, 1995. 297–328.

Lowenthal, David. "Fabricating Heritage." *History and Memory* 10.1. University of North Carolina, Chapel Hill, Walter Royal Davis Lib. 1 July 2004 www.iupjournals.org/history/ham10-1.html.

MacKethan, Lucinda H. *The Dream of Arcady: Place and Time in Southern Literature*. Baton Rouge: Louisiana State UP, 1980.

Marling, William. *The American Roman Noir: Hammett, Cain, and Chandler*. Athens: U of Georgia P, 1995.

Martin, Paul. "Antonine Maillet." *Northwest Passages: Canadian Literature Online*. 1998. Northwest Passages. 15 Nov. 2003. www.nwpassages.com/bios/maillet.asp.

Mathews, Cornelius. *Big Abel and the Little Manhattan*. New York: Wiley and Putnam, 1845.

McKee, Kathryn. "Local Color." *The Companion to Southern Literature: Themes, Genres, Places, People, Movements, and Motifs*. Ed. Joseph M. Flora and Lucinda MacKethan. Baton Rouge: Louisiana State UP, 2001. 449–52.

McKinney, Wanda. "Meet the Bayou's Mystery Man." *Southern Living* (Sept. 2005), 110–14.

Meese, Elizabeth. "What the Old Ones Know: Ada Jack Carver's Cane River Stories." *Louisiana Women Writers: New Essays and a Comprehensive Bibliography*. Ed. Dorothy H. Brown and Barbara C. Ewell. Baton Rouge: Louisiana State UP, 1992. 141–52.

Mencken, H. L. *Prejudices: A Selection*. 1919. Ed. James T. Farrell. New York: Vintage Books, 1955.

Menke, Pamela Glenn. "The Catalyst of Color and Women's Regional Writing: *At Fault, Pembroke*, and *The Awakening*." *The Southern Quarterly* 37:3–4 (1999): 9–20.

Michaels, Walter Benn. *Our America: Nativism, Modernism, and Pluralism*. Durham: Duke UP, 1995.

Miller, Perry. *The Raven and the Whale: The War of Words and Wits in the Era of Poe and Melville*. New York: Harcourt, Brace and World, Inc., 1956.

Morrison, Toni. *Playing in the Dark: Whiteness and the Literary Imagination*. Cambridge: Harvard UP, 1990.

Newitz, Annalee, and Matt Wray, eds. *White Trash: Race and Class in America*. New York: Routledge, 1997.

O' Brien, John. "Ernest J. Gaines." *Conversations with Ernest Gaines*. Ed. John Lowe. Jackson: UP of Mississippi, 1995. 25–38.

Paratte, Henri-Dominique. Foreword. *Evangeline*. By Henry Wadsworth Longfellow. Gretna, LA: Pelican Publishing, 1999.

Parker, Alice. "Evangeline's Darker Daughters: Crossing Racial Boundaries in Postwar Louisiana." *Louisiana Women Writers: New Essays and a Comprehensive Bibliography*. Ed. Dorothy H. Brown and Barbara C. Ewell. Baton Rouge: Louisiana State UP, 1992. 75–97.

Percy, Walker. *The Moviegoer*. 1960. New York: Ivy Books, 1988.

Perrin, Warren A. *Acadian Redemption: From Beausoleil Broussard to the Queen's Royal Proclamation*. 2004. Opelousas: Andrepont Publishing, 2005.

Piacentino, Ed. "Second Chances: Patterns of Failure and Redemption in Tim Gautreaux's *Same Place, Same Things*." *Southern Literary Journal* 28.1 (Fall 2005): 115–33.

Pridgen, Allen. "James Lee Burke's Dave Robicheaux: A Search for Home." *The Southern Quarterly* 41.1 (2002): 67–79.

Raphael, Morris. *Mystic Bayou*. Detroit: Harlo, 1985.

Reneaux, J. J. *Cajun Folktales*. Little Rock: August House, 1992.

"Researchers Hope to Unravel Mysteries of Cajun Genetics." *Daily News Central* 30 July 2005; *Daily News Central* 11 Jan. 2006. health.dailynewscentral. com/index.php?optioncontent&taskview&id1392.

Rickels, Milton, and Patricia Rickels. "'The Sound of My People Talking': Folk Humor in *A Gathering of Old Men*." *Critical Reflections on the Fiction of Ernest J. Gaines*. Ed. David Estes. Athens: U of Georgia P, 1994. 215–27.

Rickels, Patricia. "An Interview with Ernest Gaines." *Conversations with Ernest Gaines*. Ed. John Lowe. Jackson: UP of Mississippi, 1995. 119–36.

Roberts, Nora. *Midnight Bayou*. New York: Putnam, 2001.

Ross, Rita. "Evangeline in Louisiana: The Acadian-Cajun Connection." *Canadian Folklore* 13:2 (1991): 11–23.

Routley, Erik. *The Puritan Pleasures of the Detective Story*. London: Victor Gollancz, LTD, 1972.

Rubin, Louis D., Jr. *George Washington Cable: The Life and Times of a Southern Heretic*. New York: Pegasus, 1969.

Saeta, Elsa, and Izora Skinner. "Interview with Ernest Gaines." *Conversations with Ernest Gaines*. Ed. John Lowe. Jackson: UP of Mississippi, 1995. 241–52.

Said, Edward. *Orientalism*. New York: Pantheon Books, 1978.

Saxon, Lyle, Edward Dreyer, and Robert Tallant, eds. *Gumbo Ya-Ya*. 1945. Gretna, LA: Pelican Publishing, 1987.

Scooby-Doo on Zombie Island. Dirs. Kazumi Fukushima and Jim Stenstrum. Hanna-Barbera, 2004.

Scott, Ann Martin, ed. *Cajun Vernacular English: Informal English in French Louisiana*. Lafayette: University of Southwestern Louisiana, 1992.

Seelye, John. "Attic Shape: Dusting Off *Evangeline*." *Virginia Quarterly Review* 60 (1984): 21–44.

Segura, Chris. Editor's Notes. *Acadian Redemption: From Beausoleil Broussard to the Queen's Royal Proclamation*. By Warren A. Perrin. 2004. Opelousas: Andrepont Publishing, 2005. vii–x.

———. *Marshland Trinity*. Abbeville, LA: Win or Lose, Ink, 1997.

Semple, Lewis B. Introduction. *Evangeline*. By Henry Wadsworth Longfellow. Gretna, LA: Pelican Publishing, 1999. xiii–li.

Shaker, Bonnie James. *Coloring Locals: Racial Formation in Kate Chopin's Youth's Companion Stories*. Iowa City: U of Iowa P, 2003.

———. "'Lookin' Jis' like W'ite Folks': Coloring Locals in Kate Chopin's 'A Rude Awakening.'" *Louisiana Literature* 14:2 (Fall 1997): 116–25.

Shelton, Frank W. "James Lee Burke's Dave Robicheaux Novels." *The World Is Our Home*. Ed. Jeffery and Nancy Folks. Lexington: UP of Kentucky, 2000. 232–43.

———. "Of Machines and Men: Pastoralism in Gaines's Fiction." *Critical Reflections on the Fiction of Ernest J. Gaines*. Ed. David Estes. Athens: U of Georgia P, 1994. 12–29.

Showalter, Elaine. "Tradition and the Female Talent: *The Awakening* as a Solitary Book." *The Awakening*. Ed. Nancy A. Walker. Boston: Bedford, 2000. 202–22.

Simms, William Gilmore. *The Wigwam and the Cabin*. 1856. New York: A. C. Armstrong and Son, 1882.

Sowell, Thomas. *Ethnic America: A History*. New York: Basic Books, Inc., 1981.

Spangler, Matthew. "Of Snow and Dust: The Presence of James Joyce in Ernest Gaines's *A Lesson Before Dying*." *South Atlantic Review* 67.1 (Winter 2002): 105–28.

Stanford, Judy. "Ataxia, A Matter of Heredity: The Genetic Disease Prevalent Among Cajuns Robs People of the Ability to Move." *Daily Advertiser* 5 March 1999. *Daily Advertiser*. 11 Jan. 2006. www.1ft.k12.la.us/chs/la_studies/Cajun/Ataxia.htm.

Stepto, Robert B. *From Behind the Veil: A Study of Afro-American Narrative*. Urbana: U of Illinois P, 1979.

Still Stands the Forest Primeval. New Orleans Historic Society Exhibit. New Orleans: 2001.

Stivale, Charles. *Disenchanting Les Bons Temps: Identity and Authenticity in Cajun Music and Dance.* Durham: Duke UP, 2003.

Sollors, Werner. "Introduction: The Invention of Ethnicity." *The Invention of Ethnicity.* Ed. Werner Sollors. New York: Oxford UP, 1989. ix–xx.

———. *Neither Black nor White yet Both: Thematic Explorations of Interracial Literature.* Cambridge: Harvard UP, 1997.

Sturken, Marita. *Tangled Memories: The Vietnam War, the AIDS Epidemic, and the Politics of Remembering.* Berkeley: U of California P, 1997.

Taylor, Helen. *Gender, Race, and Region in the Writings of Grace King, Ruth McEnery Stuart, and Kate Chopin.* Baton Rouge: Louisiana State UP, 1989.

Thomas, Heather Kirk. "'What Are the Prospects for the Book?': Rewriting a Woman's Life." *Kate Chopin Reconsidered: Beyond the Bayou.* Ed. Lynda S. Boren and Sara de Saussure Davis. Baton Rouge: Louisiana State UP, 1992. 36–57.

Tidwell, Mike. *Bayou Farewell: The Rich Life and Tragic Death of Louisiana's Cajun Coast.* New York: Pantheon Books, 2003.

Tompkins, Jane. *Sensational Designs: The Cultural Work of American Fiction, 1790–1860.* New York: Oxford UP, 1985.

Toth, Emily. *Unveiling Kate Chopin.* Jackson: UP of Mississippi, 1992.

Tregle, Joseph G., Jr. "Early New Orleans Society." 1952. *At Fault: A Scholarly Edition.* Ed. Suzanne Disheroon Green and David J. Caudle. Knoxville: U of Tennessee P, 2001. 228–33.

Turner, Arlin. *George W. Cable: A Biography.* Baton Rouge: Louisiana State UP, 1966.

Tutwiler, Mary. "James Lee Burke's Acadiana: On the Trail of Detective Dave Robicheaux." Pamphlet. Lafayette Visitor Information Center.

Voorhies, Felix. *Acadian Reminiscences.* 1907. Gretna, LA: Pelican Publishing, 1998.

Wagenknecht, Edward. *Henry Wadsworth Longfellow: Portrait of an American Humanist.* New York: Oxford UP, 1966.

Walker, Nancy, ed. "Two Contemporary Reviews of *The Awakening.*" *The Awakening.* Boston: Bedford, 2000. 165–66.

The Waterboy. Dir. Frank Coraci. Touchstone, 1998.

"We Already Knew This." Online posting. 29 Sept. 2005. University of Louisiana Ragin' Cajuns. 30 Sept. 2005. forums.delphiforums.com/n/mb/message.asp?webtagRaginCajuns&ctx&cacheTa.

Webre, Stephen. "Among the Cybercajuns: Constructing Identity in the Virtual Diaspora." *Louisiana History* 39.4 (Fall 1998): 443–56.

Wells, Ken. *Junior's Leg.* New York: Random House, 2001.

———. *Logan's Storm.* 2002. New York: Random House, 2003.

———. *Meely LaBauve.* New York: Random House, 2000.

Wells, Rebecca. *Divine Secrets of the Ya-Ya Sisterhood*. 1996. New York: Harper, 1997.

White, Daniel. "'Haunted by the Idea': Fathers and Sons in *In My Father's House* and *A Gathering of Old Men*." *Critical Reflections on the Fiction of Ernest J. Gaines*. Ed. David Estes. Athens: U of Georgia P, 1994. 158–79.

Widmer, Edward. *Young America: The Flowering of Democracy in New York City*. New York: Oxford UP, 1999.

Wolff, Cynthia. "Un-Utterable Longing: The Discourse of Feminine Sexuality in Kate Chopin's *The Awakening*." *The Awakening*. Ed. Nancy A. Walker. Boston: Bedford, 2000. 376–95.

Woodward, C. Vann. *American Counterpoint: Slavery and Race in the North-South Dialogue*. Boston: Little, Brown, 1971.

Yaeger, Patricia. *Dirt and Desire: Reconstructing Southern Women's Writing, 1930–1990*. Chicago: U of Chicago P, 2000.

———. "'A Language Which Nobody Understood': Emancipatory Strategies in *The Awakening*. *The Awakening*. Ed. Nancy A. Walker. Boston: Bedford, 2000. 311–36.

INDEX